Highway 12

Highway 12 near Boynton Overlook

Highway 12

Christian Probasco

Utah State University Press
Logan, Utah

Copyright 2005 Utah State University Press
All rights reserved

Utah State University Press
Logan, Utah 84322-7800
www.usu.edu/usupress

Manufactured in the United States of America
Printed on acid-free, recycled paper

Library of Congress Cataloging-in-Publication Data

Probasco, Christian, 1967-
  Highway 12 / Christian Probasco.
        p. cm.
  Includes bibliographical references (p.).
  ISBN 0-87421-573-0 (pbk. : alk. paper)
1. Utah--Guidebooks. 2. Utah--Description and travel. 3. United States Highway 12--Guide-
books. 4. Automobile travel--Utah--Guidebooks. 5. Grand Staircase-Escalante National Monument (Utah)--Description and travel. 6. Bryce Canyon National Park (Utah)--Description and
travel. 7. Capitol Reef National Park (Utah)--Description and travel. I. Title: Highway Twelve.
II. Title.

  F824.3.P76 2005
  917.9204034--dc22

                                                                              2005001647

To Sarah

Acknowledgments

Many thanks to Leland Ford and Wade Barney for taking the time to help me understand the workings of the Highway Department. Thanks to Larry Riplinger for his input on local politics. Thanks to David Sucec, Carol Georgopoulos, and Ray Freeze for their enlightening input on rock art. Thanks to Edward A. Geary and Gayle Pollock for reviewing the manuscript; to John R. Alley, Ph.D., at Utah State University Press, for his guidance and patience; Ron Lucero for the venison; Virgil Probasco for paying the rent in April; Christine Probasco for providing contacts in southern Utah; Joshua Johnson for fixing the computer on which I am writing this; Wayne and Pat Johnson for providing the computer and for their financial help and encouragement; and my wife Sarah for supporting me, spooling a micro-cassette tape in her spare time, checking out books for me, cleaning, buying the groceries, making dinner, doing the laundry, and taking care of me in general.

Photo opposite: The Heap near Batty Caves.

Contents

Cloud over the Burr Trail

Introduction

Highway 12 and its adjoining roads traverse the last wilderness in the lower United States to be explored by European Americans. The Henry Mountains, the soot-black, bald laccolithic domes that creep across the sea of red solid rock in the frame of the eastbound driver's windshield, were the last mountains on the continent to be named. The Escalante River, which drains the wooded highlands rising in necessary opposition on that sea's far shore, was the last river on the continent to be discovered. The hamlet of Boulder in its pocket of green off the shoulder of those highlands, was once the most isolated town in the United States. To this day, it is possible to find niches and alcoves, narrow canyons and glens which no modern man has seen except from above. This is because the reach of land off Highway 12's southern edge is the most broken-up, inaccessible, intractable, inhospitable country on the face of the earth, and it is unlike anything else on the earth. It is land in the form of a mindscape, a place that shouldn't exist except as a mental construct.

I was impressed by the scenery and the isolation of Utah Route 12 the first time I traveled it back in the late eighties and over time I became interested in doing a book on it and I was encouraged in this pursuit by the superlatives I encountered in my early research. The Aquarius Plateau, the hub around which the Highway circles, for example, is the highest forested plateau in North America. Highway 12 runs through the largest exposure of cross-bedded sandstone on earth, and that sandstone is the remains of what may have been the largest sand desert in the history of the earth. The hamlet of Boulder, just off the east shoulder of the Aquarius, was the last town in the lower forty-eight states to receive its mail by pack-mule.

There are two national parks, a national monument and two state parks along Route 12's 124-mile length, and its side roads access another state park, a national recreation area, more than a dozen potential wilderness areas, and untold thousands of acres of National Forest Service and Bureau of Land Management land. It has a rich history: the San Juan Expedition came through Escalante, which is on the highway; the Civilian Conservation Corps constructed the most difficult and scenic sections of Highway 12; the Spanish explorers Francisco Antanasio Dominguez and Silvestre Velez de Escalante, John Wesley Powell, Brigham Young, John D. Lee, Mormon scout Jacob Hamblin, photographer Dorothea Lange, and the young traveler Everett Ruess, were all connected to it in some way. I found that others shared my appreciation of this jewel for all these reasons and more.

Badland formations at the end of Moody Canyon Road

Highway 12 was recently designated an All-American Road by the Federal Highway Administration (the only such designation in Utah and one of only twenty roads in the nation to receive this distinction). When it was elevated to All-American status, Highway 12 joined the ranks of the Seward Highway in Alaska, Highway 1 along the Big Sur Coast in California, and Wyoming's Beartooth Scenic Byway. In guidebooks, I found descriptions of Highway 12 like "one of the most fabulous [roads] in the nation" (Ludmer, 224), "surpasses all other highways in Southern Utah" (Rivers, 166), and "arguably the most attractive drive in the nation, and certainly one of the most diverse" (Bensen, 43). Edward A. Geary, author of *The Proper Edge of the Sky*, wrote that Highway 12 is "arguably the most scenic road in America" (145).

For all the praise that's been lavished on this highway, I learned along the way that it is really only one of many outstanding roads in this part of the West. When I began to explore this area in earnest, I had to drive down old Skutumpah Road, where John D. Lee hid from federal authorities, and Hell's Backbone Road, built over a sharp sandstone ridge, with one almost fathomless gap along its length. I had to ride down Hole-in-the-Rock Road to the high stone V at its end and drive what's come to be known as the Burr Trail down its switchbacks to the strike valley of Capitol Reef. I've included all these roads in the book; the title road, while among the most scenic in the nation, only serves as the book's unifying theme.

I compiled this narrative of my travels down the highway and its connecting roads mostly in 2002 and 2003. A few sections date back to some travels in the mid-nineties, about the time of the creation of the Grand Staircase-Escalante National Monument. I arranged the material so it would run counterclockwise, west to east with the highway, though this wasn't the order in which I collected it

Most of the photos were taken with an old but highly reliable Nikkormatt camera, with twenty-eight and fifty-millimeter lenses and polarizing filters. I digitized all the slides and put them through various filters on Photoshop to get the book's black-and-white images.

Most of the road-work was completed in an '81 CJ-5 I call the "Heap," for reasons which should become obvious in the first chapter. I came in possession of this contraption about ten years ago, and in the time I've owned it, I've changed out the engine three times; changed the radiator about three times; the starter and alternator four times at least; and the axles twice. I

have treated it roughly and it has returned the favor.

This is the story of a dream of stone and the roads that lead into it. It's a story of the people who live along those roads and those who travel and have traveled them. It's about desperate measures, loners, cowboys, ancient Indians, explorers, surveyors, pioneers, prospectors, environmentalists and modern tourists, and it's the story of a wanderer in a Jeep who would spend every minute of his life exploring that dream made real if he had the opportunity.

Lichen-covered boulders
above Bull Valley Gorge

From "Landforms of Utah in Proportional Relief." Used with permission of Merrill K. Ridd, with roads and names added by Christian Probasco.

chapter one

Photo opposite: Western portal of Highway 12

—Hoodoo Lands and the Rim—

Red and Bryce Canyons,
the Paunsaugunt Plateau and
the Road to Escalante

Red Canyon

East of Panguitch stand the Sunset Cliffs, red limestone slopes knocked back at their head and etched into steep draws and spines, bulbous pink columns known as hoodoos, flint knolls and rough walls with scree bases fanned into bajadas, and portals: mouse holes, loopholes, doorways, hallways, windows and arches, through some of which you may pass into another earth—an earth of sagebrush, pinyon and juniper and dead pine spikes and lonely roads, an anguished earth kneaded into rolls, mountains and plateaus and pinched into shark-tooth ridges and split and pried open along ragged faults and soft joints and worn down to buttes and pinnacles, washes, plains, gullies, gulches and deep, indanthrene narrows.

I'm on that revetment now, on the Arches Trail, a mile or so north of Highway 12, trudging up the hill along a well-worn and crooked path with a camera on a tripod slung over my shoulder, pausing for breath now and again and studying the rock because even with the overcast October sky, the bizarre mix of colors—the limonite yellow and rust red and jasper—is still vivid. There are arches all around me, some just barely large enough to fit my hand through (technically not arches at all, whose chord must be a foot long in any direction) some as large as my living room windows, with a view out to a neighboring slope or the rack of a broken-backed pinyon pine, and one as wide as a full-sized movie screen, today's feature being storm clouds piling against the plateau's west face and billowing into black gurges with wisps streaming off from the impact.

Near the top, I can overlook the Sevier River Valley, carpeted by bunchgrass, washed over by shadows of clouds, and the commercial row, the hotel, gas station, trading post and restaurant that line Highway 12 along its western terminus at Highway 89. The western horizon is the edge of the Markagunt Plateau, scended like a ship's bow, and beyond that lies a scorched cordillera of mafic black mountain ranges and blanched alkali flats across western Utah and the entire width of Nevada, to the Sierra's crystalline granite base.

This collection of arches is a fitting beginning for my journey. One hundred and sixty miles northeast of here there's a larger gallery of holes in the rock called Arches National Park, and within that park is a giant's garden of red fins with enormous windows worn through them. These make for the best arches because they juxtapose solidness and impenetrability with openness and wide vistas; space exploding outward from the red wall a few yards from your face into the brisance of the open earth.

Wall and window, impediment and opening, imprisonment and escape. I come to another wall, this one as big as a house side, with stiled windows and an arch as tall as a doorway. The trail passes right through it. I set up my tripod and wait for the sun to poke through the clouds but it never does and finally I pack my gear, sling it over my shoulder again, bow my head and I'm through.

On our way to the visitor's center earlier in the day, my asthmatic, scoliatic friend Gerald and I rode through what I like to think of as the western portals of Highway 12; arches blasted by highway engineers through two rock walls, now leaning like flying buttresses against the mountainside. We met a balding, middle-aged, red-faced firecracker of a volunteer ranger named Bill Shane, who set us straight as to our options—which trails to take, where to camp—and Gerald asked him if he was jealous of the rangers in nearby Bryce Canyon National Park.

"No," said Shane, "Red Canyon is more beautiful and there are fewer people here."

We followed Shane's advice and camped a half-mile up Cabin Hollow, beneath an orange clint of rock, and we had no neighbors. Shane has a talent for understatement: Bryce draws tourists like a powerful electric current. Over the course of four days and a half-dozen trails we only encountered about twelve people. Most tourists stop at the arches for photographs, pause at the visitor's center (which was little more than a wood-paneled trailer) peruse the literature, maybe use the bathroom or buy a postcard, and then they're off to the main attraction.

We hiked the Pink Ledges Trail right behind the visitor's center but it wasn't challenging enough for Gerald and he took off, with me following belatedly, up a stone-walled gully which pinched out and left us scrambling up scree, over volcanic capstone to a flat and a manzanita garden, and as I explored it, Gerald crawled over more ledges with his short legs kicking until he was lost to sight. He called me, distantly, and again I followed, until we met on the back of a red chert ridge, him with his John Deere cap cocked back and his sand-colored turban with desert motifs of camels and palm trees and pyramids wrapped over a shoulder. He pointed a stubby finger at a black lava scab a half-mile distant.

"That's the top. That is our destination."

Gerald has just been down-sized from his computer-tech job, and the jolt has radicalized and enraged him and he's been binging on pot, alcohol and Ritalin to kill the pain and bludgeon his already dull memory.

"Don't pack any more propane bottles," I told him when he'd stuffed the fourth or fifth bottle into his pack back home. "We only need one."

He just laughed at me. It took him four hours to get his things together and I finally had to drive the Heap up on his lawn to get my point across that it was *time to go*. He brought tennis balls along so we could practice juggling, and mosquito netting in case we were attacked by killer bees and a laptop computer which must be coddled and swathed in blankets like an infant, and he has spent most of the trip so far compulsively rearranging our gear.

Though I can't seem to impart the concept of "false summits" to Gerald, I do finally convince him that the volcanic ridge isn't where we need to go, but he pulls the same stunt another day and this time I find a deer trail through the hoodoos to the ledge, which is our objective, and watch him drape his short limbs and crooked back across the stone and drag himself over the rim. It's fortunate Gerald thrives so much on adversity because we've had plenty of it so far: the bike's weight on the spare tire buckled out the tailgate; I left an important lens at home and my wife had to deliver it to a point halfway between Salt Lake City and Red Canyon. The skid plate stripped out three bolt-holes on the frame's left side and had to be clamped in the rain and the holes tapped out to accept larger bolts, and a metal strap sheered and spun the gas can off the road at sixty miles-per-hour.

We spend the next several days exploring and find a side canyon of phalanges, scapulas, ribs and skulls carved from calcareous rock painted vermilion by the setting sun and we drop into an amphitheater of crumbling incarnadine clay tiers, malleiform pillars and pilasters, turrets and slanted salients, with the resemblance of rock forms to battlements becoming so uncanny at times that I realize I have it backwards: it's the castle emulating the stone formations, which have battled the elements for millions of years.

We park the Heap on the plateau top and bike down the Thunder Mountain Trail, which drops into hollows and skims over spurs and keeps its elevation for a while but then surrenders to gravity and falls in skidding, exposed switchbacks from the cool forest to the hostile, oxidized red desert, where we trade ponderosa for cedars twisted up like funnel cones and manzanita for a few struggling low patches

"Bob," a commercial fisherman on his Harley in Red Canyon.

Butte with volcanic capstone, Red Canyon

of gray brush and yucca spines. The sun bakes the earth red and bleaches it white and haze sifts off the trail in staggered waves. We drink compulsively and Gerald's asthma leaves him gasping for breath like a landed fish.

Inspiration Point, halfway down the trail, is an ancient temple. The ground falls away into a pit of jumbled red idols and monoliths toppling towards oblivion and on the far side the sunburn-colored terrain rolls up in uneven terraces towards an altar just below the sky.

At night, Gerald, stoned senseless, affects a Brooklyn accent and rails against the right wing, doctors, pharmacists, CEOs, organized religion, every corporation on earth, and working mothers.

"Economic justice," he says, "That's what I want."

Gerald makes an office of the visitor center's men's room, downloading three-hundred images from his digital camera onto his laptop, which he powers off the room's outlet.

One evening we struggle over the ridge above our campground into the next canyon, which Gerald scouted while I slept, and we find cattle vertebrae, a deep arroyo, an old road overgrown with sagebrush. We transect talus fans and plains of thistle and black sagebrush and a field of sego lilies, Indian paintbrush, columbines, asters, mats of blue penstemon. We pause before a rectangular arch high on a canyon wall and spy another, smaller one by the light of a crescent moon on our return trip, more portals into a state of mind reified into landscape.

In June of 1925 Governor Dern and James M. Sargent, mayor of Panguitch, rode into Red Canyon at the head of a procession of 315 cars to celebrate the opening of Bryce Canyon National Park and they were stopped at the second arch, at a gate manned by brownies, and then mobbed by fairies emerging from behind red rocks. "Do you believe in fairies?" asked one and, trusting his eyes, Dern answered affirmatively. "Then enter Fairyland," she told him, and they did (Newell, Talbot, 267).

That creature had it wrong. As I later discover, the highway has delivered us into a land of contrariness, a Negative Earth. Gerald boils up a pot of pasta that night and slips into an incogitant rage and flounces about, shouting, with his hands clutching at God's throat while the fire's smoke and aroma waft over me and saturate my clothes with the redolence of juniper and pinyon pine. Gerald pauses and I don't know whether he's run out of steam or if it's just for effect.

"You know," he says, "some days it's just not worth gnawing through the straps."

I crawl into my sleeping bag as the fire burns itself to embers and begin to sleep and again there is a portal before me. The stars materialize and the black dome of night rolls over me.

Volcanic boulders, Red Canyon

East Fork of the Sevier

From the turnoff onto FS 87, the earth appears to bend down to the head of the East Fork of the Sevier River, and that's troubling because the river coalesces from its tributaries twelve hundred feet above where it crosses the road. I can only ascribe this illusion to the roughly pyramidal peaks and the bare rock in the distance, where the East Fork originates. On the Colorado Plateau, such weathering usually indicates downcutting too rapid for the earth to accommodate it with gentle banks.

The road is smooth and I make time but the Heap spins a giant billowing wake of chalk-white dust into the summer sky and it coats the seats, the instruments, the steering column, my clothes, everything. I have to stop every few miles and clean my glasses and I can taste the grit on my teeth. When I look in the rearview mirror, I see a tired, gray-eyed ghost.

I pass over the end of the Tropic Ditch; further on the road narrows and begins to meander as the East Fork straightens out. Side roads curve off into Badger Creek, East Creek, Skunk Creek, Long Hollow, Blue Fly Creek, most of them coming to a dead end against the west boundary of Bryce Canyon or the backslope of the Sunset Cliffs. Pink pedregals and inchoate hoodoo columns lean from side-canyon walls.

There's a drought on and Tropic Reservoir is a shrunken remnant of itself, no anglers on its shore today. Near the road's north end, Podunk Ranger Station stands empty before the entrance to Podunk Canyon.

Who, I wonder, *would want to man the Podunk Ranger Station?*

The East Fork dries up. It's a lost stream anyway, except the portion siphoned off for the fields down in Tropic. The East Fork joins the Sevier, which evaporates or drains into Sevier Lake south of Highway 50 in the Great Basin, and never escapes from there except to sink into the mud or rise heavenward as vapor. No water in any creek or river from the East Fork westward, in fact, escapes from this basin except in a similar manner.

Beyond the East Fork, east of the Paunsaugunt Plateau's crest, the creeks join larger drainages which empty into tributaries of the Colorado and finally the great river itself. This river, too, dies out before reaching the Pacific Ocean, not because the Colorado is closed off from it but because it is put to work watering the fields of Colorado, California, Utah, Nevada and Arizona.

There's a turn-about at the end of the East Fork Road and no sign the trail ever continued beyond this point, though there are old logging roads running up the slope on my right, blocked by the Forest Service with brush and rocks. *That's fine,* I think, *there are other routes to the ridge top.* I drive back and turn into Robinson Canyon, into a tangle of roads just below the ridge, which might deliver me through the Sunset Cliffs to the town of Alton. The sun is nearly directly overhead, neither rising nor setting, and I lose my bearings. The road is narrow and rough, rutted in places and steep in others. After a half-hour chasing my tail, I see some high orange bluffs up ahead and I figure I'm nearly there, but the road drops into a gulch before I can get near them. Now I'm watching the gas gauge, a quarter tank, and I'm feeling tired and disoriented. Juniper grown over the road scratches the Heap's side.

Soon I realize my mistake: I've circled around on my path, done a 180. Those orange rocks are outcroppings of Bryce Canyon, and I'm now dropping back down to the East Fork. Then I'm there, on the road further north than where I started, facing east though my body tells me I've been traveling roughly westward the whole time.

Trying to escape from the basin of the East Fork, I've been shunted back toward it. I switch the Heap off in the middle of the road—-I haven't seen another vehicle for two hours—and in my notebook, write: "non-Euclidean space."

On my way back to town, by coincidence, I meet Wallace Ott, who's tending his herd, with this brand, on his spread of meadowland west of the road:

IX

Ott, a nonagenarian, is a little stooped, and his eyes are hidden under creased lids, but his memory, as he tells me, is "as good as it ever was."

"I've had a long life and good memories, met a lot of good people. But let me tell you, after you turn ninety, you're living on borrowed time," he says.

Ott was born in Tropic. He was on the board of the Garfield

Pines, East Fork

County School District for twelve years, and Garkane Power's board for twenty-four years and he served on the BLM's Advisory Board for thirty years. He was also County Commissioner for eight years and he still serves on the board of the Horse and Cow Association.

"Not good paying jobs," he tells me, "but they helped the county out."

Ott has nine children and about sixty grandchildren and great-grandchildren and one great, great grandchild. I ask him if it's hard keeping track of them.

"My sister was two years older than me," he says. "Died a year ago, had nine kids, just like I did and one time she was having this reunion and they had kids of all ages and sizes and I asked her, 'Do you know all those kids you've got here?' and she says, 'Let's put it this way: they all know me'."

I ask him about getting to Tropic before they put the highway through.

"The train came to Marysvale and it was horse and wagon down to Tropic. I remember when there was only one car there, a Model T Ford. A guy by the name of William Shakespeare had it. He ordered it through a catalogue and it took him two days to get to Marysvale. And I'll tell you something else that happened. My oldest brother was drafted for World War I and we didn't think we'd see him again but after he came back he married a woman from Sandy (just south of Salt Lake City) and we went to see them in an old Model T and it took us two days on that old dirt road through Sevier and Piute County, with that Model T doing one-hundred miles-per-hour."

"One hundred miles-per-hour," I say.

"Let me tell you how it done it. It was only going thirty miles-per-hour horizontally but it was doing seventy up and down."

His brother's father-in-law, a man named Charter, whom Wallace met when he was a teenager, was a Civil War veteran who'd shaken Abraham Lincoln's hand.

"Now how many people do you think are still alive who talked to someone who's seen Abraham Lincoln?" he asks.

We talk about the "drouthy" weather and the local trails and about the road running from La Verkin to Zions National Park, which *detours* around the lone grave of his great grandmother, Nancy Ferguson Ott, and about his herd and while we're talking, his middle-aged son shows up in his cowboy hat and boots and starts grumbling to him about the Forest Service cutting his range back. Apparently, all the meadow bottoms are now off limits to grazing. Then a convoy of diesel trucks pulling cow trailers comes through and the last one pulls over and I excuse myself as the driver leans out into the cloud of dust and shouts:

"It's the last roundup, Wallace!"

Bryce Canyon

Turning onto Highway 63, the only paved road into Bryce Canyon National Park, you pass the gaudy tourist row, enter a thick forest of ponderosa and limber pine, pull up to the entrance station to pay your fee (currently twenty dollars) and proceed down through a broad but shallow valley with the same feeling you'd get having paid for a carnival ride. The earth rises gently from either side of the shoulder and there are no peaks visible over the pines, so you feel you're riding along the crest of the world, with the sky more than likely overcast and morose, if not downright threatening and the clouds pressed inordinately close, as if they could be gutted by the crowns of trees.

Occasionally there's a clearing and you glimpse another huge, tilted slab of earth like the one on which you're riding, the haze and low sky elongating it along an aclinal plane. The land and heavens appear as strata of the same elements, a narrow band of blues, grays and pinks, and the further you go the more you see of those lands far-off to the east and south until you realize you're moving toward the plateau's edge.

Like the land abutting the Grand Canyon's south rim, the terrain around Bryce Canyon is heavily forested and you don't know how close you are to the edge until you're practically on top of it. In the case of Bryce, because the road doesn't initially run right along the brink and because the plateau top is bowed by the down-cutting of the East Fork of the Sevier River, you have to park your car and walk uphill a short distance to get the views you're after. You top a rise and there's a wide vacivity where the earth should be, with the main draw below: an immense, pink basin, not a canyon at all, that seems to have been burned out of the flank of the plateau by acid, filled with thousands of rock needles big as church spires. If you approached Bryce Canyon from Highway 12, you would notice similar formations as you ride up the Paunsaugunt Plateau, but here they're ubiquitous. The pink rock is also evident in the strata of the distant Table Cliffs, though at a higher elevation.

Trails divagate into the Fairyland, Tower Bridge, the Hat Shop, the Queen's Garden, through hollows and splayed arches, red limestone cities and narrow avenues of washes, with thermals sweeping up the slope and carrying hawks into the sullen gray sky without effort.

The road continues for sixteen miles with a different tableau at each stop, the declivities becoming more abrupt, the floor beneath the hoodoos steepening and the plateau itself falling away until it seems you're riding the spine of a risen chthonic beast. A salient feature of this corner of earth becomes evident—every major road and most of the minor ones will at some point follow the course of a hogback or its negative spatial equivalent, the floor of a gulch. It's the only way roads could be constructed through this land

Looking towards Navajo Mountain from Bryce Canyon

without having to scale or blast through innumerable rock barriers. A portion of the old road between Escalante and Boulder is called Hell's Backbone; Highway 12 itself rises to the Hogback; the Burr trail crests the rocky cusp of Capitol Reef and Hole-in-the-Rock Road gets its name from a narrow chute to the Colorado River, now the surface of Lake Powell.

Fifty miles to the west, in the Great Basin, the strata are wrenched up and bent over their own backs, the land shattered along faults and pried over hidden fulcrums. Traveling through that basin, however, is relatively easy because the waste plains, built from debris eroded off the surrounding mountains, are leveled to a peneplane so flat that on a vantage point over some of them you can see the earth's curve. Most of the layers of the Colorado Plateau, on the other hand, are preserved in a nearly horizontal configuration, yet in terms of travel, the terrain ranges from difficult to impassible because of the same general forces acting on the Great Basin; the land is broken and abrupt, incised, anguished.

One hundred million years ago there was a coastal swamp of deltas and bayous, jetties and hooks on the edge of an inland sea splitting the continent in two. The earth was a more violent place then, continents drifting across the abyssal plain at three times their present speed, volcanoes spewing out more lava than any age since. The climate was hot enough to melt the ice caps and giants stomped through the rivage: lizards the size of whales, crocodiles as long as buses.

About ninety million years ago, as a swollen sea advanced over this swamp, compressional forces from accelerated sea floor spreading and islands accreting to the continent cracked the crust into vast plates and pressed them over the backs of their neighbors, forcing up snow-capped highlands on the edge of the western island called the Sevier Uplift, which were cut down as they rose and carried by rivers out to sea, where their detritus began to fill the basin. The sea retreated and advanced repeatedly as the climate fluctuated; and sixty-six million years ago it was gone for good, replaced by a string of freshwater lakes as large as the modern Great Lakes, one of which, the Claron, overlaid what is now Bryce Canyon. The lakes filled with silt and lime and then the stage was set for the third act: the cretified lake basins and the land around them were lifted into the sky en masse as the highlands to the west collapsed along thousands of incipient fault lines, great unsupported slabs of earth tilting like dominoes into a jumbled heap.

Highlands erode exponentially faster as they rise. Acidic rainwater dissolves minerals and pops spall from rocks when it freezes, and steeper gradients carry more scouring sediment down slopes. More moisture also means more vegetation, with the roots of shrubs and trees attacking the rock in the same manner as ice, expanding into seams and prying it loose.

About sixteen million years ago, the rising west edge of the new upland, the Colorado Plateau, began to fracture along old lines of weakness, the Paunsaugunt and Sevier Faults, and a part of the old lake bed was tilted up into the Paunsaugunt Plateau. Fifteen miles east of Bryce Canyon, the Table Cliffs, a spur of the Aquarius Plateau, have been offset fifteen hundred feet upward from correlative layers in the Paunsaugunt. As the Table Cliffs rose, the Paria River cut down into softer sediments beneath them and wore the higher, eastern escarpment down below the lip of its once-lower neighbor, the Paunsaugunt, and exposed it, in turn, to the same forces of erosion. The end result was a huge basin called the Tropic Amphitheater, of which Bryce Canyon forms the western wall. Faulting fractured the limestone into grikes, and rain, ice and vegetation broke it down into chines, then arches, and finally stalks of soft, free-standing stone stained pink by oxidized impurities of iron and magnesium and capped by resistant finials of rock——hoodoos.

Hoodoos

I meet Gayle Pollock, a geologist and director of the Bryce Canyon Natural History Association at the park's new visitor's center and we climb in his pickup and drive south on Highway 63. He turns into the pull-off at Sunset Point and runs down the features before us like a park ranger before a crowd of tourists: there, in the distance, are the muddy Blues badlands, there is Powell Point and the Table Cliffs, there is the Kaiparowits Plateau, and down below us, in the Bryce Amphitheater, is Thor's Hammer, probably the most photographed feature of the park, and the sinking ship, a Titanic-sized chunk of tilted, straked limestone snagged by a fault scarp and dragged skyward with it.

Gayle instructs me on the geology of the High Plateaus. The Hurricane Fault, with its five to ten-thousand feet of offset, delineates the Basin and Range Province from the Colorado Plateau, but the next fault east, the Sevier, throws the strata of the Sunset Cliffs two thousand feet above correlative rock in the Sevier Valley, while the Paunsaugunt Fault has fifteen hundred feet of upthrow. Further east, it's difficult to find large faults because the more pliable rock of the central Colorado Plateau, which is further from the Basin-and-Range system, folds rather than sheers under stress. Because the High Plateaus, part of a "cryptic transition zone," (Wannamaker, 1) share faulting characteristics with the Basin and Range, they've been given their own province within the greater Colorado Plateau.

Traveling along, Pollock describes the difficulties he's up against divining a geologic history from the Claron Formation, what other geologists describe as "The Pink Crud." Early on, some geologists lumped the biolithic Claron in with the "Wasatch Formation," which is primarily sandstone and conglomerates, and it was only given the respect it deserved and classified as a completely separate entity in the early eighties. At the same time, many still considered Lake Claron to be little more than a southern bay of a larger system of lakes such as the Flagstaff and the Uinta. This isn't Gayle's thinking.

"The Claron Formation is complex," he tells me. "It may have been connected to a larger system at one time, but it definitely spent much of its history as an isolated basin."

Gayle explains the current theory; the shallow lake expanded and contracted according to the local climate, alternately filling the Claron Basin and then evaporating down to nothing. Mats of algae on the lake's edge secreted calcium carbonate, which was concentrated in the lake-bed during the dry cycles, when plant roots would have churned the soil until the layers became unrecognizable.

"When you tell people that this was a lake bed, they ask, where are the fossils of fish?" he says, "First off, those fossils may have been destroyed by bioturbation. Plant roots and burrowing animals destroy fossils directly, but they also create pathways which allow chemicals to seep in and destroy the process of fossilization. Second, we don't know if the lake waters were hospitable enough for fish even to exist. It may have been an entirely closed system, perhaps so basic, with carbonates precipitating out, that the only things that could survive well were these gastropods which can survive just about anywhere. You find them when you're hiking in the mountains now, white shells from fresh-water gastropods living in lakes."

At this point, my mind is on Pollock himself, a lucky man in my eyes because he's as familiar with the reality wrapped around Highway 12, with the geology and geography, the plant life and wildlife, the history and the ancient history, as any man living. He grew up here and his father grew up here, as did his father's father and so on, back about five generations. Gayle's great, great, great grandmother, Wallace Ott's great, great grandmother, Nancy Ferguson Ott, the woman whose grave detours the road to Zion National Park, crossed the plains from Navuoo, Illinois, with her two boys, the youngest of which she had to bury along the way. The older boy, David, then five, became Gayle's great great grandfather. There are Pollocks and Otts buried in most graveyards along Highway 12 and "Sam Pollock Arch," near Hackberry Canyon, is named for a cousin of Gayle's grandfather.

Pollock began collecting fossil shark's teeth around Tropic when he was in the fourth grade. He can't remember wanting to be anything but a geologist. Before World War II, his interest might have amounted to nothing more than a hobby.

"As a kid, prior to the war, you went through the eighth grade and then you were on the sheep herd. The only way you went out into the back country was on a horse. Then the war came along. My dad dropped out of school at sixteen, worked as a civilian for the army and guarded Italian prisoners up in Magna (just west of Salt Lake City). My grandmother worked at a defense plant there. The war opened up this place to a new economy and people started moving away to work." And the next generation, Gayle's, would also move to the cities to get an education. Gayle got his geology degree from Southern Utah University in Cedar City, kicked around in Denver for a while working for the United States Geological Survey, found a mentor, Bill Cobban, who rekindled his interest in the Tropic Shale and ammonites, picked up the job as the first full-time director of Bryce's Natural History Association and came full circle back to Tropic in 1995. As the association's director, he's given a "wish list" by the Park Service and other agencies, of projects that are within their charter but outside their budgets, and the association uses proceeds from gift shops affiliated with ranger stations and visitor's centers and from private and corporate contributions to fund these projects.

Gayle Pollock and his hoodoo kingdom

We stop at Bryce Point, above the back of the "Alligator," an ophidian mass of incipient hoodoos capped by aspects of white limestone, and he explains the life-cycle of hoodoos to me. He directs me to the matrix of fractures running northwest and northeast through the rock, where water and frost begin their attack, then to the resulting separation of the stone from narrow defiles into columns with white, dolomite caprocks. These white sentinels have an additional magnesium ion which makes them more resistant to erosion, but not immune to it, and some of the caprock wears down and coats the column with a thin, protective layer of "dripstone." Eventually this, too, is eaten back, and when the column becomes too narrow to support its caprock, the crown falls and joins others at the base of the amphitheater or initiates the birth of another hoodoo further down the slope, and the original hoodoo is left defenseless and quickly withers into nonexistence.

Earthquakes will accelerate the process but man-made events can have similar effects. Gayle tells me that several capstones were knocked from their perches by minor quakes associated with the atomic testing in Nevada.

Pollock also shows me the syncline that runs west to east across the park. It's a pervasive, subtle dip in the strata brought on by crustal compression and it would be difficult to see if you weren't looking for it. I briefly recall the paranoia I developed travelling south on Forest Service Road 87 along the East Fork of the Sevier River. Layers which appear horizontal at first glance are actually bowed and the earth is concave here rather than convex. Bizarre geologic processes manifest themselves just below the level of awareness.

Back in the truck, I ask Gayle about his feelings on the still-new national monument to the east. His relationship with the federal government and his heritage puts him in the precarious position of understanding both sides of the contention over public lands.

"If their intention was to protect the area, I'm not sure they did a good job," he says. "It used to be that you could drive the length of the Cockscomb, from Cannonville down to 89, and not see another person. Sometimes Navajos would use it as a short-cut coming up from Arizona. These days I get white knuckles coming around the corners. I pass an average of thirty cars going the other way."

He pauses for a minute and adds:

"People here can sympathize with the Native Americans. When Clinton made his declaration, he didn't bother to inform anyone in Utah, not even the governor. What that says to me is 'you're all scientifically illiterate,' and 'you're not good stewards of the land.'"

And there's the seemingly contradictory other side:

"People ask me, 'Why did they include the Kaiparowits in the monument? It's so ugly.' They don't understand its scientific value. The Kaiparowits has a fossil record like nothing else on earth and a very rich cultural history."

We arrive at the last turnout and hike out to Yovimpa Point, at the southern edge of Bryce Canyon National Park, and he introduces me to a landscape I already know but will never become entirely familiar with: the Grand Staircase. We're on the top step now, above the Pink Cliffs. He points to the lumpy shale slopes below the Claron Limestone and tells me I'm looking at the Gray Cliffs, "not really cliffs at all," he says, almost apologetically, and his finger raises over the entirety of Skutumpah Terrace, an unknown scarped-plain wilderness I could easily spend my entire life exploring, and settles on the tips of the fractured edges of huge sandstone infaces turned away from us.

"The White Cliffs," he says, and raises his hand again, "and the Vermilion and the Chocolate, which we can't see. Way out there—" there is a balk of black earth in the far distance, partially obscured by a veil of haze from a controlled burn on the Sevier Plateau behind us "—you can barely see the edge of the Grand Canyon."

No Man's Mesa is below us, and the sandstone spire aptly named Mollie's Nipple, as well as the Paria River Gorge, the Kaiparowits Plateau and the Kaibab Plateau, all part of a vast, mostly unknown land, and I have the desire to explore every nook and crevice of it, a task that would take centuries. By the time I could have compiled a catalogue of that land's canyons and side canyons, its box canyons, hanging canyons, waterfalls, gulches and buttes, arches and bridges, the first features I'd have visited would have eroded away until they were unrecognizable, and I would have to start over.

Pollock returns to the Pink Cliffs, the top of the staircase and the acme of detailed, erosive sculpting.

"The Claron is exposed in the Table Cliffs and at Cedar Breaks as well," he tells me, "But at a higher elevation, more freeze-thaw cycles break the rock down faster, before it can form high concentrations of hoodoos. Even here," and he indicates the steep slope and the meager clustering of hoodoos in the amphitheater beneath us, "the climate is less favorable for the creation of the forms we see in the Bryce Amphitheater. A thousand feet makes a lot of difference. The conditions which brought these formations into existence in such numbers are unique to Bryce Canyon alone."

Pollock sees the larger picture but attends to the geologic details of this pocket of the plateau; the exact wheres, whens and hows of the last hundred million years. In terms of the scientific terrain, Pollock is studying the rills and rivulets, all of them, but a century before him, there were others studying the major tributaries, and before them, there was Major John Wesley Powell, who studied the river.

Powell, Dutton and the Negative Earth

On August 29 of 1869, six bearded, sun-burnt men in ragged clothing for the last time pulled their battered, leaking boats to the shore of the Colorado River near the mouth of the Virgin River and limped inland with three Mormon men and a boy to the settlement of Callville, where they feasted on fish, melons and squash and related the events of their journey. They'd left Green River City, Wyoming, three months earlier and had ridden the length of the Green and Colorado Rivers from that point, down through Flaming Gorge and the forbidding Canyon of Lodore, down through Whirlpool Canyon and Desolation Canyon, Gray Canyon, Labyrinth Canyon, Cataract Canyon and the placid waters of Glen Canyon, through Marble Canyon and into the great, churning, foaming, roiling, deep, dark Vishnu-Shist madness at the bottom of the Grand Canyon. They'd fought rapids throughout all of these canyons or they'd portaged their heavy boats and their supplies around them. They'd burned themselves in a brush fire of their own making and their boats had been swamped and their supplies dumped into the river. One of their boats, the No-Name, had been smashed into the rocks. They were soaked the entire trip. Their clothes were nearly all lost or ruined and their cooking utensils, bedding, provisions and guns were even then making their way to the Gulf of California. The few rations of flour and bacon they had left were rancid. Swarms of insects had attacked them, they had become violently sick from vegetables they'd lifted from an Indian garden and their leader, Major Powell, who'd lost an arm at Shiloh, had become stranded on a cliff face, unable to climb up or down until George Bradley rescued him with his trousers dangled over a ledge to Powell's hand.

Three of their party had left the main group only two days earlier, preferring to take their chances in the wilderness rather than being dismembered by the violent boils ahead. Unbeknownst to Powell and his men as they enjoyed their feast, these three had already been riddled by Shivwits arrows on the plateau above the gorge.

In the eastern press, they were *all* rumored to be dead.

This was the remains of the Powell Expedition, the first men to have verifiably run the Colorado through the Grand Canyon. The group disbanded and afterwards Powell lost touch with the other men, except for his brother Walter. Some went on to other adventures, some published their own accounts of the endeavor, but the Major continued to run the river. He returned almost two years later better prepared for the journey, with a new crew, and he rode the current again and kept riding it all the way to Washington D.C.—his destination from the start—and an appointment as the director of a western survey that was to last until 1879.

In Powell's hand then was the tome which had secured his position, the *Exploration of the Colorado River of the West*, a condensed account of the two expeditions and an outline of the principles which had shaped the Colorado Plateau, chiefly the "recession of cliffs," the coping of stone by rain and frost at the edge of buttes rather than their centers, which accounted for the Plateau's broad shelves of rock, and the "antecedence of drainages," the rise of the Plateau around incised rivers helpless to alter their course, which explained how they could cut through mountains or highlands and across valleys "as if they were only banks of fog or smoke," as Powell's associate Clarence Dutton put it (*High Plateaus*, 287).

In time, the Major developed a second set of principles, this one concerned with the river of settlers migrating into the West, elucidated in his *Report on the Lands of the Arid Region*, and for a brief time, he tried to hold the West hostage to the vision therein: an apportioning of land based on access to water rather than raw acreage, boundary lines conforming to drainages rather than arbitrary meridians and the restriction of settlement until the West could be properly surveyed and classified according to its potential for agriculture, mining, timber or grazing.

During his tenure Powell drew able men to him to fill in the details of his vision of the West while he struggled to keep the survey funded. Thomas Moran became the survey's illustrator, as did William Henry Holmes, with his "more-than-photographic accuracy" (Stegner, illustration 6). Grove Karl

Gilbert, who jumped ship to Powell's team from George Wheeler's survey, introduced the idea of laccoliths, lenses of volcanic rock trapped beneath the earth's surface in his *Geology of the Henry Mountains*. Almon Harris Thompson, the Major's brother-in-law and leader of much of the second expedition, did the fieldwork and created the finished map of the last heretofore unexplored region of the United States so Powell could demonstrate the survey's accomplishments. And Clarence Edward Dutton deciphered the geology of the Grand Canyon and the tablelands on the west edge of the Colorado Plateau in his *Tertiary History of the Grand Canyon* and his *Geology of the High Plateaus of Utah*.

Highway 12 runs along and over many of those tablelands. It crosses the Paunsaugunt Plateau and drops through the Paria Amphitheater on the far side, then gradually rises over the flank of the Aquarius Plateau, all regions which Dutton studied in far more detail than Powell. Whereas Powell lumped the Aquarius in with the Fish Lake and Awapa Plateaus, for example, noting "All three of these plateaus are remarkable for the many lakelets found on them," (*Exploration*, 80), Dutton reveals on page five of *High Plateaus* that the Awapa, which perversely means "many waters" in Paiute, in fact, has almost no water on its surface at all. He also adds this oddly subjective description on his approach to the Aquarius Plateau:

> The ascent leads us among rugged hills, almost mountainous in size, strewn with black boulders, along precipitous ledges, and by the sides of canons. Long detours must be made to escape the chasms and to avoid the taluses of fallen blocks; deep ravines must be crossed, projecting crags doubled, and lofty battlements scaled before the summit is reached. When the broad platform is gained the story of "Jack and the beanstalk," the finding of a strange and beautiful country somewhere up in the region of the clouds, no longer seems incongruous. Yesterday we were toiling over a burning soil, where nothing grows save the ashy-colored sage, the prickly pear, and a few cedars that writhe and contort their stunted limbs under a scorching sun. To-day we are among forests of rare beauty and luxuriance; the air is moist and cool, the grasses are green and rank, and hosts of flowers deck the turf like the hues of a Persian carpet. The forest opens in wide parks and winding avenues, which the fancy can easily people with fays and woodland nymphs (*High Plateaus*, 285).

Elsewhere, he describes the Aquarius as "like the threshold of another world" (*High Plateaus*, 284). As Wallace Stegner puts it in *Beyond the Hundredth Meridian*, "Strange words in a geological monograph" (173).

Dutton also elucidates the landscape's novel aesthetic dimension in this oft-quoted passage out of *The Tertiary History*:

The lover of nature, whose perceptions have been trained in the Alps, in Italy, Germany, or New England, in the Appalachians or Cordilleras, in Scotland or Colorado, would enter this strange region with a shock, and dwell here for a time with a sense of oppression, and perhaps with horror. Whatsoever things he had learned to regard as beautiful and noble he would seldom or never see, and whatsoever he might see would appear to him as anything but beautiful and noble. Whatsoever might be bold or striking would at first seem only grotesque. The colors would be the very ones he had learned to shun as tawdry and bizarre. The tones and shades, modest and tender, subdued yet rich, in which his fancy had always taken special delight, would be the ones which are conspicuously absent. But time would bring a gradual change. Some day he would suddenly become conscious that outlines which at first seemed harsh and trivial have grace and meaning; that forms which seemed grotesque are full of dignity; that magnitudes which had added enormity to coarseness have become replete with strength, and even majesty; that color which had been esteemed unrefined, immodest, glaring, are as expressive, tender, changeful and capacious of effects as any others. Great innovations, whether in art or literature, in science or in nature, seldom take the world by storm (141).

The romantic vision had always traveled with the frontier and it was inherent in the wilderness beyond it, and here was one of the last and most obdurate remnants of that wilderness and the whole of the romantic ideal had been shoved up against it and found wanting—in fact, completely inadequate. Here was a mask of barrenness, of the "bizarre," behind which lay a new and distinct modality of sublimity. The Colorado Plateau was and is too large and too diverse, too new and strange to simply play a supporting role as a borderland or a desert wasteland in the western saga. At some point it had to be confronted on its own terms.

Dutton never tried to exactly formulate the new western aesthetic, the "great innovation in modern ideas of scenery, and in our conception of the grandeur, beauty and power of nature," (*Tertiary History*, 140), the paradigm a traveler might use to catch at some corner of the plateau country, but I think he at least pointed the way. He draws attention, for example, to the vivid colors of the plateau; a landscape which is not muted into the "modest and tender" tints of the romantic's palette but which rather bleeds into "belts of fierce staring red, yellow and toned white, which are intensified rather than alleviated by the alternating belts of dark iron gray" (*High Plateaus*, 8). And the impact of these colors is heightened by this tabescence of the landscape; they're the bright colors of fall, of death, the sharp hues of dying leaves. On a geologic scale, the Plateau is rapidly expiring, being worn down to sea level by intense erosion. From the Wasatch Plateau, the land below and beyond is "a picture of desolation and decay; of a land dead and rotten, with dissolution apparent all over its face" (*High Plateaus*, 19). And the agent of this decay? "The lessons which may be learned from this region are many, but the grandest lesson which it teaches is EROSION. It is one which is taught, indeed, by every land on earth, but nowhere so clearly as here" (*High Plateaus*, 14).

I'd like to take Dutton's argument a step further. At every level this is place where aspects of the earth have been subtracted out. It is a negative earth. Mountains used to stand where the Grand Canyon is now entrenched, and the High Plateaus, with their black lava caps, are all that remains of a level ashplain. Powell recognized that circles of erosion, of nothingness, were radiating outward from singularities like massive sinkholes, and Dutton observed them from the south end of the Aquarius Plateau:

> As we study the panorama before us, the realization of the magnitude of this process gradually takes form and conviction in the mind. The strata which are cut off successively upon the slopes formerly reached out indefinitely and covered the entire country to the remotest boundary of vision. Their fading remnants are still discernible, forming buttes and mesas scattered over the vast expanse (*High Plateaus*, 292).

These strata record dozens of regimes: an enormous sand desert, perhaps the largest in the world's history, and inland seas, lakes, sloughs and lush gardens, now long gone and their remains buried and then unearthed again and carried off.

Any argument against calling this landscape dead or dying or against characterizing it by absence might be supported with examples of the diversity and adaptability of the native fauna such as the bighorn sheep, which can go five days without water; the kangaroo rats, which can metabolize their own water; the desert tortoise, which can survive blood-salt concentrations up to twenty percent (Sowell, 86-100); the xeric, deep-rooted juniper and pinyon; the saltbrush, which can survive in poison soil; and even the soil itself, the microbiotic crust, a symbiotic community of algae and fungi and lichens. But the physiological mechanisms these organisms developed, the extreme measures they have to employ to survive, only prove how lacking the environment is in any of the resources necessary for life. The desert fox, the raven, the tadpoles that inhabit water pockets in the rock—these are all opportunists which have found a temporary refuge in the merest niche. Not much lives comfortably here. Consider the bristlecone pine with its crippled back and its roots dug in the stone, hundreds or thousands of years old but only partly alive; it's the embodiment of writhing agony.

Loss and death: these were the central paradigms of Dutton and Powell's generation, which had buried over six hundred thousand of its young soldiers. In southern Utah and the Four Corners region, there were more inhabitants in the last millenium than are there today, and archaeologists can still only hazard educated guesses as to the reasons they left. In every aspect, every nuance, in terms of geology, population, and aesthetic effect, and especially in terms of the availability of water, this was and is a land of vast, tangible, haunting absence.

The Silent City

After meeting Pollock, I decide it's time to get my money's worth, go beneath the rim. I hike a ways down Under-the-Rim Trail, descend into Wall Street and the Queen's Garden, down switchbacks, through low portals, into a slot of orange earth where the stone shines with a rutilant light and sciophilous red pines grow to slivers of sky.

I pass through tunnels and doorways, through clumps of fins and hoodoo gullies, hoodoo chambers and amphitheaters, hoodoo buttes, passes, narrows. I discover trabeated arches just around a corner from the main trail. I see knife blades and knuckles of folded phalanxes, short spires like a line of school children, broken-backed, dying demoiselles.

I pass beneath arched crestlines, spinous processes, necks of ribs, long flexor tendons, fasciculi, punctured synovial sheaths, dead myoid tissue separating from the bone.

I run my hand over the Claron walls, which are pulpy and corticiform, gravely like conglomerate and smooth as plaster and shriveled up like fried fat, and I expect some of it to crumble but it's strongly cemented so even when I pry at it, it won't break loose.

Everywhere the knobby white cap collapses there's a void and everywhere it holds a hoodoo or a spiny reptile grows beneath it. When that caprock tilts from its perch, the spell is broken and the creature rapidly rots into the earth, but the white block itself is like a hydra's tooth and it will grow a new animal downslope and if it shatters when it falls, a dozen creatures will rise up beneath it.

On top of Wall Street, the heat from the rapid decay burns the rock incandescent and melts away the border between the earth and the sky.

In the Silent City, every time the cap falls and a hoodoo withers away, a new avenue is opened up. I spend an afternoon in the City, marching up the quiet boulevards, exploring the side-streets, taking connecting alleyways, when they present themselves, to another part of town, but it's hard work because the streets are graded steep and the pavement is popcorn prill which probably acts like ball-bearings in conveying fallen debris towards

Portal and dead pine,
Bryce Canyon

the head of the Paria, and it would dispatch me just as easily if I lost my balance.

In the evening, I'm back on the rim, above the Silent City, where visitors are setting up lawn chairs on the edge to watch the sunset, and it promises to be spectacular because of the particulate matter in the air, the ash flakes settling like snow from the controlled burn in the Black Mountains to the north. When the red ball sheers the hoodoos they glare a weird, diaphanous pink, a color which could only exist on the earth once in its history, which fades rapidly, so I turn from the dull light and catch the second act, which is the cloud from the Black Mountains boiling up in massive black wracks of soot far above us and everything on earth, like an anvil cloud punching through the stratosphere.

The Black Mountains

I'm on the west bench of John's Valley watching dust sweep up from the plain above the Emery Valley, into translucent vortices which tilt eastward and unravel in the foothills of the Black Mountains. The process occurs at a regular pace; a column coalesces and unwinds every five minutes.

I ride up the south fork of Cottonwood Creek, into the dead landscape where the Forest Service held those controlled burns earlier this summer, when there was no moisture and the aspen leaves had the texture and brittleness of yellowed newsprint. A sign tells me:

WARNING
DUE TO THE 2002 FIRES, ALL AREAS BEHIND THIS SIGN ARE
SUBJECT TO THE FOLLOWING HAZARDS:

EXTREME FLOODING
FALLING ROCKS
DEBRIS FLOWS AND EROSION HAZARDS
FALLING TREES

BE RESPONSIBLE

The sky is overcast. It looks as if it could rain any minute.

I continue along the dry creek bed, past scorched aspen and ponderosa, rabbitbrush, bur sage and shadscale. The crumbly tuff is ash gray and brown or a mineral black, and some of the loose stone beneath the hills has been knapped open by the extreme heat. The ground is mottled brown and gray and soot black in places, and there are green spurts of sage growing back in spots.

At the top of the canyon, where the road runs up against the volcanic block of Adams Head and strikes east, I park the Heap and hike to that outcropping of lava, through a ghost forest—black, alligatored stalks with a vitreous

or metallic or iridescent sheen that flakes into carbon when I touch it—bare brown steeps, isolated, untouched stands of aspen and patches where the fire jumped and the trees and undergrowth have been incinerated. Tree stumps are heat-cracked there and some boles have been burnt through and are leaning on their neighbors or resting on the black forest floor.

From the brow of Adam's Head I overlook a wide, palmate basin draining to the southeast, into John's Valley. The scarpline visible from Bryce, it turns out, is just a façade, except to the west, where a headwall of buttes and pinnacles and solid crests of

Skull at the controlled
burn in the "Blacks"

The Black Mountains

old ash remain. On the west edge of my redoubt, the terrain falls into a draw where salt-white volcanic rock juts into hoodoos.

A jet cuts a negative contrail through the floor of thick clouds.

I ride down the canyon in the evening, set up camp in a living ponderosa forest below the piedmont of the Black Mountains, sleep on a thick mat of pine needles which insulates me from the forest's cold floor, and the next day I drive up the east fork of Hunt Creek, into the middle of the amphitheater, behind Casto Butte and Flat Top Butte.

Hunters come here, but that's about it. The Utah Wilderness Coalition's *Wilderness at the Edge* says nothing about these mountains and Dave Foreman's *Big Outside*, which catalogues all the land in the United States which Earth First! considers wilderness gives it less than a half-page of consideration (258). Dutton describes them as "cliffs of conglomerate fringed with buttes" (*High Plateaus*, 238), but he doesn't include them in his "Great Stairway," which we now call the "Grand Staircase," possibly because he couldn't see them from the vantage point where he conceived of the stairway, or possibly because their origins are volcanic, not sedimentary like the rest of the steps. They're not even named on my 30 x 60 minute topographic map. Yet to me, the "Blacks," as they're called locally, the brooding bulwark above the Pink Cliffs, the death's head, the "Black Cliffs," visible from most of the Paunsaugunt Plateau, are the obvious last tier of the Grand Staircase.

Ghost forest, Black Mountains

I park the Heap on top of a smooth cross-spur—an interstice of hidden hard rock with a thin soil skin, with the land sloughed away on all sides but the south—and hike up the flank of Flat Top Butte, through burnt cactus and decorticated chaparral with its wood the color of raw flesh, choosing my own line because there's no trail.

Above, the clouds are veined and curled up like old leaves.

From below, the ridge adjoining Flat Top looks like the edge of a wide butte, but that lie is put to rest when I reach its crest—only a few feet wide. On the far side, I overlook the Paunsaugunt Plateau, the galled white face of Flake Swale, the Flake Mountains, which are hills really, Mud Spring and Johnson Bench, Red Canyon, Emery Valley, Bryce Canyon Airport, Coyote Hollow, the Pine Hills, the intersection of Highways 12, 22 and 63, the rise where the East Fork of the Sevier River is born, and past that, the drop onto Skutumpah Terrace and the edge of the White Cliffs.

I climb out on a finger of lava four feet wide, the conticent earth curving away beneath me, and catch the whole dome of the sky in the periphery of my vision.

Far below me, there are lineaments, cracks in the earth's foundations, over one and a half billion years old, and thirty miles down there's an engine of crustal delamination or magmatic underplating or subducted seafloor rifting which processes the landforms above it into oblivion. The Colorado Plateau was at or near sea level during the Cretaceous, 144 million years ago and since then it has been rotated clockwise a few degrees with respect to the rest of the continent, compressed by about a percent of its width and lifted as much as three miles, most of the uplift occurring in the last five million years, the last one-tenth of one percent of the earth's history (Proussevitch, 2002).

In places, over two miles have been scraped off the top of the plateau. That vanished world is an unseen monument to the weight of absence. There are other parts of the planet where more has been taken, but nothing—loss, non-existence, the negative world—have their strongest influence on this expanse of the existential world.

Before me is a great, upside-down tableland of non being, comprised of inverse nothing steppes, conical depressions, gulches cast from divides, wide, flat, dendritic valleys and steep coteaus where the rivers run, all culminating in the great inverse mountain chain of the Grand Canyon. The past forms a template for the visible landscape and the border between the two worlds is at my feet.

The Great Western Trail

There's a blank street sign in Widstoe at the intersection of the road to Escalante and Highway 22 and there's no intersection where the last faded stop sign stands. My old map of Widstoe shows a city park, a few hotels, a post office, some stores, a couple mills, an icehouse, a ranger station and dozens of homes, and they're all gone, and the square blocks twenty rods long and streets five rods wide are all overgrown with sage. There are depressions where buildings stood and piles of lumber where those not torn down or burned during the town's evacuation finally succumbed to the snow pack, and there's rusted junk on the town's north slope and a car flipped on its metal shell roof with the linkages and wheels all frozen in place.

There are still a few standing structures. The schoolhouse/meeting hall is still here, with its bell tower and its splintered board floor, but it looks as if it won't survive many more winters. There's an adobe house in the town center plastered with "keep out" signs and riddled with bullet holes, and there are slouched shacks and barns here and there, but that's about it. In some cases, the walls of houses have buckled out and the roofs have fallen intact, so it appears the earth itself has swallowed the buildings up.

Somewhere around here is the original forty acres that Julia Adair deeded as the nucleus of the new town back in 1910. Somewhere nearby are the remains of Isaac Riddle's ranch, the first settlement in John's Valley, a stopover for pioneers on their way to Hole-in-the-Rock in 1879.

Here, too, is the story of one farming town, originally named "Houston," after James Houston, president of the LDS Church's Panguitch Stake, then Winder, after John Winder, first counselor of the First Presidency, and finally, in 1917, Widstoe, in honor of the prolific Apostle John A. Widstoe, Harvard graduate, director of the Utah Experimental Station, director of the Department of Agriculture at Brigham Young University, president of Utah State Agricultural College, chairman of the Food Production Committee of Salt Lake City during the Great War, president of the Utah State Historical Society, director of the Genealogical Society, president, in 1917, of the University of Utah and most importantly for the people of the town of Widstoe, world-renowned expert and author of several books on irrigation and dry farming.

Dry farming was Widstoe's life-blood and John Widstoe became the Utah farmer's patron saint. That shudder of horror, bewilderment and pessimism that cracked the foundations of progressive thought after the Great War and paralyzed lesser men with their own doubts never touched him. His books are fonts of willpower, directed energy. Second to the Book of Mormon, complementary to it, his gospel was the reclamation of the arid regions of the world. As he puts it:

> The work of doing this (making the desert bloom) is of true pioneer character, comparable with that done by the great explorers and discoverers of earlier days. Those who engage in the work find, as part of their reward, the joy that comes to every person engaged in the adventure of possessing new places by right of conquest. . . . It is well that we should satisfy to the full this exploring, conquering pioneering spirit of the race (*Success on Irrigation Projects*, 136).

Furthermore,

> The destiny of man is to possess the whole earth; and the destiny of the earth is to be subject to man. There can be no full conquest of the earth, and no real satisfaction to humanity, if large portions of the earth remain beyond his highest control. . . . The destiny of the arid and semi-arid regions is undoubted. They will be brought to serve man by irrigation, dry-farming and wise grazing; and the civilization thus created will take the treasures from the hills and the power from the high streams, and all the world will be helped by the conquest (*Success*, 138).

The early farmers of Widstoe put his techniques to use at seventy-two hundred feet, where the growing season was short and the winter "zero-weather" cold, and they were successful, and their success drew in more pioneer families: the Frandsens and their five children from Elsinore in 1912, the Gouldings and the Handleys that same year, the Barneys and their seven children in 1914, the Gleaves and their six children from near Antimony in 1917 and the Hermansens, Popes, Reynolds, Sandbergs, Southams, Steeds, Zabriskies and dozens of others. Widstoe's population grew to about eleven hundred, and vivid fields of alfalfa, barley, corn, rye, potatoes, oats, wheat and high-altitude lettuce covered all of John's Valley, everything you can see from the town site to the Black Mountains and the Sevier Plateau.

They turned the streams from the Aquarius Plateau to provide irrigation but the dry fields produced almost as well. They tore into the earth with horse-drawn sulky plows, cultivators and harrows, creaky-wheeled racks with concave disks, rods, springs and falcate blades, and reaped the crops with paddle-wheeled harvesters drawn by horses or monstrous steam tractors.

Lumber mills sprung up all around the valley, at Flake Bottoms, Pine Lake, South Creek and Sweetwater Canyon, not far from the town site. A developer from the Imperial Valley in California, William Franklin Holt, bought up fields and property in town and built a creamery and a summer home at Osiris in nearby Black Canyon.

Records were set for dryland oat and barley production (Nielsen, 292). When the granaries overflowed, houses were filled with grain and their occupants slept, "close to the rafters" (Nielsen, 119, 138, 212). In 1924, the grain production of John's Valley exceeded that of the rest of Garfield County, Piute County and Kane County combined (Nielson, 70). There were rumors of the county seat being moved from Panguitch to Widstoe. "It looked," said Mabel Woodard Nielsen, "as though all that was needed to be done was scratch the soil and plant" (Nielsen, 292).

That same year, 1924, at the Garfield Stake Quarterly Conference, Elder Melvin J. Ballard told the congregation, "It will remain thus so long as you stay out of debt, and keep the commandments of God; but, if you fail to keep His commandments, it will be cursed, and will be taken away from you" (Nielsen, 70).

I've never been to Widstoe on a sunny day, and this day is no exception. The clouds are bunched up and immobile and the valley is dead, gray and windless. I drive into downtown Widstoe, park the Heap, walk past piles of boards which used to be houses, knock on the doors of trailers owned by the new residents of Widstoe, who bought their lots off the state, but almost nobody is home in the middle of the afternoon. The largest house trailer is parked on a hill east of town, occupied by Bruce Osojnak and his girlfriend Valerie, in their forties, and their wily cat Little Red, age unknown, who welcome me with a glass of water, Widstoe's most precious commodity.

"There's nothing like water in the desert," says Valerie.

"That ice is made here, I want you to know," says Bruce, "You're lucky to get it."

Bruce relates how he acquired the property, sight unseen, by raising his hand at an auction.

"Did you know where Widstoe was?" I ask him.

"I knew where Bryce was. They said it was thirteen miles away."

It's a good spot with a commanding view. Bruce sweeps his hand across the horizon.

"You can look to the east, look to the west, to the north, there's twenty miles there, fifteen there, a minimum of ten there."

Bruce and Valerie are planning to build a house and they show me the staked plot of land where it will be planted. Their trailer is trimmed with Christmas lights and they've strung ornaments on pine trees. They tell me about the black frosts, the round winds, and they show me the fenced garden where they're trying to grow lettuce, tomatoes, grapes, whatever will survive. Just outside the fence, Valerie, an artist, has spread out a few tiles imbedded with porcelain shards she's picked up from the townsite.

I drive up the draw to the junkyard behind the town. I find a dump-truck fender from the thirties, rusted cans, pieces of china, a chimney flue, a soggy cardboard model rocket. I park the Heap, walk up the hill to the south of town and then down to the fields. There are crumpled buildings here and purple glass slivers, catchwaters and a ditch filled with soil, an arroyo and a dry reservoir where sunflowers turn to the dim sun, and there are black pipes which now carry dirt to a bumper crop of freakishly high rabbitbrush and sage.

Said John A. Widstoe in his seminal work *Dry Farming*: "Crop failures due to untimely frosts, blizzards, cyclones, tornadoes, or hail may perhaps be charged to Providence, but the dry-farmer must accept the responsibility for any crop injury resulting from drouth. A fairly accurate knowledge of the climatic conditions of the district, a good understanding of the principles of agriculture without irrigation under a low rainfall, and a vigorous application of these principles as adapted to the local climatic conditions will make dry-farming failures a rarity" (49).

Said Major Powell in *Lands of the Arid Region*: "The limit of successful agriculture without irrigation has been set at 20 inches, that the extent of the Arid Region should by no means be exaggerated; but at 20 inches agriculture will not be uniformly successful from season to season. Many droughts will occur; many seasons in long series will be fruitless; and it may be doubted whether, on the whole, agriculture will prove remunerative" (3).

Widstoe's graveyard is about a mile south of the townsite. The Gleaves, Adairs, Steeds, Campbells and Twitchells are the predominate residents; their headstones supply dates but no stories. Here's the grave of Lionel R. Lay, who fell forward off a wagon and was trampled by his horses in 1923. Here lies William Twitchell, whose son Augustus was picked up by a sand auger, carried over a field and deposited back on earth with only a few scratches. Here, too, among many other infants and children, is Elmer Stoddard, who spent about an hour on earth back in 1914, and Chlorine Campbell, who lived a little over three months in 1928. Nearby are Zelma Mangum and Melton Stoddard, who died of influenza in 1922, and the young Milton Desmond, dragged to his death by a spooked horse (Nielsen, 106).

There are also more recent graves: the Goulding Twins, Robert Dace and Deliverance, who died at birth in 1998, and Gerald Eugene Allen, born in 1920 and buried in 2000. After the ten-year dry cycle which crippled Widstoe, which dried up the springs and stopped the creeks, which checked the desiccated soil and turned the sky into a cobalt shield; and the Great Depression, which drove a stake through Widstoe's heart; after the Farm Security Administration convinced the few debt-ridden hangers-on in 1936 that if they didn't sell their property back into the public domain and relocate, their children would have no school to attend; after Dorothea Lange photographed Widstoe as it died that same year; after prospectors staked out the whole valley during the uranium boom in the fifties and abandoned it again, there are still Gleaves, Steeds, Twitchells and many others scattered over the west who still think of Widstoe as home. The town may be mostly gone but the graveyard lives on.

Up the road from the cemetery, there are a few shacks which have been converted to summer homes, part of the recent resurgence which threatens to send Widstoe's population back into the teens. Beyond them, there's a patchwork of old roads to fallow fields with the scattered wreckage of farming implements partially hidden in

Boots and a blank street sign, Widstoe

rabbitbrush, and cabins rotting in valley flats by another deep arroyo which is sapping the bench where the road runs. The interior of one of the cabins has been wallpapered with old newspapers, and as the sun sets I read the news, classifieds, and other ads from the *Ogden Standard Examiner* and the *Salt Lake Tribune*, circa 1914:

Furnished Apartment, $16.00/month, no children.

RELATIONS AT THE BREAKING POINT – El Paso Texas, June 29th – Announcement from Torreon that a conference would be held between General Villa and General Carahza was received here as partly explaining Villa's return with his army to Torreon and the abandonment of the campaign to the south . . .
For Rent – House, Unfurnished. 7 room brick, modern, $25/month.

LEPER TO BE LICENSED AS WIRELESS OPERATOR

$10,000 FOR AN IDEA WHICH YOU MUST TELL IN 100 WORDS OR LESS. THERE WILL BE NO SECOND PRIZE.

Selecting a Garment within Set Price – We live in a country of extremes, or as Thackery put it: It is a country where blizzards of cold are followed by blizzards of heat.

The purple light fades and by flashlight, I read names inscribed by pocketknife around the empty doorframe: Lloyd Alvey, Sept. 9, 1940, Vernon Roe Griffin, Sept. 29, 1940, Carl Trippett, Feb. 1, 1920.

I shine the light at the roof, the sagging rafters and a portion of the old ceiling with some dusty, matted black thing partially fallen through. Bones extend from it.

The clouds block the moonlight and night unfolds in a dehiscence of shadows. I drive slowly up the road, contemplating the death of settlements, where the spirit of an entire town might go. The Heap's headlights sweep across a house frame bent into the stillness on the roadside, the walls and roof gone, only the skeleton remaining. I stop the Heap and opposite the frame, next to me, is a new state marker for the Great Western Trail, a collection of roads, old trails and new trails strung together over three-thousand miles from Canada to Mexico. But the Great Western Trail could also be the road the Fremont, Anasazi and Paiute took when they left this territory. The cowboys have been plying this road in greater numbers recently, and over a half-century ago, an entire town packed up and headed down it.

Travelers

In August of 1866, a detachment of the Utah Territorial Militia, eighteen men under Second Lieutenant Joseph Fish, came up along the Indian trail through Red Canyon, intending to hook up with a larger force under the command of Captain James Andrus, who was camped in the Paria Valley, for a reconnaissance of the inner basins of the High Plateaus, which the Indians were using as staging points for their raids on Mormon settlements. Of this canyon, they relayed only that the route through it was "practicable in summer for wagons" (Crampton, 151).

In October, 1879, a wagon train of pioneers from Cedar City, Parowan and Paragonah followed Jens Nielson up Red Canyon on a "well established" wagon road (Miller, 45) bound for the Riddle Ranch where Widstoe later stood and died, then Escalante and then the rocky wasteland south of Escalante, which they hoped to traverse in six weeks, to their new home on the San Juan River.

Butch Cassidy once shook off a posse in the draw up Red Canyon now named after him.

One more recent band of travelers did not arrive on the Paunsaugunt Plateau through Red Canyon or any of the other conventional routes, for that matter. On October 24, 1947, United Airline Flight 608, a DC-6 with fifty-three people on board, bound for Chicago from Los Angeles, crashed just short of Bryce Canyon's runway, killing all on board. A heater coil had ignited fumes from a fuel tank transfer line and the plane had became a ball of flame. Bob Ott was at home in Tropic and he saw the plane come in from the southeast on fire. He followed the debris up to the airport in his Model A Ford and he knows it didn't nosedive because there was a great deal of wreckage beyond the main crash site. Maurice Cope, a ranger at Bryce Canyon, built a fence around the site. "Someone stood guard with a gun in hand night and day," he later wrote (Cope, 11). There were no large fragments of wreckage and "the bodies also were left in small pieces," which were collected and taken to the airport, where the authorities "placed a few pieces in each coffin, sealed it up tight to prevent (it) being opened and called it a day. Then they gave it a name" (12).

In October of 1934, a twenty-year old block-print artist/cook/snake-killer/wanderer/woodcutter/hitchhiker/philosopher/hobo/cliff-climber/cowboy/haycutter/shepherd named Everett Ruess rode into Bryce Canyon on the back of his mule, leading another. He was a seasoned explorer by then, having begun his wanderings when he was sixteen, having traversed much of California and the wild southwest by burro and horse, rail, car and foot. By the time Everett rode in, he'd already made friends with Edward Weston, Ansel Adams, Maynard Dixon and Dixon's wife Dorothea Lange.

He'd hitchhiked to Big Sur by then and he'd climbed and hiked Yosemite and the Sierras, he'd ridden through Monument Valley and stood by the base of the angular volcanic plug ruin of Agathla Peak. He had danced with Hopi Indians at Mishongonovi and climbed to the cliff dwellings at Canyon de Chelly and walked to the awful edge of the Grand Canyon and he had hiked up the narrows of Zion and down the narrows in Oak Creek, south of Flagstaff, Arizona.

During these travels, Ruess read Sinclair and Shaw, Emerson, Poe, Whitman, Mann, Cervantes, Ibsen, Shakespeare, Shelley, Wilde, Yeats, Nietzsche, Chekhov and Jules Verne, and his head was full of great and noble thoughts and musings and questions to which nobody ever has or ever will have the answers and his heart was filled with love and joy, anger, passion, pain, melancholy, bliss, wonder, the normal emotions of a young idealist until he starts worrying about house payments or next month's rent and every other concern "that disgusting god, money" (Rusho, 53) brings with it.

Everett kept a journal of his travels and he'd written a few dozen letters to his parents and his brother Waldo back in Los Angeles and a few of his friends before coming here. We know from his journal and letters that in July of 1932 his horse Nuflo flopped into Mancos Creek near Mesa Verde and "floundered about" until Everett jumped in and led him to safety, and then Everett had to drag his water-logged pack to shore (Rusho, 97) and we know his dog Curly deserted him forever about then and that same month, in Canyon Del Muerto, his burro Jonathan "ran sidewise like an athlete putting the shot, but his legs buckled under, and he fell to his side in a clump of cactus" and died (94).

We know something about his thoughts, his prejudices and fears, because he put them in writing. From a letter to his family in July of 1932: "The beauty of the wet desert was overpowering. I was not happy for there was no one with whom I could share it, but I thought, how much better than to be in a schoolroom with rain on the windows, or at home in my dreary bedroom. My tragedy is that I don't fit in with any class of people" (Rusho, 88).

From a letter to his father in February of 1934: "the world is hell-bent for destruction, writhing from one snare into another, becoming more and more hopelessly involved in vicious, unbreakable circles, and gaining momentum on the wretched road to Ruin" (150).

From a July, 1932 entry Everett writes this in his journal: "God, how the wild calls to me. There can be no other life for me but that of the lone wilderness wanderer. . . . The wild has an irresistible fascination for me. After all, the lone trail is best" (307).

From other entries that same month he says, " [I] remembered how I raised my cocoa to my lips and drank to the long, long dead whose bones are there above me, (in the dwellings)" (Rusho, 308), "I think I have seen too much and know too much—so much that it has put me in a dream from which I cannot waken and be like other people" (314).

Back by June of 1934, Ruess was counting butterflies on the face of Navajo Mountain, the sandstone dome opposite the southern point of the Straight Cliffs. He walked and rode down into the mazerock beneath that sleeping giant, into "as rough and impenetrable a territory as I have ever seen," where "thousands of domes and towers of sandstone lift their rounded pink tops from blue and purple shadows" (Rusho,178) and he came through the portal of Rainbow Bridge and rode south to Kayenta and then east to Tsegi Canyon, where he joined up with an archaeological expedition and scaled cliffs with them to the ruins in the alcoves as if he himself was a reckless descendent of the Anasazi. When the fieldwork was done and the team broke up, he wandered off onto the Hopi Reservation and participated in their Antelope Dance, and then he rode up to the Grand Canyon and over to Flagstaff and paid a visit to a friend he'd made on the expedition, wore out his welcome in a week and rode out to nearby Oak Creek Canyon, then returned to the Grand Canyon and then headed north to Bryce.

Ruess didn't say much about his stay at Bryce. He wrote to his father and mother that he enjoyed riding through the "grotesque and colorful formations" (Rusho,192) and that he was staying with a park ranger in Tropic. Everett was headed east, toward Escalante, but he'd already bypassed the main route. Never the easy road for Everett Ruess.

Night Road

The old alignment of the road coming down from the Paunsagunt Plateau was so steep that cars had to go up it in reverse because "the gas pump wouldn't siphon into the motor" when they went straight at it (Haymond, "Ott," 25). Now it curves down an easy eight percent grade south into Tropic Valley over what the locals call "the Dump," right through the Paunsagunt Fault, over the Tropic Ditch which brought the town of Tropic to life and into the town itself, which is surrounded by lifeless gray shale hills.

"Why would anyone try to grow anything here?" you might ask, and I don't have an answer, but the farmers and ranchers who live here, the Ahlstroms and Pollocks, Otts, Shakespeares and Mangums and many others, have at least been breaking even since the ditch came through over one-hundred years ago.

Perhaps Tropic made it by slumbering. It hibernates through the winter, like all the towns along Highway 12, and in the summer it just creeps along. Come through on Sunday and the general store and the Hungry Coyote Restaurant are closed and even the blinds on the inns and motels are drawn.

Near Cannonville

Wallace Ott lives here, and so does Gayle Pollock. Most of the government employees attached to Bryce Canyon, in fact, make their home here. Maurice Cope, the head ranger at Bryce, put Everett Ruess up for a while at his house in Tropic. Cope, who'd grown up herding sheep, was an interesting character himself, a friend of Butch Cassidy and, later, a guide for the famous geologist Herbert Gregory. He must have been haunted all his life by visions of dead sheep: three hundred head of fellow rancher William LeFevre's sheep "piled into (a) wash" and smothered by their own weight, three hundred of the herd he'd been watching on the East Fork of the Sevier killed by a winter storm, twenty-five hundred head he'd sold to a man from Ash Fork, Arizona, that all went over a five-hundred-foot cliff near Lee's Ferry, one-hundred and fifteen lambs killed by a cold spell one February, forty head lost when they got "down into the mud" in the winter, untold numbers killed off by predators or cold or disease (Cope, 3, 5-6, 8).

Four miles down the road is Cannonville, "the metropolis of Bryce Valley" (Haymond, "Pollock," 1), which is just as sleepy as Tropic, except for the campground on the edge of town and the gas station where you can fill up before you make the trip down through the Cockscomb or Skutumpah Road and the new Grand Staircase-Escalante National Monument visitor's center where green government pickups and the tourists congregate, and just south of this hamlet are the skeletons of ghost towns, among them Georgetown. Long ago, a giant of a man, a local legend named Elijah M. Moore, settled for a while in Georgetown. He had grown up with the James brothers, Jesse and Frank, and had exchanged shots with a sheriff and a posse and fought Comanches in Texas and helped bury Billy the Kid and he knew Butch Cassidy and his gang personally (Ott, 1-5).

Also long ago, in Cannonville itself, there resided a man by the name of John Henry Davis, a friend of the famous Mormon scout Jacob Hamblin and a distant ancestor of Gayle Pollock. He stayed with the Paiute tribe southeast of Bryce Canyon on occasion when he was younger and sang their songs and learned their language and employed them later when he was superintendent of the Kanarra Cattle Company, when he had two wives and fifteen children. A great friend of his, known simply as "Jim Indian," called for Davis on his deathbed and Davis came to him, and as they were reflecting on their lives, Davis couldn't resist asking him why he had never learned to speak English, and Jim answered that, "[Davis] was the only white man he ever wished to talk with, and that Davis knew how to speak Paiute" (Davis, chap. 8).

At night the ghosts of Indians, the Paiutes who used to live here and the Navajos who came up through the Paria Gulch to trade, and the older ghosts, ancestors of the Pueblo Indians and other strange tribes with no known descendents, walk the Great Western Trail, and if you come through after dark, their white-point pupils will follow you long after you've left this place.

Near Cannonville, you pass right over the Paria. South of here this sluggish puddle of a river starts to dig into the fuscous red earth, and then it entrenches itself and gnaws through rock and drills right for the center of the world. But that's south. Further along Highway 12 you pass through a roadcut portal in the Entrada Sandstone, which was left behind by the Sundance Sea a million and a half centuries ago and which behaves more like shale here than the red, eolian, arch-forming sandstone most people associate with it, and you ride out to Henrieville.

Like Cannonville, Henrieville was settled by pioneers from long-dead Clifton, but there's a lot less to it, no services, nothing to buy, just farmhouses and ranches and ranchers making it on poor soil and thin margins, same as always. Past that hamlet, on a road that wasn't put in until 1957 (Haymond, "Roundy," 1) there's coal rakes in the hills, which were mined by Mormon settlers, and there's plains of sage and scrub brush and thistle, and tumbleweeds are bunched up against the fences, and Powell Point bears down on you from the north, and a big white slab of Straight Cliffs Sandstone confronts you around a corner. Then the road climbs up a twelve percent incline, past the cutoff meanders of old road alignments, into the

Portal through Entrada Sandstone, Cannonville

Blues, the heaps and clumps of blue and purple and yellow hills, to the Upper Valley and the turnoff to Canaan Peak.

That mountain on the edge of the Kaiparowits Plateau is really an event: a massive blockslide that must have tilted the strata in such a way that it became impervious to erosion and outlived the rest of the Canaan Peak Formation that had once surrounded and enclosed it.

The forest of the Upper Valley holds in the moisture and the air is always cooler. It's a wooded, grassy paradise by day, even in winter, and at night, it's cold and lonely. I've driven Highway 12 from the turnoff south of Panguitch all the way to Escalante at night without meeting any traffic. After dark, I've noticed yellow eyes on the roadside and the tails and flanks of wild animals slipping into the sagebrush, and I've tried to make out the edge of the Cretaceous cliffs, and I've swung the brights across faltering log cabins and broken fencelines. And I've tried to illuminate some amorphous and nameless entity ahead of me on the road, or just off it, or maybe down there in the Upper Valley Creek Wash with the half-buried car frames, but it moves through the night faster than I can shine a light at it.

Layers

Humans are the most vertical of animals, stick figures totally at odds with gravity, but they lay down to die like any other animal and their constructions eventually fall as well, and so finally succumb to the earth's classification system. At mile marker 52, I pull over and look through a fixed metal scope and see a building that was constructed high in a cliff wall about seven hundred years ago, which is still upright, hasn't yet been filed away into the record. It's a Fremont granary, and without the scope I would hardly be able to differentiate it from the rubble on the thin ledge where it stands.

The record doesn't show yet whether the Fremont migrated into the Four Corners region or evolved from the indigenous population, but it does illuminate specific aspects of their lifestyles. We know that they sewed their clothes from hides and fashioned durable moccasins from deer forelegs, that they lived in flimsy wikiups and later pithouses and ate everything that was edible: rice grass, pinyon nuts, berries and roots, fish, coyotes, rabbits, squirrels, deer, antelope, bighorn sheep, even bears, and that they fashioned awls and fishhooks and game pieces from bone and strung together necklaces of bones, beads and teeth.

We know that they wandered over much of the Great Basin and all of the Colorado Plateau at one time or another. They may not have thrived but they seemed to have established themselves well in several ecological niches of the Southwest. The record shows it: their shelters are everywhere, as are their spear points and arrowheads, and their portable, mouthless, molded clay fictiles with their broad heads and applique jewelry and eyes pinched against the desert sun. So too with the shards of their pottery, the ubiquitous corrugated pots and bowls, and the other wares they decorated with phosphenic designs, panels of dots and concentric circles, black serrations and spirals and checkerboard patterns, and also their rock art, the pictographs and petroglyphs, the horned, trapezoidal anthropomorphs etched and painted all over the rock walls of the West.

They were here to stay, the record seems to show, and then, the record says, they left.

And the translators of the archaeological text don't know why they left. Even highly accurate modern archaeological dating tools and techniques will only reveal dates: when a site was abandoned, when a wall fell, not why.

South of the Fremont and contemporaneous with them, lived the Anasazi. They appeared on the scene a little earlier than the birth of Christ, lived in pithouses, used atlatls and snares and nets to catch and kill their dinner and eventually traded their individual dwellings for jacal shelters and, later, houses and towns of stone masonry and transformed their underground chambers into ceremonial dwellings, kivas, and traded their atlatls for bows and baskets for pottery. They came to rely so heavily on the corn they farmed that their backs became stooped from tending their fields and from the loss of calcium, which corn leached out of their bones, and their

Fremont petroglyphs near Fence Canyon

teeth were worn down to nubs by the grit from the manos and metates they used to grind it.

Some Anasazi built enormous conglomerations of masonry dwellings called "Great Houses," the largest of which still stand in Chaco Canyon. They aligned the houses and roads at Chaco to the paths of the sun, the moon and the stars, and on the butte at the canyon's head, they etched a spiral in stone which is stabbed through its heart by a needle of light at the summer solstice and bracketed by two such rays at the winter solstice. Simple pottery decorations evolved and diversified into dense, repeated motifs; polygons interspersed with bold lines, interlocking hatchings, solid polygons, frets and stripes and banded, oblique lines and jagged, black electric charges arcing over polished, white-slipped bowls, jars and pitchers.

The Anasazi devoted over two million man-hours of work to their great houses (Stuart, 86). They cut over two hundred thousand trees and dragged them up to fifty miles to use as vigas and firewood (Schreiber, 83). At their height, the Anasazi had cultivated almost every square foot of arable land in the Four Corners region, and then they left everything behind.

After the abandonment of Chaco there was an influx of refugees to Mesa Verde and the Little Colorado River where the modern Katsina cult rose from the ashes of the puebloans' mysterious religion, and they began to favor cliffs and other defensive locations for their dwellings. Pueblos constructed in the open were built with their keyhole doorways facing inward, toward a central plaza. Less than a century after the burgeoning of population on what had been the outskirts of Chacoan civilization, however, these areas too were abandoned, and the Anasazi retreated again to Black Mesa and the Little Colorado and Rio Grande Basins, the modern homes of the Pueblo Indians.

Again we are left with absence, the complete absence of two well-established cultures from most of their former range, but they're among the latest in the line. People first settled in the Four Corners at least twelve thousand years ago and possibly much earlier. The climate was cooler then and the fir and spruce forests which now cling to the highlands were spread everywhere.

The Paleoindians had to contend with monsters when they arrived: condors with seventeen foot wingspans, the largest birds ever to take flight, the euonymous *Smilodon fatalis* or saber-toothed cats, mountain lions one and one-half times as large as those which occasionally prey on people today, as well as long-legged, carnivorous, dog-snouted giant short-faced bears, which could, on all fours, look a man straight in the eye.

The early Utahns used atlatls and spears tipped with long, fluted Clovis points to contend with their predators and to bring down the huge prey which roamed the Colorado Plateau: mammoths about two and one-half times as large as modern elephants and smaller mastodons, ground sloths big as compact cars, and horses, musk-ox, bison and camels. Their remains and their artifacts, their hide scrapers, meat choppers and bone knives, are all neatly filed away in layers of sediment in caves like Pendejo and Pintada and Sandia in New Mexico, and their images are etched into the hidden stone pages of the Southwest.

Most of the megafauna died off as the climate began to warm, and also about the same time humans arrived on the scene, and the synchronicity of these three events has given rise to an endless controversy over the cause of their disappearance. In the context of the record of absences, however, the disappearance of these creatures is just another such vanishing in a long series and one that I am partly thankful for because as much as I'd like to see a living saber-toothed cat or giant short-faced bear, I wouldn't necessarily want to meet one in the field.

The Paleoindians adapted to the megafauna extinction by developing shorter, longer-fluted Folsom spear points for smaller prey and widening their diet to include more plants, thus transitioning into what archaeologists call the Archaic phase.

The Archaic Indians left deer, elk, antelope and sheep figurines fashioned from single willow or cottonwood twigs split down their centers all over the Four Corners region and they painted and etched the walls with horned spirit figures, often limbless, with bodies like blocks or smoke wisps and eyes like buttons.

They too laid down to fill the record and their descendents experimented with domesticated corn brought up from Mexico around 1500 BC and eventually evolved into the Anasazi and the Fremont.

And why, again, did these two groups of people leave their homes? There was a severe drought in the late thirteenth century, but it couldn't account for the Anasazi abandoning *all* of their dwellings; the land could still have supported a sizeable population through the driest years (Van West, 214). The record of bones, however, shows widespread malnutrition during this period and some evidence of warfare.

Language might provide one clue. The modern Puebloans, though they share many of the same myths and rituals, don't all speak the same language. The Hopi speak a Numic dialect and the Zuni speak Zuni, which may be distantly related to the Penutian tongue of central California, but which is otherwise unique. The inhabitants of Acoma and some other Rio Grande villages speak Keresan and the rest of the Rio Grande people speak dialects of Tanoan. Similarly, the Anasazi weren't one people: based on pottery and building styles, archaeologists can divide them, broadly, into the Kayenta, the artisans who lived in crude jacal and masonry shelters in northeast Arizona and Canyon de Chelly and southern Utah, the Chacoans on the east side of the Chuska Mountains and the Mesa Verde or San Juan, who dwelled on mesa tops or niches of cliffs from Comb Ridge to the San Juan Mountains. That the Anasazi divided along fault lines of culture and language, that they fought against each other, tribe against tribe, as was the case with most North American Indians, that they were unable to practice agriculture because of the threat of their neighbors raiding them and destroying their crops before they could be harvested, that most of the southwest became a no-man's land and the Puebloans settled in areas outside the considerable range of their enemies as a result—these are all theories currently gaining favor in academic circles.

The Navajo who now surround the Hopi Reservation like an ocean around an island key were nowhere near the Pueblos at the time of the Anasazi's exodus, but the Numic speakers, the Utes and Paiutes, were definitely moving into the area around the thirteenth century, and some scholars place the blame for the Anasazi abandonment on them. If this was the case, if the Paiutes forced the people of the San Juan and Kayenta pueblos out of their villages, they committed the perfect crime, because they left no clues of such aggression behind (Ambler, Sutton, 39-53).

The same can't be said for certain about the conflict between the Paiutes and the Fremont. One theory holds that the Fremont were pushed northward, out of Utah and southern Idaho, Ute artifacts replacing theirs every step of the way, and were probably finally assimilated into, or more likely finished off by the Shoshone in the eighteenth century (Butler, 8).

If the Utes, Paiutes and other Numic speakers were culpable in the Fremont's destruction, they certainly paid the price for it later. In the mid-1800s the emigrating Mormon pioneers appropriated most of the springs, streams, rivers and good grazing land in Utah—in short—all the best hunting, fishing and farming locations. Then, as the Numic speakers starved, they were paid by the settlers for their land with diseases such as tuberculosis. As Gary Tom and Ronald Holt write in "The Paiute Tribe of Utah:"

> It took less than twenty-five years of contact with the Mormon settlers to reduce the Paiute population by 90 percent and turn them from being peaceful, independent farmers and foragers into destitute, landless people who survived by doing seasonal and part-time work for the white settlers. Some Paiute groups even ceased to exist. (123)

The inimical landscape of southern Utah and northern Arizona kept the primitive Shivwits, Uinkarets and Unkakaniguts branches of the Paiute tribe out of harm's way long enough for John Wesley Powell to catch a glimpse of them, and he described them as peaceful people "living in shelters made of boughs piled up in circles and covered with juniper bark supported by poles" (Powell, *Exploration*, 102-107). They lived on roasted seeds, nuts and roots, deer and antelope and great quantities of rabbits and still worshipped wolves and eagles and rattlesnakes, and they believed the sky was made of ice. In the late 1800s, ranchers began to covet even these southern tribes' marginal lands, and in 1891, cattleman Anthony Ivins, self-declared "Special Indian Agent," herded the Paiutes off the Arizona Strip to a barren patch of reservation land near St. George.

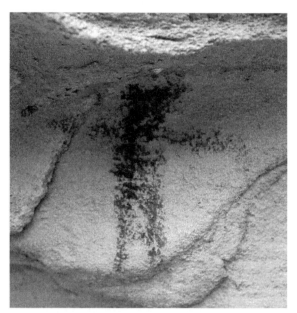

Pictograph, Alvey Wash

During the Black Hawk War, some Mormons made no distinction between the mounted Utes and Navajos and the Paiutes who mostly got by on foot. Black Hawk and his warriors raided the Mormon settlements and rode away before the pioneers could retaliate, but the Paiutes were not as mobile as their northern relatives. Some were killed just for being in the wrong place at the wrong time, and up in Circleville, a band of Piedes, a branch of the Southern Paiutes, was rounded up and held captive in the town meeting house where the men were shot down when they tried to escape and the women and children, with the exception of a few infants too young to talk, were taken upstairs one at a time to have their throats cut. About sixteen Piedes were killed that day (Winkler, 4).

The Southern Paiutes were also initially given the blame for the Mountain Meadows Massacre of the Fancher Party, a wagon train of 120 to 150 settlers bound for California in 1857, though later accounts and research lays the blame for the vast majority of the murders squarely at the Mormons' feet.

The federal government made sporadic attempts throughout the early twentieth century to move all the Paiutes onto reservations, mostly on remote, worthless land, or onto the reservations of their enemies, the Utes, but they resisted all of these efforts.

In 1954, Utah senator Arthur V. Watkins influenced the government to terminate federal recognition and all federal assistance to most of the Paiute tribes and several other tribes throughout the West, in effect "emancipating" them from government aid and "freeing" them from federal interference and allowing them to assimilate into Mormon culture. As Watkins, who later became chairman of the Indian Claims Commission, put it:

> It seems to me that the time has come for us to . . . help the Indians stand on their own two feet and become a white and delightsome people, as the Book of Mormon prophesied they would become. . . . The Gospel should be a great stimulus and I am longing and praying for the time when the Indians will accept it in overwhelming numbers. (Grattan-Aiello, 281)

The Paiutes, who weren't consulted much about their impending freedom and didn't understand all of its implications, were too poor to send a single representative to Washington to protest it, and sent telegrams instead. At a meeting in Fillmore, when one Paiute elder, Clifford Jakes, questioned whether Watkins knew the conditions Paiutes were currently living in, he was told by the senator, famously, to "sit down, and mind your own business and shut-up" (Holt, 75).

The federal government accidentally terminated the Cedar City band of Paiutes, which had never been formally recognized by the government and hence was believed to be part of the nearby Indian Peak band. It took the BIA eight years to catch this snafu and another five to inform the Cedar City band of their actual status (Holt, 126).

From termination in 1957 until the restoration of federal recognition in 1980, the Paiute were a destitute people mostly dependent on Mormon farm work, sales of their taxed landholdings and charity for subsistence. And then the federal government realized its mistake.

The Kaiparowits branch of the Paiutes used to hunt and farm here, but they've moved away, to Cedar City, Kanosh, Joseph, Richfield, and the reservations at St. George and Indian Peak. For the traveler of Highway 12, they're just another Indian tribe that's already been filed away.

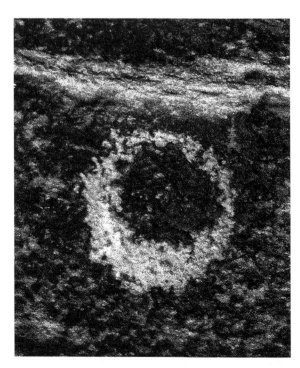

Petroglyph, Capitol Reef

chapter two

Photo opposite: Sandstone fin at entrance to Kodachrome Basin State Park

—The Western Spokes—

Skutumpah Road and
the Cockscomb

Tracks near Bull Valley Gorge

Signs and Symbols

I had a dream once where I was in a ghost town inhabited by specters from the West's past: Indians, pioneers, prospectors, cowboys, cavalrymen, even vaqueros, and they were all busy preparing for the same impending, unknown event, and a few ghost cowboys with long, wrinkled, dead faces, whose eyes I couldn't discern walked me to a building near the middle of town, near the center of the commotion, where militia detachments and bands of Indians and wagons were hurrying through at cross-directions, in clouds of dust, and inside this dirt-floored, gap-walled shack there was only a heavy old Spanish strong-box with worn, thick leather straps and tarnished silver buckles. Those ghosts waited at the door with their arms folded, watching, preternaturally still, as I approached the chest, and as I did, I somehow knew that building was the spiritual center of the West and inside that box was a mineral or a tome or some other artifact that was the cowboy West's very essence.

I woke up before I opened the box.

I spend a few hours in Torrey at the home of Ray Freeze and Carol Georgopoulos, linguists retired from the University of Utah, amateur hunters of

Indian art, listening to their theories on that art, which fit very closely with my own.

"You find the same motifs all over the world in prehistoric art," says Carol, who is confined to the couch by an ankle she'd twisted coming down a talus slope too fast, "It's a reflection of a universal cognitive structure. Human brains are the same all over the world. All cultures have art and music. But the idea of passing on art solely as a cultural expression is ridiculous. Rock art reveals a universal underlying structure."

"Our brains have a particular, inherent capacity for language," says Ray through his gray beard.

"I'll go one step further," I tell them. "I think our brains have a similar moral capacity. Nothing that can't be altered, so it's not deterministic—just an underlying framework, a capacity to acquire, like the capacity to acquire grammatical structures."

Gerald nearly went into convulsions when I mentioned this idea to him one night at our campfire in Red Canyon, and we've argued about it for hours; he's a sucker for the blank slate, but Ray and Carol seemed receptive to the concept.

I mention some ideas I have about the structural underpinnings of the present conflict over public lands and roads in the West, how opposition could arise purely from structural necessity and Carol laughs and they tell me about a big, official county sign they saw over in Wayne County which read something like, "WARNING: Roads may be impassable due to BLM and environmentalist restrictions."

Getting back to the art, what did the motifs symbolize?

"There's no way to know," said Carol.

"We just look at various elements of the art," Ray says to me, and he tells me about how in some of the panels, they could discern perspective, which would be a sophisticated concept for a rock artist.

"Are there basic, indivisible units in abstract prehistoric rock art, like phonemes?" I ask. "Could you distill it down to spirals and circles and squares and so on?"

"I don't know if you could call a spiral 'basic'," says Carol, "How many varieties of spirals are there?"

"But they may represent basic geometric universals," says Ray.

That's what I'm getting at.

I had previously spoken to David Sucec, a visual artist and vice-president of the Utah Rock Art Research Association, of which Ray and Carol are also members, over the phone. I asked him for his views on how rock art evolved. Did someone just start chiseling the rock in his spare time?

"I don't think much of it (rock art) was just doodling," he told me, "You might be able to find doodles but they're extremely rare. It's a magical act to make an image, and to make an image that resembles something in this world is even more magical. Those early people had a vocabulary of style, though some people created art we can't put in one category or another, but in general, something like the big Barrier Canyon style panels, those are probably specific spirits or deities. I was raised a Catholic and we're used to seeing pictures of the Christian God as an old white guy with a white beard and long white hair and that's the sort of thing the Native Americans were doing, and you wouldn't depart too much from that unless you had a compelling vision. It goes back to the idea of shamanism, that there were these spiritual specialists who had direct relationships or communications with the spirits.

"As for how it got started, all the early images of the spirits or the life-force are non-representational images: parallel lines, wavy lines, parallel zigzags, parallel arches, circles—those basic symbols represent basic natural forces."

Sucec believed that if the creation of rock art wasn't relegated to the tribe's shaman, the canyons would be covered with petroglyphs and pictographs, and they're not.

"Looking at the Barrier Canyon style again," he said, "It was around for almost six thousand years and there's not that many images for such a long time. You're talking about three to four hundred generations. There should be a lot more images, so I don't think these images were made casually or frivolously for the most part."

I asked David how his background as an artist helps him glean insights into rock art.

"To me, these are creations by individuals who have a vocabulary of style which is shared by other people. There's no way most archaeologists or anthropologists could ever appreciate or deal with the initiation of new images or significant changes in the imagery; it baffles them because they don't recognize individuality—they only recognize the social structure. We were just in St. George and the average high was sixty-five and the average low was thirty-seven, but we didn't have one day which was average. In fact, it rained for two days, and that's distinctly atypical. So we create these kinds of generalities and they take on a reality in our minds, but I can't abide the idea that archaeologists can only talk about every individual act as a cultural act. When you start talking about the individual, they go crazy and start using words like 'subjective' and 'imagination.' As an artist, I know that the true way to find any kind of universality is to be completely subjective, so you can break through all the influences of your mother and father and brothers, sisters, your teacher and minister and your boss and find out what truly interests you and excites you and then you can contribute a genuine point-of-view."

Edward A. Geary talks about brands in the introduction to his book on the high plateaus of southern Utah, *The Proper Edge of the Sky*, about the loyalty a cowboy felt to his brand, about how a "brand artist's flourish" could completely change a symbol's meaning. He says "These images of people taking on the identity of the things they possess, or of identities being altered by the superimposition of new elements, provide suggestive metaphors for the ways we shape and are shaped by the landscapes we inhabit (1)." And then he adds a twist whereby symbols like brands might be built into words and texts:

> The idea of landscape as text has long been part of the American consciousness. To the seventeenth-century Puritan imagination it was sacred, revealing God's designs to the elect. To nineteenth-century travelers in the West it was often a text in Manifest Destiny, or in natural law, or in the aesthetics of the picturesque and the sublime. To one whose sense of things derives from a particular place, the shape of a particular horizon that constitutes the only proper edge of the sky, it may be highly personal, a diary, even a confession (1-2).

I like Geary's approach and I identify artifacts with text as well. "A water pump," I once told my mechanic Jerry Wyrick, who created the Heap in its present incarnation, "is like a paragraph written by a mechanic for another to read. A car is like a book."

The ability to acquire the whole of a language in all its complexity at a very early age is the inherent birthright of every human being, but the deep linguistic structures which were configured by evolution specifically to allow us to achieve this remarkable feat are not just universal in the sense that Ray and Carol wish to convey, that is, universal to the human race, rather they are universal in the sense that they were shaped by natural and universal laws. Those syntactic structures are the imprint of the universe on our minds. Language is integral to the basic structure and order of the cosmos; it connects us to the universe.

Car Camping

Even with the road closures planned for the national monument, much of the terrain around Highway 12 and its connecting roads will still be accessible by day-hikes from car camps or, better yet, Jeep camps. Drive up Fortymile Road from Hole-in-the-Rock Road and from one camp, you'll have access to Jacob Hamblin Arch, Cliff Arch, Steven's Arch, Coyote Natural

Bridge and Coyote Gulch, or you can park your vehicle just off the Early Weed Bench Road and walk down into Peek-a-boo, Spooky, and Brimstone Gulches.

I always look for spots which are just out of sight of the main roads, where somebody has driven before, where there is plenty of firewood and preferably where there's an old fire-pit already established. If I'm only going to be at that location a day or two I'll sometimes forego the fire because it usually takes me about half-an-hour to collect enough wood for the night and get the fire going, and it only takes me ten minutes to roll out the sleeping pad and bag and set up the stove for the night's meal.

Paraffin is great to get a steady fire going but I can usually make do with a few scraps of newspaper underneath some old bark and tinder. The secret to getting moist wood to burn is to create an intense rather than dispersed flame. I wad some papers up, but not too tightly, and place strips of bark over them and small branches and tinder over the bark, teepee-style, allowing room between the sticks for the fire to breath.

When it comes to meals, the simpler the better. I know people who will pack away a portable kitchen to create exotic multi-course meals in the desert just to prove it can be done. I can cook up boil-in-bag rice or some canned vegetables and canned chili in about twenty minutes on my stove, and when I'm through I boil up a little water and wash out the aluminum mess kit and the snap-together metal fork, knife and spoon in about five minutes and then I throw it all back in the duffel bag I keep on the passenger seat and I'm ready to sleep or take a night hike.

The camp stove is a disposable propane tank and screw-on burner, and if it fails, and it has only failed once, I've got a campfire grill I can position over the embers which will heat up my food just as fast. Cooking in this manner requires a little care, however, so you don't dump your dinner in the fire or burn it and cause the grill and the cooking utensils to eventually become blackened with carbon, which has to be scrubbed off or it will stain everything it touches.

A few years back I bought an army intermediate sleeping bag from a war surplus catalogue. Its bulk and weight aren't serious drawbacks when I'm car-camping. I keep it in a heavy-duty rubber bag I bought for almost nothing out of the same catalogue. My philosophy is that equipment designed for war, the harshest environment imaginable other than space, has to be strong and durable. The sleeping bag's heavy-duty metal zipper doesn't snag and the straps that allow me to tie it up in thirty seconds haven't worn out or come loose. In the wintertime I stuff a wool liner in the bag and drape a wool blanket over the top and I'm comfortable even when the temperature drops into the lower twenties. War surplus equipment is also, paradoxically, dirt cheap.

I don't use a tent. I've always felt that setting up a conventional tent took far too much time. Years ago I told friends I'd be rich if I could invent a tent that would unfold when you tossed it in the air, like metal-sprung windshield shades which collapse to fit into one-foot diameter circular covers, and now that these tents have been developed, I find most are too flimsy. If the ground is wet, I throw a cheap tarp down and unroll my cheap sleeping pad over it. If it looks like it's going to rain, I tie the tarp to the Heap and sleep beneath it.

Whenever possible, I choose natural fiber over synthetic clothing, which will melt if brought near open flame, and on cold nights I like to get as close as possible to the fire without actually burning myself. Wool and cotton also retain the aroma of pinyon and juniper better than synthetics. In *Desert Solitaire*, Edward Abbey said, "The odor of burning juniper is the sweetest fragrance on the face of the earth, in my honest judgement; I doubt if all the smoking censers of Dante's paradise could equal it. One breath of juniper smoke, like the perfume of sagebrush after rain, evokes in magical catalysis, like certain music, the space and light and clarity and piercing strangeness of the American West. Long may it burn" (13). Often when I'm driving home or when I'm unpacking my gear I can smell the fire I built days before on my sleeping bag and my jacket and jeans and it can lull me into a dangerous reverie.

I wear leather gloves with cotton liners in the winter and I used to have Gore-tex shells for them but I never used them, so they stay at home. If I haven't used a certain item for a few trips, I will try to find a way to make do without it, not to reduce weight but to eliminate clutter.

The parka is one of the exceptions I make with regard to synthetic material and I doubt it will melt unless exposed to very high heat. It conforms to military specifications, has a thick metal zipper with a wide clip and fat plastic buttons that can be done up while I'm wearing gloves and it has an integral coyote fur-lined snorkel hood. It's heavy and bulky, almost like wearing a sleeping bag, and it was expensive but it was designed for arctic conditions. So too are my Sorel boots, rated for seventy degrees below zero. I even bought a pair of mickey boots once; they're the huge, inflatable rubber boots soldiers wear in the winter up in Alaska and beyond, which will make your feet sweat at fifty below, but those were too extreme even for me, a person who has a serious aversion to being cold.

In the mornings I usually pack up and have a couple bagels and get some photographs while the sun is low in the sky. Around noon, when it's warmest and the light is bad, I'll heat a pot of water and throw the floor mat from the Heap's passenger side next to the hood so my bare feet don't get dirty, pour some dish soap on a washcloth and dampen it with a half-cup of water and give myself a bath and change, by which time the rest of the water is boiling and I can make myself some instant coffee. In the winter I'll stay near the campfire while changing. I've tried a few different approaches to staying clean and this method seems to be the most efficient.

I prop my six-gallon water jug on the spare tire. Six gallons will usually last me three or four days.

Maglite flashlights are tough, and if you've got one of the larger models you can club a hostile Gila monster with it. I use the shorter version that takes two AA batteries, with a headband to free up my hands to gather wood and start a fire, and once that's going I can usually make do with firelight. The only complaint I have with Maglites is that the bulbs are sometimes hard to come by.

Before I start driving to the next camp, I'll have a look around to make sure I haven't forgotten something and I'll try to get all my junk in its proper place within the Heap so nothing comes loose and, say, rolls under the brake pedal. An ounce of prevention, as they say, is worth a pound of cure.

Georgetown

Georgetown is one of several abandoned settlements south of Cannonville and it's named for the same person as the modern town, George Q. Cannon, my great-great-great grandfather, who had five wives, God help him. Clifton and Stringtown, now gone, overlapped geographically and temporally with the present town and with Georgetown, but the latter had the greatest presence of all the ghost towns in the area, and it still does. There are ruins here, ghosts, and a cemetery with a few graves reserved for the still-living, that can be accessed through a white turnstile, a revolving gate.

I walk through and stroll by the graves and jot down a few names: William Henry Dutton, August 30, 1877 to January 25, 1957, lived to the age of eighty-nine, not a bad accomplishment, even today. Bessie Patterson Ott, June 2 1907 to September 3, 1994—eighty-six years, also not bad. Mary Ann Adair Mangum, July 5, 1824 through May 5, 1892, sixty-eight years old when she passed on. There are a lot of Littlefields, Mangums, Otts, Johnsons, Twitchells and a few Heaps and Asays who lived full lives buried here but they are outnumbered again, as in all old cemeteries, by their children. Nephi and Zina G. Johnson's children, Clara, Jessie and Lydia, for example, were born and died in 1895, 1896 and 1924, respectively. Of Geo. W. and Henrietta G. Johnson's children, Seth Geo. Johnson lived three days beginning in January 15, 1889; Daniel H. Johnson lasted from March 16, 1892 until April 3 of the same year; and David P. Johnson lived for two days, June 27 and 28, 1895.

Byron Clark survived from February 15, 1900 until the first of May. His tombstone reads: "Budded on earth to bloom in heaven."

Also there's Joseph, Alfred and Karma Asay, the children of Susan S. Johnson Asay and Joseph Edward Asay, all of whom died short of their first birthday, and Norma D. Dutton and John N. Clark, Elijah Pinney, Matilda Pinney, James Mangum, George Mangum, Little Holley Mangum, Randolph Twitchell and many more who died as infants. Inscribed on young Jessie Johnson's gravestone: "Of such is the kingdom of heaven."

The gate creaks as I walk out, and I have to wonder at the symbolism of it— whether it's just another manifestation of Mormon practicality meant for that future day when the dead will rise and gather up their children and march back through the gate—or whether it's a more mundane, contemporary convenience for the departed, so they can come and go as they please, so they can turn that gate on its hinges in the night and visit with the living for a while.

Not far from the fork in the road to Sheep Creek, there's a wash with a few crushed cars in it; a white, sixties-vintage Pontiac with a shiny chrome grill and trim, a V8 engine in its open compartment with the valve covers taken and the radiator cap also missing (which is significant because the cap on the Heap's radiator is malfunctioning and could use replacing) and there's a blue car beneath it, partially buried by gravel—I can't figure out what make or model it is—on the side of which is scrawled "Al Gore Wins," and another car with its nose beneath the second and otherwise almost completely buried beneath the gravel bar, so I can only make out its color, which is also blue.

I might add that in addition to a shot radiator cap, the Heap has a hole poked through its canvas roof and the left tail light is gone and the brights are shorted out, the tuner on the radio doesn't work and the rear brakes don't engage at all. I consider leaving it here with the other wrecks.

Up the road, the front wall of an old line shack has been bashed in, so I can see its insides: stacked-up moldy mattresses and bed frames. I find another shack not too far away and within are old parts on shelves, covered with cobwebs: a stator, a truck flywheel, hinges, pulleys, brake shoes, engine bearings, hoses, pipes, nuts, bolts, washers—all neatly arranged as if the owner left and expected to be right back. I find a radiator cap but the rubber gasket is gone—probably eaten by mice whose nests are everywhere.

I pass a sign that says "Road Damage," and come to an arroyo about 250-feet wide and maybe one-tenth as deep, which is lapping away at the road's shoulder one stem-winder at a time.

Further on new hay ricks are stacked in an old corral and there are roller-sprinklers and a fairly new tractor parked in an alfalfa field, so somebody is still doing business in Georgetown, and that somebody turns out to be squinty-eyed old Bob Ott, cousin of Wallace Ott, and his wife Mira and son, Bob Ott, who are driving up the canyon ahead of me in their two pickups and who stop to say hello and find out who's exploring the roads on their range. They're working on an irrigation canal and running out of daylight, so they don't have much time to talk but Bob Ott senior and Mira invite me up to their trailer south of Cannonville later on.

I continue up the road, headed directly for the hoodoos of Bryce now, past fallen fence posts tangled in knots of rusted barbed wire, leaning cabins, a few pickup campers the locals use as line camps, a big reservoir that's perhaps ten percent full, a field of yellow grass and black dots of cattle, hidden dells, empty earthen tanks, terminal moraines of chained juniper and pinyon, a ranch beneath the Pink Cliffs where longhorns and buffalo graze, and llamas and goats and a braying jackass.

Driving back in the evening light, there's Navajo Mountain, distant and dim, a ghost mountain.

"That's the Stubbs' Ranch," Bob Ott says of the operation with the llamas and bison and so on. "It's a zoo. He wants to charge people to come in and see exotic animals."

Ott's trailer is parked up in the red pinnacles west of Skutumpah Road and from his living room, he's got a good view of his ranch, the sagebrush prairie above the road, the barn and horse corral on the roadside. The Otts have had a presence here for generations, as the graves attest, all the way back to when Stringtown and Clifton, Losee, Georgetown and Woodenshoe were going concerns. All of these except Georgetown were prospective settlements, the kind that Powell wanted to avoid, the kind that just dried up and blew away when the precipitation fell below average. Mira was born in New Clifton, a.k.a. Loseeville, a.k.a. Losee, pronounced "Low-see," northeast of Tropic and I've driven up the road to that settlement, past the big white "BV," which stands for "Bryce Valley," on the hill at the edge of town, and there isn't much left, just some leaning shacks and a gutted farmhouse built after the exodus, a couple old cars and a cemetery with seven graves. A plaque near the graveyard details Ebenezer Bryce and Daniel Goulding's attempts to bring water down to that spot from Pine Creek and the subsequent settlement founded by Isaac H. Losee and a few Mormon families, which survived there for about ten years.

The settlers of New Clifton sold their water rights to Widstoe, which would run into troubles of its own a half-century later, and that was the end of that settlement. The Paria dried up, according to Mira, and that killed Clifton and Georgetown. You needed at least fifteen inches of precipitation for dry farming, Bob tells me, and some years the average dips well below that level. It was beginning to look like Powell's prophecies would be fulfilled again for Cannonville and the valley would die from thirst and the settlers would have to move to greener pastures, but the Mormon pioneers came together in 1889 and decided to revive a project Ebenezer Bryce had initiated years earlier, which was to divert the East Fork of the Sevier River over the edge of the Paunsaugunt Plateau, from the drainage of the Great Basin to the Colorado Plateau and Tropic Valley, "under the Dump." The newly incorporated water district sold one and one-quarter acre lots in the future town of Tropic to raise the necessary capital and divvied out stock based on the labor and capital expenditure each family put into the Tropic Ditch. By spring of 1892, the nine and three-quarters mile diversion was nearly ready to receive the waters of the East Fork. Andrew Hansen, chairman of the incorporated water district records, coming across Jack Thompson of Henrieville and his family and some cattle, who were all on their way to the head of the East Fork, wrote:

> There were several men and a number of women and children. It was a beautiful evening, and they were scattered about all over the flat on the green grass. I was asked about the canal. Did I think it would ever be completed?. . . I told them I expected the water along here to the end of the ditch tonight, and I feared that it would disturb their camp. They only just laughed out loud at me. They said that they'd heard about the water coming along in that canal for years, and that they would like to see some of that water. . . . They spread their beds out all over the flat and went to bed, and in their dreams no doubt had visions of the follies of men such as I, who was spending my time trying to make water run up hill.
>
> Being camped only about one quarter mile distant, I could not help but get a "kick" out of the scene that followed at about 2 a.m. . . . when the water having reached the end of the finished part of the ditch, backed up and ran over,

spreading itself over the grassy flat where these good people were sleeping in peaceful ignorance of what was "pendin." Their first warning came, of course, when someone woke up finding himself floating in water. (Hansen, 5)

Up until that stream ran over the edge of the plateau, the settlers had mostly followed the water, and then they made it come to them. According to Mira, the populations of all the smaller settlements "aggregated" into Tropic, Cannonville and Henrieville not only because of the water but because that's where the schools, stores and churches were. When she says "aggregated" I immediately think of the Anasazi who "aggregated" into larger villages and cliff dwellings as the drought at the end of the twelfth century wore on.

And what effect has the current drought, in its fourth year, had on Bob Ott's ranch?

"It's had a severe effect," he says, "Henderson Creek runs year-round eight out of ten years and now it's completely dry. We got two alfalfa crops last year and the second was poor and we generally get three good crops. The livestock numbers on our range are half to twenty-five percent normal. We've had to sell about a third of our cattle and we've put another twenty percent on other pastures in Nevada and other parts of Utah."

"What did you get for your cattle?" I ask impolitely.

"Cattle prices weren't unreasonably bad, not as low as we expected" he tells me, "But they've stayed at about the same level since 1955. Most operations have some kind of supplemental income."

And that includes Bob, who worked in the maintenance department at Bryce Canyon for twenty-seven years and who owns the concessions in Kodachrome State Park.

"There weren't any rich ranchers until recently," he tells me. "Now we've got some big ranchers coming in from out-of-state and they might generate some employment, but really they're investing in real estate. There's always a demand for property. When a rancher sells out, the price always goes up and you take private land out of the local economics."

"Why would any young person get into the business?" I ask him. "It's pretty hard work."

"It's very hard work," he agrees, "And it's turning into a hobby, but you get the free agency of farming and ranching. You get to raise your kids in an agricultural environment and that means a lot to me. Kids learn the value of work and it makes them appreciate the easy city life."

I ask him how ranching has changed over his lifetime. For one thing, he tells me, he and his children and grandchildren don't ride horses nearly as much as they used to. Traffic and speed limits have steadily increased on Highway 12, where they used to trail their cattle, so now they load them up in trailers to move them from one range to another. And then there's the roads themselves. Travelers used to have to ride up to Widstoe and over the Escalante Mountains on the Sweetwater Road to get to Escalante.

"There was a trail to Escalante from Henrieville," says Bob, "But it was harsh, not even a wagon trail."

Then there was the Paria River, whose wash is still used by ATVs and four-wheel drives to get down to Paria Town and back, though usually not in winter.

"You can use it from early spring until late fall," he tells me, "when the floods are over. The headwaters of the Paria are diverted from the first of April until the first of November, so it's dry then. It used to be one of the only routes out of here. It's a beautiful drive."

The Skutumpah Road, which abuts Ott's property, was constructed in the early forties, when a bridge was finally built across Bull Valley Gorge. About a decade and a half later, in the mid-fifties when construction began on Glen Canyon Dam, the "Cottonwood Cutoff" was put through the Cockscomb, and at one time the state was considering making that road, rather than the route through Long Valley and Kanab and the base of the Vermilion Cliffs, the main thoroughfare, and if that had been the case, modern Highway 12 up to Cannonville would now be Highway 89, but Utah's Division of Transportation decided the latter route, though longer, would be more economical to service.

Back to ranching. Ott tells me when times get tough ranchers will sell their cattle down to a core of good stock, the bare minimum of good genes they can use to rebuild their herd in better years, and Ott is drifting toward that point. Recently they've had trouble with predators.

"Calves under two-hundred pounds have trouble with coyotes," he says, "We lost two calves to coyotes last year. There used to be a bounty on coyotes but that's gone. And there's mountain lions. We had one come onto our front porch in February and kill three of our cats in one night. It was a young lion, couldn't kill deer, so it went after our cats. When you sell a critter [cow] you pay a 'predator control fee' but there's been an increase in the predator population."

Years ago, they had a bear killed right in their back yard but they haven't been bothered by bears much since, at least "not the kind that want to come into town and raise hell," according to Bob.

Pretty soon it's time for me to hit the road.

"What's your brand?" I ask.

"Ranch cross on the left hip," says Bob, and he sketches it.

$$\overline{\top}$$

"Twitchell's ranch, near us, is MF combined".

$$M\overline{F}$$

"The Dunham's on Skutumpah Road is bar IV".

$$\overline{IV}$$

"My son Robert's is OTT on the left ribs and my other son, Kowan's, is on the right ribs."

"Hope you get some rain before long," I tell them.

"We're so far overdue," says Bob, "it can't help but do something."

Names

The place names along Highway 12 and its connecting roads have no more consistency or coherence than the landforms they signify. Dutton, as Wallace Stegner notes, disliked the long, tongue-twisting Paiute names and so he stuck romantic descriptors like Temple of Isis and Osiris and Vulcan's Throne onto the various buttes, spires and monoliths of the Grand Canyon. Fortunately, he didn't name too many features around the highway and its offshoots, but he did influence some of the nomenclature of Bryce Canyon by his example—Thor's Hammer, Inspiration Point, Fairyland Point, Rainbow Point—these didn't come from Dutton but could have. Powell, ironically, was more down to earth. He saw Vermilion Cliffs, a Waterpocket Fold, a Marble Canyon, a Split Mountain, and that's what he called them, unless he was paying a compliment to someone who had been or could be influential to his career, such as Doctor Joseph Henry, secretary of the Smithsonian Institute (who got an entire mountain range named after him). Other explorers followed suit. Grosvenor Arch (pronounced Growvenor), for example, honored the president of the National Geographic Society.

Thompson was thoughtful and practical. He called what's now known as Harris Wash, False Creek because it wasn't the creek he was after. He stuck his wife's name, Ellen, on the Henry's highest peak—a wise decision—and his photographer's name, Hillers, on another of the Henry's summits. His choice of Escalante for the Unknown River and the valley it flowed through and ultimately the town near its head, carries a lot more cachet than Potato Valley or Spud Valley or Potato Creek or Potato City. He often referred to the Henrys, by the way, as the Dirty Devil Mountains, which sounds more

Bob Ott

appealing than their present name, though it's less appealing or mysterious than the original Unknown Mountains.

Some of the shorter Paiute place names survived to convey the other-worldliness of the landscape: Paunsaugunt, Skutumpah, Paria, Kaiparowits, Awapa. But such names are few and far-between. The pioneers couldn't get their tongues around most Paiute names any better than Dutton could, and they had to have a handle on the land's features because the land was their livelihood, so they slapped on the name of the person who was living in the place or running cattle there: John's Valley, Spencer Flats, King Bench, Kerchaball Canyon, Alvey Wash, etc., or they settled for simple but effective descriptors: The Gulch, The Spring, The Flat, The Gut, The Gap, The Blues, the Cockscomb, Big Flat, Red Rocks, Horse Spring, Horse Canyon, Meadow Canyon, Camp Flat, Big Sage. Here they were often following the same age-old process the Paiutes had employed of telling a quick story with the name, but they simply did it with fewer syllables. Cowboys corralled wild horses in Trap Canyon and avoided the den on Rattlesnake Point. Model Ts bogged down at Ford Stuck. A sheepherder out by the Entrada Sandstone clumps near the bottom of Hole-in-the-Rock Road mentioned he'd "sooner be home than here" and that outcropping became "Sooner Rocks."

The problem with pioneer place names not hitched to surnames is that they got duplicated. There's Sweetwater Canyons above Boulder and Widstoe, a Big Hollow west of Boulder, northwest of the Aquarius Plateau, in the Sunset Cliffs, and near Coyote Gulch southeast of Escalante. There's a Cockscomb near Teasdale and a larger version south of Cannonville. There's a Birch Creek west of Escalante and one just below the Pink Cliffs, a Fourmile Bench east of Wahweap Creek and another in the Circle Cliffs, a Long Canyon on the Burr Trail and east of Capitol Reef, near Hall's Mesa and near the (southern) Cockscomb and there's one just off Johnson Canyon (there's another Johnson Canyon, too, in the Sunset Cliffs). Highway 12 is surrounded by Willow Creeks and Oak Creeks, Cottonwood Creeks, Red Canyons, Dry Hollows, Dry Benches, Wide Hollows, Death Hollows, Muley Twists and Little Valleys.

There are two Dry Creeks within eleven miles of each other near Widstoe and there are two Sulphur Creeks in Capitol Reef within eight miles of each other. There is another No-Man's Mesa on the south side of the Colorado River. There's an Escalante Desert and another Escalante Valley in Iron County about ninety miles west of the town of Escalante.

Isolated as they were, the farmers and ranchers often twisted pronunciations to suit their own tastes. Thus Escalante is still sometimes called "Escalant," when, as Nethella Woolsey notes, "There is no authority for the omission of the final syllable" (29). They also stuck their own labels on features which had already been named. According to Charles B. Hunt, author of *The Geology of the Henry Mountains*,

> Some local people had objected to the name Dirty Devil for the principal stream in the area (east of the Henry Mountains). When the Board of Geographic Names was told by a postmistress that "the nicer people call it Fremont," the name Powell had given to the stream was dropped. . . . I was interested in restoring Powell's name. . . . When I found that most local people still used the name "Dirty Devil," I related the earlier protest and was told, "Oh, the nicer people moved away from here a long time ago." (6)

Here are a few of those terms which might give newcomers problems, especially those who would try to follow the routes of the early explorers.

Aquarius Plateau: Simply called the Mountain by locals. Its eastern volcanic crown is known as Boulder Mountain or Boulder Top. Thompson referred to the Aquarius as Wasatch Mountain.

Canaan Peak, or Kaiparowits Peak: Nine-thousand, two-hundred and twenty-three foot peak southeast of the Table Cliffs. According to Woolsey, it was named by Thompson "for (a) Hebrew word meaning low mountain" (452).

Collett Wash: The single break in the entire fifty-five mile length of the Straight Cliffs. Thompson called this wash Last Chance Creek and it was later re-named after Rueben Collett, an Escalante rancher (Alvey, 3).

Escalante Rim: Northern end of the Straight Cliffs.

Fifty Mile Mountain, or the Fifty: South end of the Straight Cliffs, beginning about fifty miles south of Escalante, but often used interchangeably with the Straight Cliffs.

Grosvenor Arch, or Butler Valley Arch: Wallace Ott relates that the cowboys who ranged near the arch were well aware of its existence before Jack Breed "discovered" it but they hadn't named it (see next section).

Harris Wash: Thompson calls this drainage False Creek and Rocky Gulch but the locals renamed it for cattleman Jimmy L. Harris (Alvey, 6). According to Woolsey (454), it was named for Llewellyn Harris.

Impracticable Cliffs: Name on George Wheeler's map for the east side of the Escalante drainage.

John's Valley: (Plateau Valley on Wheeler's map) Thompson calls John's Valley the Panguitch Hayfield. Nobody seems to know the exact reason for the present derivation.

Kaiparowits: (pronounced Kay-PAR-o-witz) Paiute for "Big Mountain's Little Brother," as it originally applied to Caanan Peak, the "little brother" of the nearby Table Cliffs. Thompson expanded the term to include the plateau on which it stands. Wheeler's map labels the Kaiparowits Plateau the Linear Plateau.

Mollie's Nipple: (labeled White Cone on some early maps) On Wheeler's map called Nipple Peak, it was named for a rancher's wife.

Paria: (pronounced Pah-REAH) Also spelled Pahreah. Paiute for elk.

Skutumpah Road: (pronounced SKOO-tum-pah) Also called Skumpah, meaning "rabbitbrush" in Paiute (Gregory, *Paunsaugunt*, 19).

Straight Cliffs: Cliff-line south of Escalante, also sometimes known as the Kaiparowits, though it only forms that plateau's eastern edge, including Fifty Mile Mountain.

Table Cliffs: Southern escarpments of the Escalante Mountains, which are outliers of the Aquarius Plateau. Marked Last Bluff on Wheeler's map and called by Thompson Table Ridge or Table Mountain. The promontory at the south end of the Table Cliffs—Powell Point—is also called Pink Point.

Ten Mile Wash, Spring, Flat; Twenty Mile Point, Flat, etc.: These landmarks along Hole-in-the-Rock Road were all named for their distance from Escalante.

Other common terms used in the area need slight translation as well.

A *dump* as in Schow Dump, (east of Hole-in-the-Rock Road) is a declivity where water can dump off the edge. A *holler* is a hollow, a *crick* is a creek, a *cayoat* is a coyote, a *drouth* is a drought and *flippers*, according to Tom Shakespeare, the supervisor of Kodachrome Basin and Escalante State Park, were the slingshots children used to shoot their eyes out before they got hold of

Angel's Palace, Kodachrome Basin

BB guns. They are also the Forest Service and BLM's "No Vehicle" and "Wilderness Study Area" signs that flip back up when you drive over them, though these are also referred to as *flippies*.

Kodachrome Basin

The road lifts gently to the entrance of Kodachrome Basin, with a ledgy, lavender bluff on the right and a row of fins like broken teeth on the left, revealing a peppermint-rock-wasteland valley (a microcosm of the Colorado Plateau isolated from it by Entrada ridges and ramparts of white Henrieville Sandstone) with an uneven floor of grass and tumbleweed. I park the Heap and hike down the line of rusty sandstone shards on the Panorama Trail, clamber up narrow passes in the late-morning summer sun, rest and drink deeply in the monoliths' shadows, and then the path curves around and brings me back and across the road to the Grand Parade Trail. I follow it around the base of a spur ridge, through a tight side passage into a finger canyon where the skin of the land, draped in thick stalactite-like folds, has been flensed back, exposing gristle and sinew.

I take a connection not shown on the map, between the Grand Parade and the Angel's Palace Trails. The route runs along the east wall and wraps back into thin stem-canyons, one of which opens into the amphitheater for which the latter trail was named. The air thins as the side walls recede and the terrain opens up. The embankments in the distance are far enough away to be hazy in the hard noonday sun. There's a mudstone cathead jutting from the slope and there's a mountain of bones on my left with a pinnacled summit.

I take a break, drive the Heap up to the north end of the park, cook a meal on the hood and refill my water bottle, and then start up to Eagle View on a path which often approaches forty-five degrees, chopped into the side of a cinerous shale declivity and held in place by spiles. By the time I get to the top, half-an-hour later, my shirt is soaked, my temples are throbbing and my heart's

ventricles are thumping on my chest like sledge hammers, but the reward is a horizon falling to the brilliant white Navajo Sandstone rim of the Skutumpah Terrace on the south and the lovely, lonely, slanting, black, back-lit Markagunt Plateau to the west. The trail circles down into an adjacent canyon without the spectacular colors or topography and then it swings north to Henrieville, which is so close it looks as if I could walk there in an hour.

The cars on the road, the RVs berthed in the campground below

Petroglyph near
Fence Canyon

me, those people making slow progress along cracks in the tumbleweed plain, they can't be of consequence to me; when I turn my eyes from them, the evidence of their presence ascends to my aerie only as disjointed shouts and motor growl. The coherence of the terrain is lost from this vantage point; the cliff line vacillates and wanders. The banded rock is worn back unevenly, tilts fifteen degrees to the northeast along a gentle syncline, and towers tip from the banked red sandstone like the superstructures of battleships settling on choppy seas.

Near the base of the trail stands a tall, thick red sill, like a sandstone fin, and there's another red "pipe" made up of similar materials, about fifty feet tall, in the center of the basin, and there are sixty-five others scattered in and around the park. These dikes and pipes are unique to Kodachrome Basin; they're conglomerations of sand and gravel and other debris that have been forced up as slurry from the underlying Winsor and Paria River Members of the Carmel Formation, some blunted and some so thin and suggestively shaped that they could best be described as phallic.

There are no geophysical laws to explain the existence of these columns. Geologists believe they may have been formed by cold water springs percolating through the Entrada Sandstone and/or that the ancestral Paria River saturated the sand long enough for an earthquake to liquefy it and squeeze it into its present configurations or even that the weight of the overlying rock forced the lighter sand to erupt as "boils" but these are all speculations. Scientists aren't even sure when the pipes formed, though it was probably earlier than, or possibly contemporaneous with, the deposition of the Henrieville Sandstone.

It's been a long day of exploring and I drive back a ways down Skutumpah Road in the evening, find some bare ground screened by junipers and set up camp. I make dinner, excavate an old fire pit and spend the next hour and a half searching for wood. It should be all over here but the place has been stripped of it. Another mystery. I have to circle a half-mile out from camp to find enough brush to sustain me through the cool night, and then I'm almost too tired to light the fire.

In the morning, the sun warms my sleeping bag and I crawl out into the still heat, shovel sand on the embers, heave my junk into the Heap's bed and set out for Grosvenor Arch, a few miles south.

The arch is another inexplicable feature. Ranchers had been running cattle through this area for the better part of a century when a National Geographic expedition came through in 1949 and right off the bat, according to author Jack Breed, discovered a 152-foot high arch carved in the same Henrieville Sandstone which might possibly have pressured the pipes up north into existence. Apparently none of the local cowboys knew it existed. The expedition's guide, John Johnson, told them that he'd heard of undiscovered natural bridges and arches in the area but "In my 40 years here I've never seen any. I'm always too busy looking for stray cattle or good grass feed to notice the scenery" (Breed, 369).

Too busy to look up once in a while, even to scan the sky for storm clouds? Didn't any of the hundreds of cattlemen who ranged through here ever chase a stray into the vicinity of this arch? It sounds like a cover-up to me, and according to Wallace Ott, the local cowboys knew the arch was there long before Jack Breed "discovered" it and dubbed it for National Geographic Society president Gilbert Grosvenor. I sometimes wonder what the cattlemen would have called the arch if they'd been asked. Perhaps they'd have called it The Socket for its resemblance to a skull orbit or Double Arch because there's a much smaller hole, maybe fifteen feet high, in a spandrel to the left of the main opening.

In the distance, Grosvenor looks like a nasal septum, and as you get closer, it separates out from the cliff. Standing right below it, the arch appears as a hollow that might indeed once have been occupied by an eye, a huge, oval, unblinking eye, fixed for a thousand millennia on the prairie, waiting for a metagnostic event to occur, at the conclusion of which, a scaly lid would finally press over the pupil and it would sleep and die and rot out, leaving no trace behind.

What might it have been waiting for? I turn around but there's nothing; only sage and the road and distant domical hills.

Grosvenor Arch

Entrance to Kodachrome Basin State Park

On my way back to Kodachrome Basin, I detour to Chimney Rock, an eight-story tall sand-gall stele out in the middle of a desert flat. A road runs around it and there's an older couple peering out from the artificial climate of their hermetically sealed late-model Buick, wondering what to make of it

It's just a big white thumb of rock, I think. *Or it's a fossil for which the entire formation of Entrada Sandstone acted as template, a cenotaph for a plain or it's the antithesis of the level, featureless valley floor, arisen from logical necessity. Or it's a fluke.*

Probably the latter.

The couple drives off and I walk up to the monolith, the pocked, pull-crack lined face which became desiccated like a mummy's and recoiled from the walls of its prison before those walls were worn away and carried off to the sea. I feel the urge to kick it.

Shouldn't be here, I think, but Chimney Rock is a little more solid than I, and it will still be standing here, without logic and any proven geologic principles to prop it up, long after my bones, the element of my body which most closely resembles stone, have broken down into their constituent elements.

Next, I drive out to Shakespeare Arch, which is beyond the state park's boundaries. Director Tom Shakespeare discovered it in the seventies while chasing down a coyote. A short trail curves around a lonely Entrada plug to a cuneiform window beneath a rock-span shaped like a flat-decked bridge. I watch for a while as high emissary clouds disintegrate across the portal, tipping it toward me.

I return briefly to Kodachrome Basin and when I drive back, the arch is directly in line with the road. I can't see the sky through it, but the curved base is unmistakable. How many tourists must have looked straight at that arch without seeing it? How many more undiscovered arches are out there?

While I'm looking for "Probasco Arch," heading back to camp, my portable tape player dies. I've been listening to various genres of music, whatever I can get my hands on, trying to find pieces which resonate with the same rhythm as the landscape. The player goes defunct right after the Police's "When the World is Running Down"—a poor choice, I admit—and it's a serious malfunction: the spindles won't engage, won't turn at all. I mess with the power cord and then load it with batteries but it makes no difference. A tape player is actually a fairly complex piece of equipment—a thin plastic shell surrounding a delicate circuit board, with plenty of tiny plastic and metal gearing to translate potential energy and magnetic imprints into the slow, even spinning of small reels and a recognizable sound pattern. This particular machine has been with me and the Heap, on and off, for about seven years and it's scratched and covered with dust and has probably been shaken to failure. It, too, is out of place.

I pull over to an abandoned line camp—a corral, a crumpled single-axle trailer and a warped-plank shack—and set the player in front of a sun-faded green plastic bucket on a mound of dirt, load the automatic pistol and fire at it from about fifteen feet. At first the bullets pass right through it but after four or five shots, the plastic carapace cracks and the electronic guts shatter satisfactorily. I gather up the shards and toss them in the Heap's garbage bag, and then I'm on my way again.

520

"Walk this way," screams Steve Tyler, and the Heap does walk and skid up drifts, and then fishtails and tips around junipers at blind corners so its vector and the direction I have it pointed become completely disentangled. The first leg of 520 was hard and uneven; frozen mud and potholes across a chained pygmy forest, but then I came to soft sand and the road began writhing into loose knots and wicked, high-banked bows of blow sand, so I can't help but push the Heap as fast it will go, which is twenty-five miles-per-hour, maybe, and if anybody was coming the other way, we'd wreck for sure. But I am travelling in the fall and haven't seen any traffic for two days.

The road finally comes to a turnabout and at the edge of it, where the trail begins up to the overlook to the confluence of Sheep Creek and the Paria River, somebody has stacked four coyotes belly-to-back. All their skin and fur is gone except for the paws, so it looks like they are wearing fur slippers, and their eyes are open and some sand sticks to their smooth white and blue muscle.

I study the bodies for a while, the banded musculature and the tendons, and then I walk down the trail as the clouds drift over the sun. I see yellow swells and crags and red sandstone blisters and deep-runneled convolutions like a brain's sulci on the far side of either chasm and the vermilion Paria Gorge and the line of cliffs bent back from it and waves of clouds back to the sky horizon. I climb and leap down the ledges and outcroppings of white sandstone until I come to the red edge of an overcliff. I toss a fist-sized rock off and it takes five seconds to hit bottom, so I calculate the distance: one-half acceleration (thirty-two feet per second per second) multiplied by the square of the time (five seconds) and that equals four-hundred. Four hundred feet down if I slip or if the wind blows me off or if the overhang I'm standing on snaps. I step back.

The red sun flares and sets and a crescent moon fades in directly above Mollie's Nipple. In my journal I write "sinkhole world—something fell out of the bottom of this place." It's not just absence I feel but contraction, the earth receding from its own skin, contracting from meaning. You can pile a column of words on it and make a virtual reality around it while the actual earth slips away, carried by that trickle of water at the bottom of the gorge to a real river and then out to sea.

Expeditions

Before Red Canyon, Johnson Canyon was the main entry route to the headwaters of the Paria. In 1872, two years after John D. Lee settled Skutumpah, Almon H. Thompson led an expedition up Johnson Canyon, through that last outpost of "civilization" toward the Dirty Devil River, the upper stretch of which is now known as the Fremont River, in an attempt to retrieve a boat cached there on Powell's second journey down the Colorado. Soon afterward, Lieutenant William L Marshall, Edwin E. Howell and Grove Karl Gilbert, who were attached to a rival survey under Captain George Wheeler, followed in Thompson's footsteps, and their illustrator, John E. Weyss, sketched the first known depiction of the head of the Paria and Bryce Canyon (Scrattish, 350).

Lee's sawmill at Skutumpah was a result of an expedition from Parowan that Brigham Young had authorized in 1870, the purpose of which was to reconnoiter the Sevier Valley, Johnson Valley and the Paria River Basin for sites that would be favorable for settlement. Lee and Major Powell were both part of this expedition.

None of these explorations could have actually occurred and Skutumpah certainly could not have been settled in the face of determined Indian resistance. Only a few years beforehand, nearby Kanab stood abandoned and relations between the Mormons and the natives were quite different.

Fourteen miles southeast of Cannonville, I come to Averett Canyon and I walk down river from the road in the cold evening dark along a creek with a poisonous yellow mineral tint to it, with the banks rising up into teepee buttes and bluffs and cliffs banded with badland hues: desert reds and shale green, white and uranium yellow. There's a silent, scintillant aluminum speck crossing the cloudless sky beneath a crescent moon and I come to a copse of pinyon and cottonwood on a bank and there I find Elijah Averett's gravestones, the first just a circle of stone half-sunk in the sand with "E.A. 1866" inscribed, and the second, larger one, behind it, built of cobblestone and cement, which reads: IN MEMORY OF ELIJAH EVERETT JR. KILLED HERE BY INDIANS IN 1866: BURIED BY HIS COMRADES OF THE CAPT. JAMES ANDRUS CO., U.S. CAVALRY.

The Indian war which claimed a life in this lonely spot began on April 9, 1865, at a peace negotiation in Manti, when John Lowry grabbed the hair of Jake Arapeen, son of Chief Arapeen, and yanked him off his horse. The main protagonist was a friend of Arapeen, a man named Black Hawk, who was thirty-five or thirty-nine or forty-five or well over fifty at the time of his death, who stood 5'6", 5'7½", 5'10" or 6'1½" according to various reports, who was pure Ute or Ute and Navajo or Ute and Sioux. His warriors ambushed a detachment of the Utah Militia in an abra near Manti soon after the altercation and then they set about raiding settlements and killing isolated homesteaders for the next seven years, running off with thousands of head of cattle and horses, until Black Hawk took a bullet in the gut at a place called Gravelly Ford, which crippled him and adjusted his disposition and finally killed him.

The Mormons abandoned their outlying settlements and consolidated their populations into defensible towns of 150 or more people during Black Hawk's raids and they fought back and chased after their attackers, killing a fair share but only going so far because the wilderness remained perilously close to the outskirts of their settlements, just over the next mountain range, usually, and the Mormons' determination to rectify their ignorance of that frontier explains how Averett eventually found his way here.

Captain James Andrus's expedition of sixty-two men set out from Saint George on August 15, 1866 to explore north and east of Kanab, specifically to map the terrain up to the mouth of the Green River, to locate all crossings of the Colorado River below that point and punish any hostile Indians they met along the way. Andrus had proven his abilities in the last capacity during an earlier reconnaissance, where his men had killed eight Kaibab Paiute warriors he believed were complicit in the murder of a couple ranchers from Pipe Springs.

Andrus's command rode up the eastern rampart of the Kaibab Plateau known as "Buckskin Mountain," through the Vermilion Cliffs at Johnson Canyon to the flat where the town of Skutumpah was later established, then northeast to the amphitheater at the headwaters of the Paria River, roughly following the route of present-day Skutumpah Road. Though they must have seen the entablature which makes up Bryce Canyon, Adjutant Franklin Woolley, who kept a chronicle of the expedition, makes no mention of it.

On the 26th they were joined by Lieutenant Fish's detachment of eighteen men who'd come up through Red Canyon and over the top of the Paunsaugunt Plateau. Here, at "Camp Seven," somewhere near present-day Henrieville, Andrus detailed six men to return to Kanab with fourteen of their animals that were "unfit for service." Averett, dismounted, lead the party into the canyon which bears his name and was killed by gunfire from two Indians hiding behind a tree before he knew what was happening. The man behind him, George Isom, took an arrow in his left shoulder. Hiram Pollack, third in line, emptied his revolver at the attackers and took cover while the last three, supposing themselves to be outnumbered, retreated to camp.

From his vantage point, Pollack watched the Indians gather up their horses and lead them toward Paria Canyon. He, too, began to return to camp, leaving Isom hidden in the brush until he could return with help, but when he met up with a contingent of twenty-five soldiers, rallied by the other three men, they all rode off through the darkness after the Indians who, though initially holed up in a cave and surrounded, managed to slip by their pursuers in the night and "escape to the mountain" (Crampton, 152).

They recovered twelve of their horses and found Isom, shivering in his hiding spot, the next morning; and they buried Averett and moved on, riding east where Highway 12 now runs.

Willis Creek

The walls are covered in black stains and gray lichen, they are scored with multiple transverse fractures and hackle striations and weathering pits and they close in tight and raise up in overhangs and then waver out into cold, lightless, dead-sound chambers where I can hear the keys jangling in my pocket and the pat of my boots on mud and the strike of them on gravel, and the chambers go smooth and fracture again into red protuberances and buttons and noses and chins and constrict again into narrows where the rock winks and grimaces. The passageway turns ninety degrees and a diffused amber light falls in and gets carried downstream, over shriveled and sagging old-flesh walls waved into ripples that are the shape of water, over the old sandshale horizons, around black waste pockets, over the dead channel floor and footprint confusions, thistle drowned in a mud sheet and gravel bars, pine cones trapped in the pearl-ice, ponderosas with red-plate bark, and chockstones with water shadows fanned out behind them. This goes on until the light slants away and the walls turn purple like old glass and crack into stalks and crosses and alcoves and recesses of side-canyons where landslide maws empty onto the rotten ice floor and I come to the end, where the rock boils red.

Bull Valley Gorge

I had been warned by various officials and cowboys last week about taking Skutumpah Road down to Kanab as a shortcut. They said that it was wet and slick in places, that the clab pan had turned to gumbo, and their warnings sounded a lot like Michael Kelsey's, at the beginning of his book on hiking the Paria River, which I should pass along.

> When heavy rains soak the area, it may be a one or two day wait in the warmer season; maybe a week's wait in the winter, before [Skutumpah Road] is passable. . . .
>
> Warning: Don't blame me if you get into trouble in some canyon or out in the desert! It's Your Choice and Your Responsibility!
>
> . . . roads can be washed out by a sudden thunderstorm, or a big snow storm might make it impossible to drive a section of road. Things change! So it's up to each person to anticipate problems and go as well-prepared as possible.
>
> If you go out along the Skutumpah Road in mid-winter without proper clothing or tire chains, and get stuck and freeze to death, don't blame this writer! (Kelsey, 6, 17)

Bull Valley Gorge has a reputation: your vehicle might spin out or slide into a ditch or flip down a hill if you negotiate the drop into some other gulch wrong but Bull Valley Gorge will kill you outright, and the people of Garfield County will bury your vehicle beneath tons of rubble—trees, boulders and dirt—to expand the bridge you missed and make the crossing safer for future travelers.

Kelsey provides more details why you should be cautious on this particular stretch of road, and I pull off just above the bridge on this winter day

Bull Valley Gorge

when the road *is* frozen and walk out and see one of those details: a bent-up, but still gleaming chrome grill on a pickup truck lodged fifty feet down, looking straight up at me and the sky. Max Henderson, Hart Johnson and Clark Smith all died in the mishap that left that pickup stuck there back in 1954. The Sheriff believed the truck made it across the original log-and-plank bridge to the south side and then stalled and rolled back, fell in and got wedged where the walls narrowed to less than the cab's width. One of the bodies was ejected to the floor of the gulch nearly two hundred feet further down.

Skutumpah road winds down through a hundred washes and Bull Valley looks like just another gulch in a long series, and there are no warning signs, but this canyon is less than five feet wide in places and over 250 feet deep. There are now speed limit signs on Skutumpah Road, which I don't pay much attention to, but you'd be advised at least to follow the limit approaching the bridge over this gorge.

I grab my writing pad out of the Heap and some peanuts, my camera bag and a water bottle. I'd planned to wear my new Stearn's plastic green rain slicker, which I paid twelve dollars for, over a sweatshirt to stay warm but the right arm tears off when I grab it, so I don the seven-pound extreme weather parka instead. I have about fifteen pounds of equipment draped over me, so

I'm not very well outfitted for hiking narrows, but it's December and these narrows are cold and I won't regret bringing the parka.

At least I won't regret it later. Now I walk a quarter-mile upriver to where the gorge cuts into the Navajo Sandstone and climb down a flood-smoothed pinyon trunk, a Moqui ladder, and walk into the abyss, to the edge of an eight-foot drop-off with a mud hole beneath it. I take off my equipment and lean over the side and see it's an overhang—no way to climb back up, and there are no Moqui ladders beyond the mud hole.

I climb back out of the slot, find a pinyon log and drag it to the edge of the gorge, where it's maybe a fifty-foot drop and I slide on my belly to the curved rim, to the limits where friction will hold me and spot the drop-off almost directly below. The log goes over the side and shatters, so I find another, heavier one, maybe a hundred pounds, and send it down, and it shatters too, but a five-foot section survives intact.

I'm sweating but I cool off fast enough as I hike back down into the shadows. I shove the log over the drop-off and swing down myself and cross over the mud hole on it. Now I can come back this way if I have to.

The upper gorge's floor is a rocky wreck. There are more drop-offs and there are chockstones to negotiate, and mud holes and ice terraces and high driftwood piles. There are empty potholes where the water has seeped into the sand and left a translucent ice shell behind and there are stretches of creek frozen slick and opaque like sinter. There is a tree wedged across the gulch with the bark hanging in ragged strips and the trunk polished to a sheen by gravel and water, seventy feet above the floor.

An old knotted climbing rope tied to a trunk wedged against the cold wall allows me to climb down another overhang, this one about fifteen feet high. I crawl beneath a ten-ton chockstone and then I'm below the bridge.

It's a step-side pickup trapped up there, covered with mud inside and out except for the grill, and the bias tires still look full. I take photographs, leaning against the wall to keep the camera steady rather than pushing the film, and my hands begin to go numb and my ears ache. Crossing beneath the bridge, I pull my hood up and as I do a thumb-sized rock bounces off it from two-hundred feet above.

A dirt bike is half-buried in the sand. Ahead, there's relucent womb-light on the canyon walls, and then an obscene white blaze where the sun reaches the floor. I stand in that light, where it's twenty degrees warmer, where I can breath, with my eyes closed but turned to the sun and then I start down again past plinths of old dunes, sandstone walls painted black, across channels, eddies and antidunes, miniature embouchures and deltas where steep, sometimes vertical side canyons have joined the main branch, over

Bull Valley Gorge

boulders and more frozen puddles and chocolate-syrup mud and frozen mud and beazed mud cracked into prisms and spokes.

The walls close in to seven feet and there's a church hush here and a red cathedral light far above me, and then the walls widen again and the light reaches down to a garden of Fremont barberry, gamma grass and serviceberry and stalks of thistle on a bank against the sandstone. The protogenic white line above me eats the edge back; where the sun shines, I can discern no details.

Sandstone bands converge at buried loci. I take my glasses off and from six inches away, examine the ripiculous orange spores and colonies of lichen and the shiny, dead patina on this page of rock and the terra cotta stains, the ancient, oxidized reds, the hues of the primordial earth.

I come to another chamber of harsh white light and a garden of buffalo berry, scrub oak, more thistle. There's a huge fir in the creek bed with spread-eagled two-inch-thick roots tangled up in the air and there's a snath-shaped stalk of fir projecting out and then up from a foot-wide sandstone ledge one hundred feet above me. The gulch widens and I pass through walls of sun and shadows with my shoes caked in gault and come to a dell of tall firs straight and sharp as toothpicks. The stone turns blue, as if starved for oxygen, and becomes clathrate and spalled with massive crescentric seams where elements of overhanging rock have snapped clean.

At 1:30 I decide to climb out. I find a rockfall which has spread out to the creek bed and though the slide has blocked my view of the upper part of the wash where it originated and it might very well cliff-out, I start climbing anyway, slowly, one step per deep breath. When I get to the border of daylight I have to tie the parka around my neck and hike in my T-shirt.

It does cliff-out at the top, the last thirty feet or so, but by then I've spotted a dozen alternate routes out. I scramble up a crevice and then a fifteen foot slickrock face with a seventy degree slope, which isn't steep enough to break traction, and I get to the top of a nameless mesa of sand and red ledges and microbiotic soil, manzanita, juniper, pinyon and yucca. When I get a few hundred feet from the edge, it's hard to tell the gorge is there; looking west, the forested terrain rolls gently out to a high horizon with no indication of the gulches and stone valleys in between.

I find an old jeep trail—I knew I would—and follow it up to a ridge top where I can see the low bulwarks of Powell Point and Canaan Peak. I walk the road and its two tracks deepen and soon I have the Pink Cliffs over my left shoulder and I can view the whole circumference of the Paria Valley, which seems like a level plain from my vantage point at its epicenter.

Rills run to creeks which empty to "rivers" like the Paria which wind to the Colorado which used to, and someday will again, run to the sea. In a like manner, faint jeep tracks lead to graveled and graded roads which lead to paved roads which run to highways. I follow the trail and coyote and deer tracks up to Skutumpah Road and then back to the Heap, and then I'm off to another rill of road, a tributary of a tributary of Highway 12.

No Man's Land

For his starring role in the Mountain Meadows Massacre, John D. Lee was excommunicated from the Mormon Church on October 8, 1870, while he was living in Skutumpah trying to set up a sawmill to provide Kanab, newly resettled after the Black Hawk War, with lumber. He continued his work and built four homes there for his wives and then he was advised by Jacob Hamblin, on authority of the church, to set up a ferry operation on the Colorado River where the Paria River empties into it, a place his wife Emma, who accompanied him, named Lonely Dell. The Clarks families moved next door to the community he'd previously founded and named the place Clarksdale or Clarkston, and it appears under that name on Thompson's map but doesn't appear on any modern maps because it was abandoned in the late 1800s.

I've searched for Skutumpah, found nothing. It was apparently lifted off the earth without a single nail left behind.

Toothed discs, Deer Springs Ranch

When I lived in northern Arizona, the dry climate preserved old trucks for decades, even those left out in fields. You'd commonly see trucks a half-century old or older hauling water, still in use because there was still a use for them. And you could find road cuts a century old without much difficulty, just from the gap in the ponderosas, but cabins or even concrete structures a half-century old were leveled, gone, and it's the same way in southern Utah. A well-built but uncared-for log cabin will fall in a few decades and all traces of its existence may be eradicated in less than a century.

I am concentrating on this difficulty as I drive down Skutumpah Road, on how quickly things change, how quickly snow breaks down the roofs of houses and pushes over the walls and how fast a person's fortunes reverse, how fast the wind can fill in the footprints of a man like Lee, who worked at a feverish pitch all his later life buying and selling land and building houses for his wives, as the church directed him in one direction and then another until his past caught up with him in Panguitch and he was taken out to the meadow where he supposedly ordered the execution of the Fancher Party and finally shared their fate, and how he never did get to see the fruits of his labor, see Kanab thrive and Skutumpah die.

Down Skutumpah Road, there are plenty of failed or abandoned enterprises, lots of sage where there were once alfalfa fields, lots of old tractors being swallowed up in rabbitbrush or disassembled by seasonal floods and scattered for miles down arroyos. There are quarries and mines falling in on themselves and fallen fence posts, creaking shacks, busted bunkhouses, road-cuts filled in by rockslides, silted-in irrigation canals and metal gates buried in mud. Dried-up no-man's lands.

I've been down to Deer Springs Ranch, no town but a loose association of retirees and absentee homeowners which probably has a higher population in the summer than Skutumpah ever did. There I found a huge arroyo cut deep into the soil, and there were rusted farm implements on the edge of it, sinister-looking multi-toothed shredders, drawn scythes, choppers, bailers. These tools, all in a neat line, tell a history of country life all over the nation, one very good reason rural populations have declined and employment out here gets harder to find every year: because one man running a modern harvester or a shovel or a chainsaw or a feed lot can do the work of ten or a hundred men. The rural population has become so efficient at harvesting resources, it's taken itself out of the equation.

Down there at Deer Springs Ranch, there's a coop where chickens still roost, a shower shack for guests, a small country store, closed now in the off-season, a rabbit hutch and blacksmith shop, reminders of the way things used to be when the world was bigger, before electricity, interstate highways, telephones, television, the Internet.

Taylor Button is the operator and interim manager of Deer Springs Ranch, as the regular, hired manager left last season and the board of directors is still looking for a replacement. He told me about the amenities in the guest cabins and they're few.

"You leave the tap dripping in winter," he said, "or you won't have any water. The cabins are lit up by gaslight. It's comfortable and cozy but there's no cable. It's quiet."

The brand of Deer Springs Ranch is:

$$\begin{array}{c} D \\ \bigvee \\ S \mid R \end{array}$$

And I found other brands on the side of the general store.

Further down the road is Johnson, another minute Mormon farming community that never did amount to much, where Lee and other polygamists occasionally hid out from the law, where movie stars later sauntered down the main street of a fake clapboard town and where every resident of Kanab over fifty, it seems, came out at least once to get shot or fall off a horse or drive a stage coach or get dressed up as an Indian and get chased by the cavalry. The movie set is still there and so are a few farms, but I'm sticking to No-Man's Land today and I finally find that unmarked, unnumbered side route the BLM will some day turn into an administrative road, and follow it east past a corral, through a gate, past an earth tank filling with bull rushes, to Swallow Park where a house built by Sears Riggs is still standing, amazingly enough, and in fairly good shape, probably due to the roof which was patched up and taken good care of until the place was let go. The glass windows are still intact and there are chairs at the table and two gas ranges and tin cans left on the kitchen counter. The garage over the trailer looks better than the trailer itself, which has been broken wide open.

Further on, there are a few leaning shacks, some fence line and there's the remnant of Adair Lake, about a fourth its normal size, right up against a blackened thrust-nappe of cross-bedded Navajo Sandstone, and then just beyond the lake, the road comes to a pass and drops along the fault scarp down a sandy pitch, through a forest of limber pine and fir and then into the rabbitbrush, Mormon tea, yucca, scrub oak, manzanita and dried sunflowers lining the road in Park Wash; and then it runs by No Man's Mesa, a giant block of Navajo Sandstone, an outlier of the White Cliffs cut off from Calf Pasture Point to the northwest, and capped with Carmel Sandstone and inaccessible except for two steep trails, one of which got Lewis Jepson's goat herd to the top in 1927. It hasn't been grazed since then and its significance to biologists lies in that fact; it's a relict area and tells them what the countryside looked like before it was overgrazed and on top it looks pretty much like the surrounding scrubland but with grasses interspersed between the juniper and pinyon, yucca and sagebrush. Grand Staircase-Escalante National Monument is valuable to researchers in part for the same reasons No-Man's Mesa is valuable to them, the absence and the fading traces of mankind, with the exception of the names: Johnson Canyon, Thompson Creek, Ford Pasture, Dunhan Wash and Mollie's Nipple.

The Nipple

Mollie's Nipple is a towering, whitish Navajo Sandstone plug that local rancher John Kitchen named after his wife, Martha, a.k.a. Mollie, and I'm curious about the Nipple and I'm here to climb it.

No Man's Mesa and the White Cliffs, both carved from the same material, are miles distant and nobody can say why this adjunct is still here while

On the Nipple

the whole plain around it is on its way out to sea. What's so different about
the Carmel caprock on Mollie's Nipple?

The road to the Nipple is just as crooked and wild as the last mile of 520.
The Nipple is right there; you could walk to it in an hour or two but the
road wraps back, switchbacks for no reason, goes straight for the Nipple
then veers off towards Highway 89 or Starlight Canyon, so you don't know
if you're on the right route until it finally gets close enough in a sideways
manner that you know Mollie's Nipple has to be its destination. When I
park the Heap at the base, I've gone at least twice the straight-line distance
from the main road.

I can scratch sand off the white stone with my fingernail but I can't do
the same to the fallen redrock slabs with my knife. White sand has washed
down from the butte like water from a fountain; it's formed the dunes I had
to drive over to get here, but there was no red sand. There are, however, a
few squat red hoodoos; red caps on foot-high pedestals projecting weirdly
from the white rock.

I start climbing late in the afternoon of a winter's day. There are limber
pines at the base and Mormon tea and the usual juniper and pinyon, and as I
get higher there's some thistle and sage clinging to the sugar-white rock. As

Brush and rock on Mollie's Nipple

the pitch steepens, blocks of the heavier red sandstone lean away from the slope as if the butte was rising and pushing them out. I walk straight up the side and I try to pace myself but the approach still leaves me winded and I've got to rest every twenty or thirty feet.

The top is a castlerock formation, rubiginous red and black and sheer, spotted with lichen that is such a pure and radioactive neon green that it actually glows, illuminates. I find a crack that I can chimney up, thinking, *this is what I promised my wife I wouldn't do* and I drag myself onto the top where the wind slaps my face and I throw on my windbreaker and the wind adheres it to my skin and flaps the loose edges like canvas. I climb around the exposed edges of the crag like a sloth, towards the highest point. The rock around me is rain-fractured, rimose, so some of the knobs and even the boulders I reach for let loose and tumble down towards the Heap, generally keeping their integrity or slinging off a few pebbles as they go and I'm very quick and agile when that happens so I can watch them spin rather than becoming part of the spectacle.

The highest point overhangs the south side of the Nipple like it could slide any minute. Mollie's Nipple's giant gnomon shadow is aimed at the northern Cockscomb and also a dim and distant peak that's mostly mist now in the straight-on light of the sun. The Cockscomb is an echinate Chinese dragon's back twenty miles long with its head buried in the earth; God help us should it rear up. Far to the south, past the Vermilion Cliffs and the highway and House Rock Valley and Buckskin Mountain, past the Grand Canyon, I believe, right on the edge of what Dutton called the Dreamland, right on the edge of visible reality and rapidly fading out of it, there's this tiny bump, this irregularity that just might be the San Francisco Mountains, which are actually one mountain, Navatekiaoui to the Hopis, from which the kachinas will descend every winter solstice to enter the bodies of the Hopi dancers in their ceremonies and draw the rains and renew the earth until the Blue Star Kachina leads them to the Fifth World.

The wind is picking up and it's freezing me. Closer to the Nipple, I see clusters of haystack buttes that I must explore and I record their location in my notebook, take a few photos and make a hasty retreat. I slide down the steep upper slope of the Nipple in twilight, get out of the wind and back to the Heap, put the parka on, warm up some chili for dinner and pack up and head out on the road, into darkness.

The whole radio dial was static during the day but AM 570 fades in and out now. George Norry, is "somewhere out there" and his guest is talking about "intelligent signal processing" and neural networks hooked to cameras which would rewire themselves through trial and error until they could tell by looking at a person's face whether he was lying or not. And this guy says maybe we should move beyond equating God with an "energy" that somehow permeates everything and pay attention to numbers; God may manifest himself through the mathematical relations which dictate the behavior of matter and energy.

While I'm listening, the full moon silhouettes Mollie's Nipple, which is the hub of this corner of southern Utah, hub of an epicycle of Highway 12.

I wake up next morning at the pass above the ruins in the West Swag and I follow Michael Kelsey's directions and hike down to the box canyon with a dozen decussate contrails frozen still above me like white rafters snugged down on the walls, to the remains of jacal dwellings—a few foundations and a low, circular wall covered with graffiti. There are tiny corn cobs scattered around, and charcoal, shards of "crudware," a metate, and shrubs growing upside-down from seeps in the alcove's ceiling. Nearby, there are big cat tracks in the sand.

Kelsey's directions later bring me past the scattered remnants of Nipple Lake, to the "Monkey House" in Kitchen Canyon, once the home of Dick Woolsey and his wife and a screeching monkey in a cage, built right into a bulging sandstone barnacle so it looks like the structure is under attack from a cancerous growth. The lintel is about five feet high and the only place I can stand upright inside is beneath the highest rafter, which is about a foot over my head. Two doorways four feet tall lead into narrow spaces between the house walls and the rock, which I'm supposing Woolsey used for storage. Again, there are cowboyglyphs on every surface you could scratch with a knife. Dale and Lloyd LeFevre were here and Wallace Ott, and WR was here in 1916. Otherwise, I find these:

H Ē ℝ Ł Ĥ Ṽ Ж Ħ Ẳ P2

I move on to something which isn't in Kelsey's book: the teepee buttes of Wilsey Canyon, which I spotted from the top of Mollie's Nipple, and as I walk upcanyon, I come to an arroyo fifty feet deep, and there are green cutworms climbing the side of this arroyo in great numbers, maybe twenty per square foot in places. I walk down and watch them in their slow progress up the sand slope, leaving faint tracks which are wiped away by the wind, which also knocks them loose once in a while so they slip back two or three or ten feet and lose a morning's worth of hard work in a second or two.

Down the arroyo and up a canyon side, I'm in the land of milk-bottle buttes, pot-bellied buttes, bulliform buttes, candy-cane rocks—a geometric barrens, algebraic functions made tangible—hyperbolic slopes, parabolic chambers, lofted bridges. I cross a rock saddle to a turban dome capped with a five-foot hoodoo sculpture, stacked and tipping over and somehow balanced by its own offsets. Nearby buttes are capped by similar art forms. These buttes are all grotesquely overweight, three feet of caprock protecting a campanular sandstone splay with a three-hundred foot base.

Across the gully there's a double-prowed battleship of bombous gray sandstone, like cassideous organic growths mounted on a ship's hull. When I get further up, I spot a columnar red rock garden way out to the east, above Paria, with a light speck through a fin, which must be Starlight Arch. The clouds have been gathering and breaking up all day but now there's a solid black deck just above Mollie's Nipple, which has itself turned dark and menacing, turned into the incarnation of Mount Doom. Open Tolkein's *Hobbit* to the map, to Smog's mountain and you'll see what I'm seeing.

Above the milk bottles there's a shell-white sandstone shelf weathered into funicular polygons, what I will come to call hadrosaur skin, and above that, I find marble-sized iron concretions on a creeping dune and then a waxing slope where they are precipitating from the rock like polyps, and then plates of hematite, rough with rattails on one side and smooth on the other, like fragments of a smashed, cast-iron statue, and then I come to their source: globular ironstone outcroppings, thin shelled, like tree rings. Some of them have been split open to their solid blue cores.

The sky darkens, the sun vanishes, and shadows wash over the ridge like a fast wind and it gets cold so I walk back down into the arroyo where the cutworms have ceased to struggle

Now I'm headed for that town beneath Starlight Arch. Concretions will form layers around anything solid: a branch, a piece of bone, but usually something as simple as a grain of sand, all those hard layers to protect a

Wilsey Canyon

speck of quartzite. Trees, too, grow in rings out from the pith and the Colo-rado Plateau was built up in layers from a granite heart. Around here the settlements grew in layers from the hearts of streams and rivers, which sometimes beat too weak, sometimes too strong.

The Muddy River and Yellow Rock

It's a winter night and I'm parked near Highway 89 with the engine off, listening, on AM 570, to John Hogue, an authority on Nostradamus, who's talking about twenty-seven-thousand-year cycles of time, about reaping and sowing and the yin/yang energies which permeate history. I'm also reading, going over maps to plan out my itinerary, and I hear a high-pitched whine coming from the east which rapidly becomes a rumble and then a roar that threatens to shake the Heap into the ditch off the side of the road; it sounds like a 747 skimming the earth and it passes about a quarter-mile behind me and the sound quickly diminishes. I look out the passenger side window in time to see a yellow light flickering westward.

This is a military flight zone. I feel sorry for the Iraqi soldiers.

An hour later, a few miles down the highway, the Heap's lights cross a plaque set in a blade of ripplerock, symbolic of the water that made the

The Paria movie set

nearby town and wrecked it, I suppose. "Repeated floods destroyed property, forcing the inhabitants to leave," says the plaque.

I drive up the road to the first town of Paria, the movie set, which is nothing like I remember it. I park the Heap in the middle of town, grab my flashlight, saunter into the empty saloon through new doors swinging on bright new brass hinges. The inside smells like a lumberyard; it's all new, even the upstairs, not a warped board in the building. The other buildings are the same. I drive north again a short ways and the Heap's lights fall on the Paria signpost and a movie poster with Clint Eastwood holding those enormous six-guns he carried in *The Outlaw Josey Wales*, part of which was filmed here. It tells me "Flooding undermined, damaged and destroyed the original buildings, creating a safety hazard," so the BLM and some of the locals tore down the set on the wash and built a replica here. A photograph shows the sad state of the movie-set town—I don't want to say New Paria because I hear there's an inhabited town by that name south of Highway 89—just before they tore it down: buildings listing over into the ditch running down main street.

I drive north until I find level ground and set up camp. There are no pinyon or juniper trees around so there'll be no fire tonight. The clouds have dissolved, dried up, and the big dipper is standing on end with its handle resting on the horizon.

In the morning I see I've camped within a stone's throw of the graveyard which has also been fixed up. There's a new cast-iron fence around it, for one thing, and the old headstones are gone, replaced with thirteen blank ripplerock markers. A monument at the gate lists the names of the dead.

Past the Paria, which is running thirty feet wide and six inches deep, past the BLM marker which reads "ENJOY BUT DO NOT DESTROY YOUR AMERICAN HERITAGE," nestled in the banded badlands beneath Carlo Ridge, is the real Paria and the most impressive structure of the home and headquarters of Charles H. Spencer, the West's Fitzcaraldo, a prospector and promoter with the ear of some wealthy Midwestern investors, whose operation, the American Placer Company, constructed a paddle-wheeled steamboat in San Francisco, disassembled it, and shipped it by train and then wagon, down to Warm Creek Canyon where the company reassembled it on the banks of the Colorado.

Spencer's scheme to recover gold from the Chinle formation above the river didn't pan out, so to speak; the specks of gold were and are too fine to separate from the host rock, and the steamboat was left to rot on the Colorado's banks. His other ideas came to similar ends. The mining equipment scattered around Paria, the concrete blocks and cables and the old sluice, is a testimony to his failure to extract gold from the same formation here.

Spencer also planned to build a dam in The Box, the portal where the river breaches the Cockscomb just downstream from Paria, and that also never came to fruition.

If Charles Spencer built the house of rock at Paria, or even if he just designed it, it would be his one success to count against all of his failures. The beams in the back rooms have fallen in and the roof's gone but the well-chinked slabstone front walls are still standing. The doors and windows are framed with boards or ripplerock lintels; these openings and the walls are still square.

This building is one of Paria's later structures. The houses built by the early settlers, the ones who came here around 1873, are just chimneys and foundations now. By the time Spencer got here in 1912 the town was practically dead. Up in Widstoe the streams dried up, and down here, the creek grew to ten times its normal size, slithered out of its banks and swallowed homes and drowned crops and probably carried off a cow or two. It busted loose in 1883 and '84 and turned the fields into washes and most of the townspeople left the next year. Some stayed on to ranch, some to supply the ranchers but the town was wholly deserted by the middle of the last century.

Spencer's Cabin

Yellow Rock

"Pahreah," the word from which "Paria" derives, was commonly and incorrectly thought to be Paiute for "muddy water." In fact, it actually means "elk." But the mistake is understandable because the stream gets a muddy appearance from the banks of silt it tears away at flood stage and carries with it to the Colorado.

According to Kelsey, there's a weirdland on top of Carlo Ridge, the red wall the town was knocked against when the river came to life. There's crazyrock up there. I drive downstream in the Paria to the edge of The Box's sheer walls. An old cattle trail takes me to the top of the ridge and heads for the rock garden above the ghost town but I take a right and hike out to the dome Kelsey calls Red Top, from which the Kayenta Sandstone washes down in waves and the Navajo shoots up in spikes and spires and sphenic buttes, one of which has a curved face where a circular block of stone has sloughed off, and cracks and desert varnish have spread from the center of a clock with no hands, seventy feet across. Every landform is hunched over, clumped, swollen. This is the west edge of the Cockscomb, a monocline where the rock folded to relieve compressional stress on the Colorado Plateau sixty or so million years back, the surface trace of a deep, oblique, reverse fault.

Kelsey's book leads me north from Red Top and the Cockscomb into a dark valley choked with scrub oak and thistle, boulders and dead and living cottonwoods, where it's cool and damp and it smells like rain and earth, and there's still snow in niches the sun never reaches, and I climb out to the sunlight again and the skullcap and beetle-shell domes on the north end of the valley, beyond which is Yellow Rock.

Reality bends around the singularity of this risen dome of Navajo Sandstone and the sky circles it, the fabric of space curves across its xanthous face and pulls time through it like a pump and spits it back out in shock waves of minutes and seconds and minutes. Yellow Rock won't fit into my viewfinder at any distance and I can't find anything nearby to relay its physical presence; a photograph would only show one dimension of it anyway, the visible aspect of something that extends beyond its physical boundaries, into the sky, out to the horizon, into a deep and unknown earth, down into hypogeal recesses of the psyche.

There's a redrock altar in front of Yellow Rock—there's always an altar near such temples—and there's a pothole of about the same volume nearby and if I read the symbolism right, this is something which encompasses and transcends opposites: yin and yang, positive and negative, male and female, good and evil.

I climb up the northeast face and wander over the rock and fanned, damascened, sandstone bands and tawny-red rivulose streaks, graticulated surfaces peeled back from the red musculature beneath.

Yellow Rock bleeds colored stone across a plain and over the rim of a side canyon of the Cockscomb.

I hike back when the sun is low, over the same tilted shelves of Kayenta Sandstone and I get into trouble on a shortcut. I'm crossing a platform of stone that's all askew and there's a section where I have to lay down on a sandstone ramp and reach for a handhold or else I'll have to spend five minutes going around. I reach the hold but my feet lose purchase on slickrock that really is slick and I slide sideways until four fingers on a half-inch sill are all that's keeping me from sliding another six feet down the face and picking up speed and falling ten more feet to the rock floor. I might not break any bones if I can land right but I certainly will if I don't, and my camera will get smashed either way.

I remember telling my wife I would be on Skutumpah Road.

While I'm hanging there the silence draws in and I hear a hissing that grows plangent and my chest starts vibrating like a speaker cone and shortly thereafter comes the loudest sound I have ever heard. It's as if somebody had mounted a redlined stratofortress engine two feet from my left ear. My grip tightens and I yell something obscene and inaudible and then this gray dart is flung through the periphery of my vision and I turn my head as far as I can the other way and see a B-1 Bomber—I know one when I see one—banking south, close enough that the pilot should be able to read my lips.

Before the sound has faded out I spin my feet like wheels until I reach the next hold, from which I haul myself off the ledge.

Up the River

I end up stumbling into Deer Creek Canyon. The night before, I had parked the Heap just downriver, within sight of the canyon, but I didn't know where I was. Kelsey describes a number of nonexistent ranches on the Paria—Carlo, and Kirby, and the Dugout, the Hogeye Ranch at an abandoned meander that I missed, and Seven Mile Flat Ranch—all these are gone, sometimes completely gone, swallowed up by the Paria, and it's hard to know how far I've come up towards Cannonville.

I spent the evening of the previous day exploring old mining roads at the mouth of Dugout Canyon without ever finding the mine shafts and then I found the petroglyphs near Kitchen Canyon; handprints, wave lines and wedge figures with arms raised and hands joined in some ancient ritual. Then I drove on as the sun set and the dusk light withered out, over ATV tracks when I could follow them, or down the riverbank—the river being about six inches deep in September—until it was no use to go any further, and I set up camp. About eight-o-clock it rained enough to make me consider packing my things in and sleeping in the Heap, but then it dried up and there was a fierce wind for a span of about five minutes and the clouds moved on, the stars came out, and it became perfectly still.

If I would have headed downstream from Paria Town instead of up, if I'd hiked down the exquisite narrows south of Highway 89, I would have come to the spot where the Domínguez-Escalante party, which had set out from Santa Fe in July of 1776 to find a route through what would become Utah to Monterey, California, languished for days while scouts tried to find a ford across the Colorado River. They had taken a roundabout way to get that far, coming up through what's now Colorado, around the San Juan Mountains, turning west and crossing the modern border into Utah near where Vernal is now and dropping down through Spanish Fork to Utah Lake and then roughly following the course of present-day Interstate 15 south along the edge of the West Desert, with the intention of crossing it, until their guide deserted them in early October and winter storms blew in and they drew lots to see whether they should still attempt to make it across the desert or return to Santa Fe by way of a southern route. God or chance instructed them to go back and while two more of their guides deserted them, they came east into the land of the Kaibab Paiute, crossed the Kaibab Plateau, skirted the Paria Plateau and met up with the Colorado just south of where John D. Lee later established his ferry. There, at the mouth of the Paria, which they called the Santa Teresa, they sent two strong swimmers across the river. The results were disappointing:

It was so deep and wide that the swimmers, in spite of their prowess, were barely able to reach the other side, leaving in midstream their clothing, which they never saw again. And since they became so exhausted getting there, nude and barefoot, they were unable to walk far enough to do said exploring, coming back across after having paused a while to catch their breath (Warner, 113).

They named their camp near the Paria "San Benito de Salsipuedes," *San Benito* referring to a robe which was the color of the "mesas and big hogbacks impossible to climb" (Warner, 113), which were imprisoning them, and *Salsipuedes* meaning "get out if you can." Here one Don Juan Pedro Cisneros tried to scout a path out of the Paria River Gorge while others built a raft that was blown back to shore "without getting even as far as the river's middle" (114). They killed a horse for meat and sent out more scouts and finally decided to go up the Paria River to a seissure where they could ascend, with difficulty, to the rim of the gorge, from which they could again proceed northeast towards the ford on the Colorado.

I park the Heap at a turnaround and walk into Deer Creek Canyon from there, just far enough to have a look at the petroglyphs and pictographs; wheels, suns, rows of dots, sideways ladders, snakes and block and stick figures. One panel has a spoked wheel and two vertical figures with lines etched across them like tabulations and a sun off to the right, and it looks like a calendar to me but otherwise I can't decipher it. Further up, there's more handprints, the largest about a three-quarters as large as my own hand, the smallest an infant's, and bichromatic figures beneath a high overhang. One figure is split down the middle: fugitive red on one side, yellow on the other.
Every plant in the canyon is in bloom: dandelions, cryptanths, yucca, wirelettuce. Even the otherworldly desert trumpets whose pod-stem design is the best evidence I've seen so far that life on our planet may have originated somewhere else, are sprouting tiny yellow flowers. A giant cottonwood has fallen on its side, straddling the creek bed and I can see from the cryptogamic soil built up around its roots that the mishap wasn't recent, but amazingly, though it's perfectly horizontal, it's still alive and has a healthy crown of green leaves. The canyon is suffused with life; it would take an effort to expire here. Parasitic paintbrushes have got their underground haustoria locked onto sagebrush roots and their bracts are blooming bright red and the yellow petals of the prickly pear have opened to invite my attention, which proves to be detrimental to one of them. I carefully cut it open and scoop out the succulent insides with my knife. It tastes like melon.

Calendar, Deer Creek Canyon

Monsters, Deer Creek Canyon

Upper Cockscomb

The insects are out as well. I have to keep moving or the swarm of gnats around my head will settle on me and red ants will crawl up my pant legs. I find a big darkling beetle with only one antenna crawling along a ledge beneath one of the panels and I flick it into the canyon before it can raise its back and spray me.

I haven't seen anybody else since I left Paria Town, but as I exit the side-canyon, I'm confronted by wildlife in the form of a helicopter flying down-canyon maybe 150 feet above the deck and well below the cliffline.

Watch the skies, I think.

The Cockscomb

North from Highway 89 on the Cottonwood Wash Road, you get into black badlands and washboard. When it rains the road turns to a chocolate clay marl sludge so thick and slick you may be trapped for a day or a week if you stop or get stuck. As Gayle Pollock said, "People see it (Cottonwood Wash) on the map and they think it's a shortcut but they don't know what it's like when it gets wet." Even vehicles with four-wheel drive have trouble making headway in this gumbo which will coat mud and snow tires up to an inch thick.

Spring rains came through yesterday, but they weren't heavy, so the mud isn't deep now and my tires get some traction on level stretches. The bluffs and hills and washes in this black shale gunk are ghost formations; they could change shape in a day, they might be gone tomorrow, they are not anchored by any vegetation save some sickly, pale saltbrush.

Something small glimmers off the roadside near the edge of the alcove-lands and I stop and pick it up. It's a smooth, egg-shaped rock in a clear plastic bag on which someone has written "water, wind and sand."

A side road cuts off to an overlook on the Paria River and the settlement of still-inhabited Adairville, where some of Paria's settlers moved after the town died. There's a tractor down there in the valley and some old pickup trucks, a few ricks of hay, a corral, a gravel quarry, some ranch houses.

Further on, the road runs next to a cliff and Cottonwood Creek swings around to it and curves out and back in tighter loops as the Cockscomb closes on it until it's incised in sandbanks. I stop where the canyon opens up, near a grotto Kelsey says may have sheltered the hamlet of Rock House. Jacob Hamblin, the Mormon scout Powell employed on a few occasions, may have settled here with a few other missionaries and a few Indians back in 1870 to raise squash and corn, until floods forced them out a few years later. Kelsey thinks this is a likely spot for the town because of the straight lines of tamarisk here which form a Y when seen from above, but he's been unable to find any other evidence to support his theory. I get out and walk around, walk up the short connecting canyon to its box head as Kelsey must have done, walk along the rock slope's base on the supposition that if the pioneers built a rock house here, they would have erected it close to the source material, walk *through* the southern tamarisk thicket because the north one has been burned, but the only artifact I find is a bathtub-shaped hole in the ground which might have been excavated for an outhouse. There's no foundations, no rusted cans, no metal at all or stacked rocks or old garbage, nothing that would indicate Rock House was here besides those lines of tamarisk and a hole in the ground.

Continuing north I pass The Box and the road cuts northeast, climbs a muddy pass, drops into a valley of "flatirons," giant ramps of Dakota Sandstone. I come to the mouth of Hackberry Canyon, with Yellow Rock right above it but decide I'll explore that canyon tomorrow and I drive east into a thick gray slop formation, the Tropic Shale, which requires me to put the Heap in four-wheel-drive. I slip and slide up switchbacks until I'm on the crest of the Cockscomb, over the strike valley, over the flatirons, following this seam with my eyes a few miles north and south, but the surface trace extends much further than I can see: north at least to the head of the Paria River, south to House Rock Valley where it bifurcates and then joins together again, south through the Grand Canyon where it splits and joins once again and finally down through northern Arizona, where it forks one last time and dies out near the San Francisco Mountains (Tindall, 630).

Dutton called the East Kaibab Monocline, of which the Cockscomb is the tip, "the longest line of displacement of which I have ever heard" (*High Plateaus*, 32) and he observed the fault-at-depth structure that underlies the upper, folded strata where it crossed the Grand Canyon. That fault emerges from the basement of Precambrian rock; it was formed in the earth's azoic

Stream ripples, Hackberry Canyon

ages and "reactivated" by tectonic compression sometime between fifty and eighty million years ago. Oddly enough, the monocline runs right through the spot where one theory has the ancestral Colorado River altering its course from the bed of the Little Colorado River—it would have flowed "up" the Little Colorado to a basin in eastern Arizona or would have joined another river system—to the channel where it runs today. I've always wondered if the East Kaibab Monocline had anything to do with this alteration in its course.

The sun sets on the Cockscomb and a night wind blows in. I drive down into the Brigham Plains, which are of the typical Kaiparowits variety—incised brown hills and chaparral—and I pull off the road only a short ways and set up camp beneath liver-colored badland rock, and in the morning, I drive back down to the base and hike up Hackberry Canyon.

The Canyon cuts through the Kayenta Formation and is suffused with its dark vermilion light. Where the trail comes close to the wall, I can study the tilted, sinusoidal layers—a year of deposition here and then five years or ten; here a lazy river; there an oxbow or a levee or ephemeral lake—pressed flat as a dime's edge. This is what time looks like.

The stream cuts around a rockfall and curves northeast, parallel to the Cockscomb. I find flood debris four feet up the rock bank and barbed wire wrapped around a boulder by a mad current. It's hard to believe the tiny

Mud ripples, Hackberry Canyon

stream I can cross without getting the tops of my shoes wet could have been responsible for the carnage along its banks, much less for cutting this canyon down to its present level.

Further on, the canyon widens and the stream is caught between sand banks, and old meanders wander from wall to wall. Cottonwood crowns branch into an albescent incoherence and the rushes take on the same purple, gold and red hues that are beginning to appear in the shale slopes beneath the Kayenta.

I hear the echo of the brontides of a B-1 Bomber but can't find it by sight.

I come to my destination, the cabin build by Frank Watson near the turn of the last century. According to Gayle Pollock, Watson was involved in a few of Charles Spencer's schemes and when they went south, he built this cabin and did some prospecting of his own, with the same results as Spencer obtained. Watson moved on to herding sheep and then selling provisions and bootlegging whiskey from a small store near Henrieville.

Cactus grows on the cabin's dirt roof. The inside is gutted and muddy but the walls look like they could hold up for another half-century and the chimney is still in good shape. There are cowboyglyphs all over it:

GW   Ā   J   9̀   V̄F   +   A̶

+̄   4̄   4G   ⋔N   ☆   W4   ⱧF

Coming back, I try to follow my tracks through the creek, especially near the mouth, which is thick with quicksand. You're never really in danger from

Cottonwood, Hackberry Canyon

quicksand unless you drive into it, but there's something repellant about the way the surface oozes smooth seconds after you walk through it, erasing all evidence of your passing.

North again, I pass beneath the power lines coming up from the dam that would "ruin" a lot of the pictures I want to take. Wallace Ott helped put those in. In fact, he helped survey Cottonwood Road. Wallace's take on those power lines is that they're the "prettiest part of (the) canyon" (Haymond, "Ott," 32).

I come to a stretch of road where the Navajo Sandstone, and the Carmel Formation, and the Entrada Sandstone have been everted into red and white and yellow cones and there's a roll-cloud bank right over the strike valley being undermined by a front so the cloud walls are deformed and skewed at the same angle as the strata, and the sunlight is shining beneath the deck and lighting the rock against the black sky into hues I've never seen before.

Not too long ago, Gayle Pollock went to Hong Kong to oversee the printing of a book on the national monument. The Chinese had desaturated the colors of the photographs because they didn't look real to them, and it took him some time to convince them that, "Yes, in southern Utah, the colors really are that intense." He told me, "That trip had a profound effect on me. They had no idea there were places like this."

Those colors are before me now, but they are too rich to last long, and they don't. The light fades and so do I. Though it was nearly a level hike up Hackberry Canyon, I'm worn out and I fall asleep behind the wheel. The menacing clouds that looked as if they might let loose a torrent dissipate instead and when I wake up late at night, the sky is clear.

No sense waiting until morning. I grab the flashlight and a spare and hike down into the narrows on the far side of the road. The rock on my right is cross-bedded and the wall on the left is darkly stained, and white veins run through it like branched lightning. The slot quickly sinks deeper than I'd expected and narrows until I can almost reach out and touch both walls and the light just barely reveals the overhanging rock far above me.

The walls are literally crawling with green caterpillars. When I point my flashlight at them, their tiny eyes shine back with a metallic glow. When I switch the light off, I can hear them moving through the leaves that have dropped into the slot. Otherwise, it's so still that the universe seems to have ceased its rotation. My eyes adjust until I can see the stars and the faint

Middle Cockscomb

Cottonwoods, Hackberry Canyon

galactic light through the crack in the darkness but the walls don't resolve themselves at all except at the edges of the fissure.

I know a modern-day prospector who lives in the ghost town of Gold Hill, Utah, whose flashlight failed while he was deep in an old mine, and he used his watch light to find his way out. When I try that trick, the feeble green glow illuminates about a square foot of rock face. If my batteries died here and the second flashlight didn't work, I would just sit down and wait for morning.

Ahead, the canyon floor narrows to a foot wide and becomes muddy, so I have to stem through in order to clear the mud holes. Near the end, it tilts to the same crooked angle as the Cockscomb and so, at last, do I.

The mouth of Hackberry Canyon

Creekbed pattern, Cottonwood Wash

chapter three

Photo opposite: The Heap near Hole-in-the-Rock

—Hard Roads—

Highway 12 to Boulder,
Hell's Backbone,
Smoky Mountain Road,
and Hole-in-the-Rock Road

The Searcher

I'm traveling east on Highway 12 with Doctor Alan Titus, a paleontologist with the Grand Staircase Escalante National Monument. I'm on the passenger side of his cavernous government-issue Ford Expedition, and we're talking about the work he's been doing lately on permits throughout the monument.

"I'm working on twelve permits right now, some for paleontological research, some for oil and gas exploration. The larger ones, where they're going to significantly disturb the surface, require environmental impact statements and input from a lot of experts—archaeologists, paleontologists, biologists, geologists."

Titus has spent the last several days checking up on a number of uranium mining operations in the Circle Cliffs, administrative work I get the feeling he'd rather leave to someone else. Alan Titus is a searcher and an educator. He's hiked all over the Southwest and he discovered one of the two specimens of dinosaur skin impressions unearthed in Utah. Alan has authored or co-authored dozens of papers on paleontology with zippy titles like "Discovery and Excavation of a Therizinosaurid Dinosaur from the Upper Cretaceous Tropic Shale (Early Turonian), Kane County, Utah" and "New Records of Vertebrates from the Late Cretaceous Tropic Shale of Southern Utah." He's also written a book about ammonites called *Late Mississippian (Arnsbergian Stage-E2 Chronozone) Biostratigraphy of the Antler Foreland Basin, California, Nevada, Utah* (the Antler Basin was an ocean basin on the east side of an island mountain back in the Late carboniferous Era, about three hundred million years ago). I've leafed through this catalogue of ammonites and it's a little dry to me, but it pretty accurately demonstrates Alan's mindset.

"The truth is, only those who make paleontology the entire focus of their lives are going to make it," says Titus, "and I can't really imagine doing anything else."

The doctor is an intense individual, the kind who can talk about developments in his field for hours on end, and in his former incarnation as a college professor at Snow College and the College of Southern Idaho—that's exactly what he was paid to do. His passion about ancient life has kept him young; he's three years older than me but he looks five younger, like he's barely pushing thirty, and he has the energy level of an excited seven-year-old. He calls the new monument the "frontier."

We turn onto Hole-in-the-Rock Road and his truck skims over the washboard at forty or fifty miles per hour with no problem. I point to the brush off the roadside.

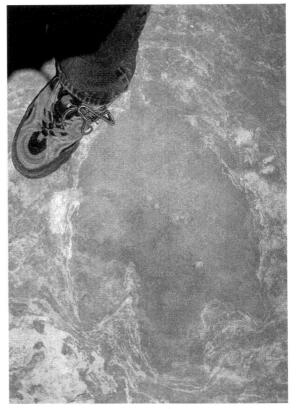

Dinosaur "undertrack,"
Twenty-Mile Wash

"If we were in the Heap, we'd be over there by now," I say.

We talk about the politics surrounding the monument's creation and about an organization called the Grand Canyon Trust, which until recently was buying up grazing permits for permanent retirement in riparian areas of the monument.

"We're required to treat their applications with the same objectivity we would anyone else's," he says.

Titus is well aware of the local sentiment toward the new monument, but he had nothing to do with its creation. Like most government workers in the area, he's caught in the middle of a dispute he had no part in raising.

We drive by cud-chewing cattle—"wild cows" I call them, "slow elk," he says—and take a side road toward Left-Hand Collett Canyon and pull over by a white lobe of Entrada Sandstone and begin hiking up the side.

I've heard Entrada called the "stuff which dreams are made of." The arches and windows and fins of Arches National Park and the fins near Moab, are formed from Entrada Sandstone, though they have more red pigment to them than the rock we're climbing. Navajo Sandstone will usually erode into high precipices and narrows but Entrada has a different genetic tendency and it weathers into standing waves and potholes, portals and locules, whorls and knots, knobs and hoodoos and shapes that don't yet have names.

We pass small lattices in an outcropping, something I would never have paid attention to if Alan weren't with me. "Bee colonies," he says. Then he points to faint, tangled etchings in the rock face and says, "worm trails."

During the middle Jurassic, what's now Twenty Mile Wash was a sand desert, like the Sahara, arid and mostly lifeless. But some things large and carnivorous walked across its edge and we find their tracks, or rather their "undertracks," the sand displaced from beneath the prints, along a bench near the top of the fossil dunes. They were discovered in 1997 by Josh Smith, a colleague of Alan's, who was looking for a place to ride his mountain bike.

"There's a major road coming down Right-Hand Collett Canyon" he tells me, "It runs right past here, but these tracks were discovered less than five years ago."

This *is* the frontier. We take turns walking in the prints, making long strides to match the dinosaur's leisurely gait. Alan thinks these prints, which have their own fossil name, *Megalosauripus*, were either made by *Allosaurus*, meat eaters whose remains are the state fossil and which each weighed as much as a car and had scythe-like teeth, or by a creature much like them. He shows me another print where I can discern the impression of the pads on its feet, which are about three times the size of my own feet.

"And remember," says Alan, "it was leaning into its stride, so we don't see an impression of the whole foot."

He shows me some more prints, called *Brontopodus*, made by a smaller sauropod: hand-sized impressions left by the front feet, larger ones made by the rear feet and a snake-like pattern down the middle left by the tail.

The BLM is mapping the Entrada outcropping with a camera mounted on an eighteen-foot-long, tethered blimp, which drifts high and surreally over the terrain.

The eolian, or windblown, sand which made up the Entrada was deposited at the edge of an inland sea, the Middle Jurassic Seaway, which slowly withdrew north beginning about 170 million years ago. The continent had been split off from Europe and the great island of Pangaea and as it rode over the Pacific plate, the western edge was compressed and later, during the Cretaceous, eraginated by thrust faults and piled up to form the Sevier Orogenic Belt. The relatively dense rock of the Pacific Basin slipped down toward the asthenosphere at a shallow angle and the resulting magma forced its way up through weak spots in the crust to form volcanoes. The Sierra Nevada was forming deep within the earth at this time from a solidifying pool of magma which would later be exposed by erosion.

Sediments from west and south of Highway 12 washed down through embouchures to fill the basin from which the sea had retreated, and dinosaurs roamed this new plain, which became the Morrison Formation. Paleontologists find the bones of herds of massive, ophic-necked, bulb-headed sauropods, the largest of which weighed as much as three loaded semi-trailers, and of armored *Stegosaurs* with their egg-sized brain pans and of *Allosaurs* and smaller predators like *Ceratosaurus*, which were seven feet tall at the hip.

The sediments immediately above the Morrison Formation were eroded away, leaving a gap in the record, which picks up again about one hundred million years ago when eastern Utah was a lush, forested lowland, much like present-day Louisiana, rife with fast lizard predators. Alan believes that while the sauropods like 120-plus ton *Ultrasaurus* may not have needed a high metabolism and were probably cold-blooded; theropod hunters like *Allosaurus* may well have been warm blooded, i.e. capable of sustained, rather than just explosive bursts of speed. The latter were probably fairly bright even by the standards of today's predators and they had a top speed of perhaps twenty-five to thirty-five miles per hour. What's more, they may have hunted in packs, so even if you could outrun one, which a human couldn't, it's brother or cousin might be waiting for you up ahead.

The early Cretaceous is preserved in the Dakota Formation. Above it, the Tropic Shale records the return of the inland sea and the temporary exodus of dinosaurs, and this is where Alan and I pick up the trail again. He drives me to another site not far from the first, and we hike up onto a crumbly shelf of rock covered with paleocurrents, into the sandstones and mudstones and siltstones that once lay at the sea bottom. Before I can catch my breath or get my bearings, Alan has shown me a half-dozen petrified oyster and clam shells, distant ancestors of the kind we pry open today for dinner and pearls, with names like *Cardium curtum* and *Exogyra olisiponensis*. When I ask about a certain type of shell once known as *Gryphaea* and now as *Pycnodonte*, he provides an example within about fifteen seconds.

We also find fragments of ammonite shells. He holds them up to me and as I try to see the cross section, he examines them for such exotic characteristics as "suture lines," "whorl sections," "umbilical shoulders," and "ventral prongs." Ammonites, relatives of the chambered nautilus, appeared on the scene about 390 million years ago and were wildly successful and prolific during the Cretaceous. Their ubiquity throughout the Paleozoic and Mesozoic Eras makes them a perfect index fossil for the correlation of strata. When the dinosaurs died off sixty-five million years ago, about two-dozen genera of these creatures went with them. This last fact makes Titus skeptical of theories that rely on super-germs or climatic changes to wipe them and the dinosaurs off the earth. The ammonites had three hundred thousand *millennia* to adapt to pathological organisms and they had endured gradual climate changes just as powerful as anything in the late Cretaceous. Whatever killed them all had to have been sudden, violent and global.

Occasionally the Tropic Shale will offer up something more than clam, turtle and ammonite shells. Paleontologists have recovered fossils from sharks which hunted in the shallows and forty-foot-long marine reptiles with four-foot skulls and jaws which could unhinge like a snake's to swallow large prey whole.

We climb back in the behemoth and drive west, through Escalante, to another outcropping off the side of Highway 12, this one belonging to the John Henry Member of the Straight Cliffs Formation. When this formation was laid down the sea was withdrawing from southern Utah, though it wasn't a straightforward retreat; the Interior Seaway would draw back then flood over the basin again, withdraw and advance, and this happened at least twenty-three times, until, at the Drip Tank Member of the Straight Cliffs Formation, which was deposited about eighty-four million years ago, it made its final departure from this place. During this time, the shoreline of the Interior Seaway and the outwash plain from the Sevier Highlands alternated between swampland and river plain, depending on the proximity of the sea.

We climb up a narrow wash to a crumbling cliff face in the Wahweap Formation and Alan begins finding fossils immediately, some still entombed in rock, some free: fish scales, snail shells, a beautifully preserved crab claw, dinosaur bone marrow and ammonite shells. We find a clamshell still closed on itself.

"He's still in there," says Titus, handing me the rock.

"You've got to break it open to get at the soft part," I tell him.

We examine the cliff face closely and it turns out to be composed of millions of frangible layers of paper shale, sheets of sediment like freshwater varves, deposited by spring runoff each year.

It's the completeness of the geologic record which draws scientists from around the world to the national monument. Alan tells me there may be better examples of certain types of fossils in Mongolia or the badlands of Alberta but the monument's record of the late Cretaceous terrestrial ecology is the most comprehensive on earth. Each layer is like another page and each fossil like a written word to those who can read the text.

"You can only get the whole story here," Titus tells me.

We drive on and Alan talks about dinosaur skin, specifically *Hadrosaur* skin. I would imagine it looks something like elephant hide but I'd be wrong. *Hadrosaur* integument was a tessellation of "polygonal tubercles," discrete, thick, raised pentagonal or hexagonal plates, the largest about one and one-half inches across, which radiated off into smaller, increasingly diamond-shaped polygons, especially toward the underside and along the tail.

The idea of being able to run my hand along dinosaur skin fascinates me. The rock seems to have preserved everything but the living reptile itself. From Alan's point of view, fossil remains like these make the monument a gold mine, and that's why he gets so upset about the illegally operating, amateur fossil hunters he has to compete with. Dinosaur bones tell only part of the story; much of the data paleontologists collect comes from the fossil's context: nearby fossils which could date the find, gastroliths (also known as "gizzard stones"), which dinosaurs ate to help grind up foliage in their stomachs, and the strata from which the dinosaur emerged. Some fossil hunters use picks and dynamite to free their wares and sell them by the pound. The contextual elements are completely lost, and fossils like skin impressions are almost always destroyed in the extraction process. To Alan it's like "going through the Louvre and stealing the pedestals and lights."

There are currently no federal laws dealing specifically with fossil theft from national parks and monuments. On the rare occasions where fossil hunters are actually apprehended in the act on federal land, they're charged with "theft of government property."

Still traveling west, we come to the Kaiparowits Formation, known locally as The Blues. In terms of scenic value, The Blues are rather mediocre; they're badlands but not the colorful variety. In fact they're a uniform, drab allcharite-gray, and the strata are slumped and streaked with brown stains and studded with pinyon and juniper and wiry saltbrush. Most travelers on Highway 12 breeze past the ugly gray slopes without giving them a second thought, but Alan's eyes light up as we approach them. This landscape is currently ground-zero for worldwide paleontological research.

Much of the Kaiparowits's blue-gray hue was imparted by carbon from decomposed vegetation. The soil itself was alive at one time. We walk along the bottom of a wash and Alan studies the vergence of sediment; sharp lines indicate a steep gradient and vigorous river activity while horizontal current-bedding relates to a more languid pace. Riverwash and point bars accumulated along slow-running streams and rivers, and so did dinosaur carcasses, settling out of the purling current like a heavy element, like gold. Alan points out rust-colored circles in the claystone—petrified wood. Then we come to a block of stone with a huge bone stuck out obliquely.

"That's a *Hadrosaur* femur," Alan says, almost nonchalantly.

Judging from the coxa at the end, which is as large as a soccer ball, it must be at least four feet long, and the detail is perfectly preserved; it's museum quality.

Further on, Alan shows me where he found a fossilized, seventy-five million-year-old turtle shell that had fallen right out of the cutbank after a hard storm, where it had bounced off a wall and come to rest. Apparently, this sort of thing happens all the time. The soft sediments of The Blues are constantly eroding, and this process is constantly unearthing fossils.

In the Kaiparowits, paleontologists have recently discovered a specimen representing an entirely new genus of Ceratopsia, a category of monsters which includes the *Triceratops* and the even larger *Torosaurus*, a horned plant eater with a huge, plated neck frill and a skull over nine feet long, and a parrot-like beak for slicing through tough vegetation.

Sparrows dart past us at eye level. The dinosaurs are still among us, though in an altered form. Modern birds evolved from dinosaurs; some "terrible lizards" survived the great extinction by learning to fly. Though they walk with the same posture as dinosaurs and have the same footprint as some dinosaurs, it's hard to connect something like a sparrow or a hummingbird with an *Ultrasaurus*.

The dinosaurs are extinct, and they're here, reincarnated in a different form. When you follow something which you thought was familiar far enough back, you may find the bizarre, the grotesque.

The mountains through which we ride were once sea floors. The abyss has been raised up, and it's all around us. I think about the layers of the Straight Cliffs Formation, the millions of pages of geologic text, each recording the subtlest changes in dinosaur skeleton morphology, and I think about how that text has itself been transformed and metamorphosed by time, how layers of sediment laid down parallel to the earth's core could be wrapped and bent into folds. Time exists in layers as well.

Escalante

Back in August of 1866, Andrus's men were struggling through the same gray muck, turned slick by a thunderstorm that would later prove a bonanza for paleontologists. They emerged from The Blues, what adjutant Franklin Woolley describes as "deep almost perpendicular gullies worn in the mountain side by the storms of ages" into the Upper Valley of the Escalante, "a beautiful park, green grassy meadows, groves of timber on Sloping hill sides, streams of clear, cold mountain water shedding into a Small open Valley forming the Centre of the picture" (Crampton, 153). This valley they followed until they encountered "a succession of deep hollows with Steep rough rocky sides almost impracticable at first and worse as we proceeded," where they were forced to detour back down to the valley bottom. In the process of getting there, one of their horses tumbled down the slope and broke its shoulder, necessitating them to shoot it.

They camped in the valley and the next day shook off the frost which had settled on them and crossed the icy North Creek and came into what was then called Potato Valley, for the wild tubers which grew there, and they camped that night at the present site of Escalante. Woolley wrote that the area was "level, easy to irrigate, fertile, facilities surrounding it for the support of a thriving settlement of one hundred and fifty families. . . . Fuel and timber abundant, excellent range for cattle, hay accessible in valley at Timber Park, within a distance of 10 to 12 miles" (154).

Andrus and his men tried to continue east but they found the "whole of this country from the mountains to the River . . . cut up in all directions by these narrow deep perpendicular crevices, Some of which are hundreds of feet in depth and but a rod or two in width" (Crampton,154), and were obliged to detour again up Pine Creek, through "Steep rough difficult kanyons, and side hills" (154) to the sublime, montane uplands of the Aquarius Plateau and Boulder Mountain.

John Wesley Powell's Mormon scout, Jacob Hamblin, came to Potato Valley in 1871 by the military expedition's route from the Paria through Tropic Valley and over The Blues. He mistook the Escalante River for the Dirty Devil, which actually ran about forty miles to the northeast and proceeded south through the slickrock toward the Colorado, where he was to cache Powell's supplies, for fifty miles before quicksand and impassable ravines turned him back. When he reported the failure, Powell decided to have him leave the provisions at the Crossing of the Fathers downstream.

Next year, Almon Harris Thompson, who was in charge of the second expedition down the Colorado during Powell's frequent absences, tried to reach one of the expedition's boats, the *Canonita*, cached at the mouth of the Dirty Devil River, by an overland route, and in the process he corrected Hamblin's mistake. Thompson arrived at Potato Valley by the same tedious route as Andrus and Hamblin, up a "horribly steep" trail through the "steep gulches and steep ridges" of The Blues (Gregory, "Diary," 80), to Birch Creek and then Hamblin's "Dirty Devil." Thompson climbed to a vantage point in Harris Wash where he could see the Henrys, then called the "Dirty Devil" or "Unknown" Mountains, and the tips of the Abajos and the crestline of the Aquarius Plateau, and he saw the "Dirty Devil" Hamblin had described for what it was: an unmapped, unnamed, unknown river which the Colorado expedition had completely missed because the canyon through which it ran narrowed to insignificance at its mouth. This was the last river in the contiguous United States to be named by a European-American and he called it the Escalante, in honor of Father Silvestre Vélez de Escalante, the Spanish explorer whose party crossed the Colorado, nearly one hundred years earlier, sixty or so miles due south of where Thompson was overlooking the river.

Returning four years later by a northern route, Thompson met four Mormon scouts in that valley and he suggested they call the town they were planning by the same name as the river, and they apparently thought it was a good idea. The names of the pioneers who settled into Escalante those first few seasons are now the names on the landscape: Barney Top, Griffin Top, Roundy Reservoir, Alvey Wash, Allen Creek, Heaps Canyon, Shurtz Bush Creek, Hall Creek, Twitchell Creek, Joe Lay Reservoir, Liston Flat, Collet

Top. They dug canals the first year, returned to Panguitch for the winter and came again to settle, living in dugouts with whitewashed walls and rock-pile fireplaces and roofs of dirt shoveled over poles. Lacking a flag, they saluted an Indian blanket on the Fourth of July, 1876, and when they had harvested the crops that year, they got down to the business of building a Mormon town.

The settlement was originally laid out on the north side of the Escalante River but that was good farmland, so the townsite was moved to the opposite bank. The pioneers' original dam on the Escalante gave out so they dammed it again two miles upstream, and when that dam breached in a flood two years later, they moved upstream and built a pile dam. When the stream changed channels, they moved another quarter-mile upstream and threw five-thousand wagonloads of rock into the bed and poured one-thousand sacks worth of cement on top of them. That dam held the river in check (Woolsey, 97).

They set up a sawmill in 1877 at North Creek and built a schoolhouse that doubled as a church. They quarried clay adobe from the creek's north side and fired it into brick to build their houses and they turned their dugouts into "backhouses" for storage. In 1879, they built a gristmill two miles northwest of town and in 1885 they started putting up a proper two-story sandstone church. They wove their own rugs and carpets and sewed their own clothes, raised bees to make honey and planted molasses cane at the mouth of Calf Creek so their children could have sweets (Chidester, 94).

Settlers from the San Juan Expedition began arriving in late 1879 and the townspeople shared their supplies and their knowledge of the surrounding terrain and some of the men left off work improving their own lands to help build the road down to Hole-in-the-Rock. Charles Hall, Bishop Andrew P. Schow and Reuben Collett became scouts for the mission, and Hall's sons, John and Reed, helped him build a raft to carry the pioneers across the Colorado.

In 1902, a year before Escalante was officially incorporated, the townspeople blasted a 380-foot tunnel through a sandstone ledge past one of their canals to bring water to the southern reach of Escalante. They later built two reservoirs: the North Creek Reservoir, completed in 1938 with WPA labor, and the Wide Hollow Reservoir which had five times the capacity of its predecessor (Woolsey, 98-101, Chidester, 99).

The settlers brought in cattle to graze the slopes of the Aquarius Plateau and the Upper Valley, prizing milk above beef because Escalante's early trade economy ran off butter and cheese. As time went by and more mills were built, timber was added to the mix, and wool, too. The sheep herd brought in from Kanarraville in 1876 was wiped out by the winter cold but Joseph and Earnest Griffin brought more in the fall of 1877. Joseph Barney brought three separate herds of sheep into Escalante, one of over two thousand head (Woolsey, 130).

The combined grazing of huge herds of sheep and cattle was more than the range could handle and half the livestock on the range starved to death in the four-year drought that began in 1896 (Chidester, 161). With no grass to hold it, the gullied land washed down to the Escalante.

The ranchers knew their woes had been caused by overgrazing and poor range management and when the federal government set the Aquarius Plateau and much of the land around Escalante aside as a forest reserve, they petitioned it to add more lands between Main Canyon and Upper Valley as well. In 1907, local ranchers formed a cattlemen's association, with a charter to:

> promote and protect the business of raising cattle and horses upon and adjacent to Powell National Forest, to work in cooperation with the Forest Service in administration and use of the National Forest grazing lands and to work in cooperation with the Grazing Service in the administration of the Public Domain. (Woolsey,148)

Livestock was threatened by lions and wolves and by a giant, sheep-eating grizzly bear named Bruno, who finally went down after a three-hour running battle with hunters who'd riddled him with thirty rounds (Woolsey, 397-401).

A five-year ban on hunting and a bounty on predators in the early twentieth century turned deer from a scarce commodity into hungry pests which competed with livestock for forage, and the pioneers reversed the ban to cut down their numbers.

Black Hills beetles destroyed tens of millions of board feet of timber in three major infestations between 1919 and 1954, and the Engleman spruce beetle killed tens of thousands of acres of spruce around Escalante between 1916 and 1928, with some of the loss recouped by the sale of downed trees mines for timber frameworks. Joyce Muench wrote about the "Ghost Forests of the Aquarius Plateau" in *Westways* magazine in 1956, when there were still large swaths of dead stands. The local timber industry fought back by cutting and burning infected trees, then by spraying uninfected trees with insecticides.

When the pioneers had turned the creek to do their bidding and created reservoirs to slake their thirst and water their fields in drought and when they had killed the wildlife that preyed on their stock and brought the exploding deer population back under control, when they had built their schools and churches and stores and two-story brick homes and helped the missionaries on their way to the San Juan River and Bluff and had harvested the timber and successfully fought off the Black Hills beetle and the Engleman spruce beetle and saved the rangeland from overgrazing by their own cattle and sheep, that's about when their little town of Escalante began to die from within. Each drought, each fall in the price of wool, milk, beef or timber would shake some family loose to look for better pastures up in the Snake River Plain of Idaho or Wyoming's wide-open horizons or even the fast-growing cities along the Wasatch Front. Often it was the young who left in this fashion, seeing as they grew up that there was no place for them in Escalante. As Nethella Griffin Woolsey writes in *Escalante Story*, "Escalante has long been engaged in exporting a great many of her people, particularly her youth" (363).

Prices for beef and wool skyrocketed during the First World War, but financial gains were offset by other losses in 1918 when Escalante, like every other town in Utah except Boulder, was hit by the Spanish influenza. Some ranches were left short-handed and couldn't move their stock to the winter ranges. There was a hard winter and the ranchers found nearly all the cattle left on Fifty Mile Mountain "dead in piles" (Woolsey, 137). Then the market plunged, and the cattle left alive and the wool gathered that spring became worthless.

Ranchers went bankrupt and many left for good. Those who stayed behind mortgaged their spreads to rebuild their herds while the market slowly recovered, the prices for wool and beef steadily improving until 1929, when the combination of the great crash which knocked prices below nothing and a severe drought obliterated all the gains the stockmen had made over the previous decade.

The ranchers who kept on tried to make up their losses by pushing more sheep and cattle on the already overcrowded range. Melvin Alvey estimates there were as many as forty thousand sheep grazing around Escalante prior to the Taylor Grazing Act of 1934, and he characterized the range as a "dust bowl" (Haymond, "Alvey," 12). That same year was the "driest of record in the history of Utah on all watershed(s) in the state" (Cannon, 310), and up north, near Grantsville, Utah, stock were actually smothering to death on the dust (312).

When the government stepped in to save the dusty range from overgrazing, it received no gratitude from the Livestock Association, which petitioned to "have nearly every ranger removed over a period of twenty years" (Woolsey, 138). This was the beginning of a deep enmity between rancher and ranger, often between brother and brother and father and son.

Escalante was a wreck of a town during the Depression, with its old rip-gut fences and rutted roads, leaning plank shacks and children in rags and dust clouds blowing in from the desert. Nearly all the range around town was "severely eroded and badly overgrazed" (Cannon, 314) and the crops had all failed (315). There were two Civilian Conservation Corps camps nearby and nearly three-quarters of the population was on some type of welfare. It was the sort of place you'd expect to see in a Dorothea Lange picture, and in fact she visited the town and photographed downtown Escalante, some of the farmhouses and a few of the pioneers still trying to eke out a living.

But that was over a year after Everett Ruess came through in 1934, at the height of the calamity. Ruess spent a couple of weeks exploring side canyons of the Escalante River and camping on its banks, participating in a dance or two and attending church, socializing with the children from town, even taking a couple of them to *Death Takes a Holiday* at the cinema. Then he wrote a letter to his brother Waldo and another to his parents. He wrote them he wasn't sure which way he would go next: north to Boulder, south by way of the Kaiparowits Plateau and Smoky Mountain or down along the scarpline of the Straight Cliffs and across the Colorado to the Navajo Reservation. In the end, he chose the last option, loading his burros Chocolatero and Cockleburr and setting out along the old Mormon trail for Hole-in-the-Rock where, he wrote, "no one lives" (Rusho, 196).

Death Ridge

The headline in the March 6, 2003 edition of the *Garfield County News* read "Woman Dies, Man Survives Week-Long Challenge in GSENM." Down past the lead, the article quotes the driver, a Londoner: "On the map, it looked like an easy trip to Escalante."

Traveling east from Kodachrome Basin, they got their Jeep stuck in the mud near Death Ridge, which got its name from the cattle that froze there one winter, and they waited a week for someone to rescue them. They survived on sunflower seeds and Skittles and ran the Jeep occasionally to stay warm, and meanwhile a spring storm dumped almost a foot of snow on them. Finally they decided to walk out, heading back the way they came, but the girlfriend could only make it four miles and the driver left her beneath a tree and kept walking all day and through the night and met up with a couple locals near Kodachrome State Park the next morning. By that time the girlfriend had frozen to death.

I'm on that road now and I'd planned to be there at the same time that couple was traveling through, but the water pump went out on my wife's Mitsubishi and I tried to fix it and failed (in my defense, you have to take the whole front of the engine off, including the timing belt, to get at the water pump). We had to spend the money I was going to use for the trip to get the car fixed and the trip was delayed by a week.

Could I have helped them? If the mud didn't turn me back, then yes. Could they have helped themselves? According to the locals I grilled on the subject, absolutely. They could have helped themselves by bringing water along and something more substantial than light jackets, and they could have brought more food, and they could have helped themselves by knowing how their vehicle worked. From what I understand, when the rescuers got to their Jeep, it wasn't even engaged in four-wheel drive. Furthermore, I doubt they tried airing down the tires or driving out at night when the mud froze up. And it sounds like they had no idea how to get a fire going with wet tinder, and the guy should have walked his girlfriend back to the Jeep before going after help, or he shouldn't have brought her along when he tried to walk out, no matter what she said.

This is the kind of story locals love to tell: ignorant city-folk getting lost in the boondocks. But having talked to a few members of the Search and Rescue team in Escalante, I understand it's not the typical scenario. Most travelers on these roads and most backpackers have some idea what they're getting into and take the necessary precautions and only run into trouble when they get injured. Or mauled by wildlife, maybe.

I park the Heap at the top of Trap Canyon, probably less than a mile from where those two got stuck, and walk into the narrows, and the first thing I come across is fresh bear tracks, one large set and one small, both headed down-canyon. I've met a black bear with a cub before in the woods and we all just went our separate ways, but I wonder what would happen if I came across bears in the narrows. What if these two forgot something and they were coming back and we all met? Would we pass without incident, them grunting and me tipping my hat?

Horses must think this way because the canyon was named by ranchers who corralled wild horses here. Apparently horses didn't have much use for such tight passageways. The narrows only continue for about a mile and then the canyon opens up and becomes thick with vegetation: ponderosas and limber pine, cottonwoods and shaggy spruces and scrub oak thickets, purple thistle, serviceberry, mountain mahogany, buffalo berry, the ubiquitous yuccas, barrel cactus and prickly pears bearing red flowers from areoles. Such a profusion of life is unusual on the Colorado Plateau, except at higher elevations. The narrows themselves are unusual for the Kaiparowits Plateau in that the Wahweap Formation, which makes up most of the plateau, normally crumbles under its own weight before the walls get this steep.

I find more bear tracks and some wild turkey tracks but no bears or turkeys. The sky is an even gray sheet, obviously full of moisture, but it's been that way all morning and it hasn't let go yet. I return to the Heap and drive

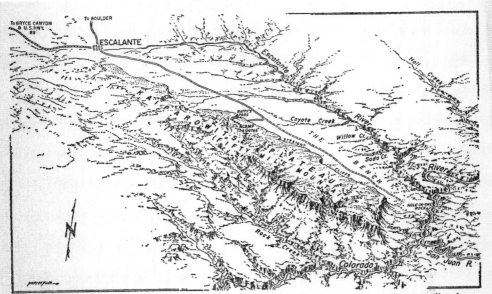

Kaiparowits Plateau, overlooking the Colorado River in southern Utah, rises from the floor of the surrounding desert with an almost vertical escarpment. Prehistoric Indians found their way to the top in a cleft where the ancient trail is used by an occasional visitor.

Illustration by Norton Allen, from Henderson, *On Desert Trails*, 142 (Used with permission of Westernlore Press)

up a steadily worsening road to Death Ridge. Hunters can continue along the ridge for miles but I just came for the view. The overcast sky doesn't make the Kaiparowits any prettier; it's mostly slumped, gravel-gray hills and scab-brown scrublands and crumbly yellow ramparts. The one thing it has going for it is that it smells like pine after a rainstorm.

A wall of rain, filmy like smoke, breaks over the next, heavily-timbered ridgeline and for a moment this place looks like the Cascades.

The rain curtain drifts north and the view opens up. There are supposed to be several north-trending anticlines around here but the covering of vegetation makes it impossible to read the strata. Out on the plains of the Kaiparowits, the geologic text is closed to my eye.

But others could still decipher it. Dutton gave the Kaiparowits only a cursory treatment and neither Thompson nor Gilbert spent much time on it, but geologist Herbert Gregory brought a pack train through the trackless eastern half of the Kaiparowits in 1915 and returned in 1918, 1922, 1925 and 1927 to continue his studies, and what he and his associate, Raymond Moore found, as they relate it in their 1931 work *The Kaiparowits Region, A Geographic and Geologic Reconnaissance of Parts of Utah and Arizona*, was coal.

I drive out to Four Mile Bench and the colors and landforms are the same, and the ground cover is too thick with sage and pinyon and the geology too spineless for my tastes. The bench itself is a rolling plain with an occasional arroyo feeding into the dry forks that feed into major canyons where the vegetation is stripped away, like Warm and Wahweap Creeks. Had certain interests prevailed, that bedraggled Londoner would have come to a five-thousand megawatt, coal burning plant here, but those plans died off in the mid-seventies. The Utah Wilderness Coalition blames poor economics (UWC,148) but the locals blame them, and I don't know why they wouldn't want to take credit. According to their literature,

> Nine thousand acres of vegetation would have been destroyed during construction. A network of roads, power lines, pipelines, pumping stations, and coal slurry lines would have blanketed the western half of the Kaiparowits Plateau. A new road 67 miles long would have cut the Plateau in half, bringing the thunder of heavy truck traffic rolling across the heart of the area. . . . One hundred and twenty million tons of solid waste would have been dumped in a 1,550-acre disposal area on Fourmile and John Henry Benches. A new town of 20,000 would have wiped out 4,000 acres of critical antelope habitat on East Clark Bench (147).

Not to mention the tremendous amount of air pollution that would be generated, which they do.

But there's more. Two days later, I find myself at the other end of the Kaiparowits, at a place called the Burning Hills, and that's no misnomer. I spent most of the previous day crawling down the Croton Road, which is a slow journey even when the road has been graded, which it was. I crawled from Big Sage past the huge green backslopes of Fifty Mile Mountain, past an old rock shelter in an alcove right next to the road, past fasciate taupe cliffs, past Navajo Canyon and East of the Navajo, with the wind blowing strong in every direction while two weather systems battled for possession of the plateau, as they had for the last week, with the light on those massive plains narrowing to a promise and then blinking out and Navajo Mountain glowing white, then red, then fading into the blue airglow, down to where the land finally started falling away from the plateau into dead gray ash plains, and I could see the tops of the three huge smokestacks of the power plant at Page, Arizona. I camped on a ridge where giant black bats swooped through the night, unaware of how close I was to my goal, and in the morning I saw the smoke rising from a butte not two miles distant.

I get as close as I can on the blackened mining roads, but the roads themselves have been cut by vents, which are ringed with chemical hues of yellow and orange and a crusty, neon-green fungus, and smell like hot asphalt. I test the ground as I pick my way around them and I get up to one vent that's exhaling a steady column of poisonous black fumes. Closer in, I can hear the draw of air. It's the same sound a gas furnace makes. Closer still, I feel the heat and see an orange glow like a sunrise in the chamber beneath me.

From the slope, I can see how the ground around this butte is slumped. It gets even worse seven miles west, around Smoky Mountain, where the land is incised by deep fissures and the slaked sandstone cap cracks loose into massive slip blocks which settle towards the bottom of Last Chance Creek. The coal is so abundant here that it spontaneously combusts and burns the mountains from the inside out, and then the mountains crumble.

Most of the mining would have taken place at the south end of the Kaiparowits, where the coal-bearing seams of the John Henry Member of the Straight Cliffs Formation have the least overburden. There's about sixty-two billion tons of coal beneath my feet and it would be economically feasible with present mining techniques, to extract about 11.3 billion tons, which would translate into about 223 to 330 billion dollars (Blackett, 1997).

In 1991, Dutch-owned Andalex revived plans to mine into Smoky Hollow after those billions of dollars of coal. The amount of surface disturbance created by their mine would have been small, but it would have been necessary to create a new road or improve Smoky Mountain Road to the point where it could be taken over by double and triple trailer trucks running all hours down to Cedar City, Utah or Moapa, Nevada. This is the operation President Clinton effectively killed by declaring the creation of the Grand-Staircase-Escalante National Monument in 1996. And the curious thing is that the same environmental movement which had worked so hard to stop the mining project had been most responsible for reviving it in the first place. The coal beneath this plateau is known as "compliance" coal because it allows power plants to comply with sulfur emission standards set by the Federal Clean Air Act of 1990, which had been heavily promoted by the environmental lobby.

And here's another curious thing: the Southern Utah Wilderness Alliance, which was instrumental in killing the proposed mine, continues, to this day, to downplay the quantity and value of the coal under the Kaiparowits. SUWA was one of the prime movers in bringing a big project worth an unearthly amount of money, which had a lot of momentum, to a complete halt, and that's nothing to be modest about. So I can only assume they are actually trying to sway their constituents to the view that the government overpaid Andalex to give up its mining claims on the plateau.

This sort of behavior isn't limited to one side. Politicians routinely employ phrases like "over a trillion dollars of coal," being "locked up" beneath the Kaiparowits when in fact the *recoverable* coal amounts to mere hundreds of billions of dollars. The purpose for these overstatements, by the way, is to get the coal field excluded from the monument's boundaries, which would add another strange twist to the saga because the whole purpose behind the establishment of the monument was to protect from exploitation the land over those coal fields.

The mine's absence contributes more to the current political rhetoric than the mine itself ever could. As long as it remains in the realm of potentiality, it will continue to grow in value and infamy.

As for the plateau which was spared by Clinton's proclamation, its worthlessness has more value now than the hundreds of billions of dollars that lay beneath it. In this sense, the battle to "save" the Kaiparowits is similar to another environmental battle taking place out on the West Desert, near the Deep Creek Mountains, where a faction of the Goshute Indians, who are related to the Paiutes, are fighting the state for the privilege of storing nuclear waste on their reservation. Somehow the Goshutes ended up being shuffled onto some of the most economically worthless land in the state, and the land around them was worthless in the same respect—so worthless, in fact, that nobody else really wanted to live out that way, which also made the Goshutes' reservation so isolated that a corporation specializing in waste disposal now considers it a prime candidate to receive lots of radioactive waste, and lots of money, too.

So, too, has the Kaiparowits become worth so much by sheer dint of the fact that it has been shunned by most people for most of recent history. It is part of the last, largest de facto wilderness left in the lower forty-eight, and now that someone's found a use for it other than scientific study, it's too late.

Or maybe it's not. As Alan Titus said, "that coal isn't going anywhere anytime soon." If we as a nation decide sometime in the future that the value of the coal beneath the Kaiparowits outweighs the plateau's scenic and scientific value, it will always be there.

In my case, the Kaiparowits is valuable because it's a wilderness—not a wilderness *area* but a true wilderness, a true refuge from civilization, from the city, from rules and regulations and prejudices whereby we're all guilty until proven innocent. I'm drawn to it because it's one place where the good Samaritans who would free me from want and fear, from cigarettes, drugs, guns, religion, meat, fast food, my parents, low taxes, high speed limits, high blood pressure, my own bad attitude and my own car have not yet penetrated, though they are, at present, massing on the border.

The Kelly Grade at the south end of Smoky Mountain

The Lost

One winter day, I travel down to the pictographs in Alvey Wash. I look into the pinpoint eyes of a wedge figure who guards over the main route onto the plateau. I discover three individuals with their arms raised up as if they were greeting me, or perhaps, as the recumbent figure in the corner of the mural suggests, they are armed and ready to mete out the same punishment to me, and I find a red man with his arms outstretched beneath an overhang, faded.

I camp in Camp Flat, as seems appropriate, and read a few passages by firelight from *Wild Horse Mesa*, which is the name Zane Grey gave to the Kaiparowits. What he wrote is pretty much what I see.

> Low down the distant rock surfaces were gold; above them the sky was yellow. Canopying this band of pale sky stretched a roof of cloud, an extension of that

Formation on Nipple Bench

canopy enshrouding the mesa, and it had begun to be affected by the sinking sun. At first the influence was gradual; then suddenly occurred swift changes, beautiful and evanescent—white clouds turning to rose, with centers of opal, like a coral shell. . . . The flat roof of the cloud took on a fiery vermilion; the west end of the shroud became a flame, and mesa, sky, mountain slope and canyon depths seemed transfigured with a glory that was not of earth. (12-13)

Next day I hurry down through Pete's Cove and Dry Bench and Reynolds Point and get beaten up by the Heap because the weak-willed, rocky road wraps around every hill and sinks through every draw and accommodates every other landform in the vicinity in some way, and I continue to Ship Mountain Point where I lose time looking for a route that will get me closer to that thin white ridge so I can climb it some day, and then the road straightens out on the back of Smoky Mountain, and I can open it up a little because the washboard isn't bad enough yet to shake the Heap into the sagebrush.

There's only scrub brush here; no trees, no shade. I pass by the Smoky Hollows—there are two of them, actually, one on each side of Smoky Mountain. Over the edge of the plateau I see Navajo Mountain, which Domínguez and Escalante called "the Black Mountain," with the sun right over it and its face, which looks to the sky rather than the horizon, shining like a full moon, and beneath it, on the near side of the lake, I can see the beginnings of the dead white rock oddity plain where those two explorers and their retinue scrambled around for days like trapped rats, but before I get to that, there's something else I want to investigate. I pull off the main road and drive only a short ways out and there's a vent belching mephitic black vapor like a smokestack and everything within a radius of one-hundred feet except me is dead. I hold my breath and get in close but there's nothing to see, just more of the same, and no sound, so this soot is coming from deep inside the mountain.

No sense in saturating my clothes with this smell, so I keep going, right off the edge of the plateau, down the Kelly Grade, which points the Heap's nose into the plain and circles down an old dugway from the prospecting days like the path of a fighter jet in a death spiral.

There's no vegetation here, either, just towering smoke-gray shale deadwalls around the amphitheater where Squaw Canyon and the "dry arroyo" of Warm Creek (Warner, 117) empty out. The badlands on the piedmonts are beautiful to my eyes, as is all of the lifeless wasteland on this side of the plateau. Every day the sunlight burns these crags and plains clean and every evening the wind picks up and the night comes over them like a storm, filling the washes with shadow rivers. I've spent days

Bluff on Nipple Bench

Sand ripples near Kitchen Canyon

down on these benches, exploring the shale waves, and I find myself drawn to them now, but there are other places I want to explore. The road splits for Big Water and Sit Down Bench, and I head for the latter, traveling along the base of the plateau.

A side road takes me out to Alstrom Point, which the map says is about five miles away, and five miles is an hour in this terrain. The view is worth the trip. Alstrom Point is on a peninsula of rock jutting out in the middle of Lake Powell. From its edge, I can see an expansive island flat that shouldn't be there, with scrub starting to grow on it and past the sand bank that's nine-hundred feet below me, I spy the tops of stone buttes about to peek through the surface, but menacing the toy boats down there in the meantime.

The low brush on top of the butte is parched, and nine hundred feet below, Glen Canyon is drowned. Widstoe died of thirst and Paria was destroyed by floods. The washes which feed the lake run as torrents or run dry. The days are hot and the nights are bitterly cold. There are very few in-betweens.

Domínguez and Escalante circled around the base of Romana Mesa, which is before me, and got caught up in a "strong blizzard and tempest consisting of rain and thick hailstones amid horrendous thunder claps and lightning flashes" (Warner, 118) in Gunsight Canyon, which is just east of me. They prayed and the storm abated and they continued east past the base of Gunsight Butte to Padre Canyon, where they chopped notches into the rock for their horses and descended and crossed the Colorado at a point which is now over five hundred feet beneath the surface of the lake (120).

Beneath the lake, in a drowned layer. It's interesting for me to read the father's names for their camps and compare them to what's there now. Levan, Utah, for example, was San Bernardino, Scipio was Oje de Cisneros, Milford was San Rustico and the Valle de Nuestra Senora de la Luz, "The Valley of Our Lady of the Light," is now the Beaver River Valley. But those earlier names are gone now, except in Escalante's journal, just as the Paiute names are nearly all gone. Just as the lake covered the place of the father's crossing, so have the names been covered over, again and again.

Hole-in-the-Rock Road

The Heap and I are about to be strafed by a Stealth Fighter. It's a thumb-sized parallelogram a hundred feet over the desert right now but its black matte surfaces are shifting and its vector altering until there's no horizontal gain; it just gets bigger. The Heap sputters and rattles a bit; the engine is tied to its mounts with electrical wire and the radiator is spitting fluid and the whole mess could fall apart if driven over seven miles per hour. But there's a seventy-million-dollar killing machine sighted squarely on us and approaching at a hundred times our speed and I'm thinking about hitting the accelerator anyway and taking my chances.

The stealth fighter attack is just the latest mishap on a journey filled with bad luck. It began the day before when I dropped into Left-Hand Collett Canyon on the rocky bed of a gulch, what the map described as a road. The road it connected to (Hole-in-the-Rock) was washboard, which Jeeps have a hard time negotiating, their wheelbases being just short enough and their suspensions just stiff enough for it to literally shake them apart at any speed between seven and forty miles per

Washboard south of the Cockscomb

hour. Being in a hurry, I chose the above-forty option and came to regret it; a pothole sent the Heap airborne and upon landing, the drivetrain sheared off its mounts and sprang forward and imbedded the fan in the radiator.

The fighter veers at the last moment, crossing the road about a hundred yards in front of the Heap, and it's followed a few seconds later by a low rumble, like thunder coming over a ridge. I count twenty-eight seconds before the pilot clears Fifty Mile Mountain, by inches, and consult the map and do some quick math and figure he's doing about 650 miles per hour.

With this black angel alighting on me, I have to question the frame of mind and series of events which brought me here. *Where*, I wonder, *did I go wrong?*

The most important axiom of four-wheeling, which could apply to any activity in the wilderness and which I've consistently flouted, is 'never go alone.' Witness my descent into Left-Hand Collett Canyon: the initial grade was so steep and the spring weather had turned it so muddy that I wasn't sure the Heap could crawl back out again if the trail downstream had been blocked. Two writers, Edward Abbey and Mark Taylor, author of *Sandstone Sunsets*, both nearly met their ends by dropping into narrow, unscalable canyons from which there was no obvious exit; Abbey was fortunate enough to have a walking stick along and he used it as a makeshift ladder to gain a tenuous purchase and drag himself, by his fingertips, out of a stone draw (*Desert Solitaire*, 227). Taylor just yelled until someone found him (12). Both could have avoided the predicament they found themselves in if they'd had a partner with a rope on the lip of the canyon.

If the trail down Collett Canyon had been blocked and if the Heap couldn't make it back up, I could have walked out, but a friend with a winch on his vehicle at the top of the canyon would have given me peace of mind.

Then, too, I was on a tight schedule. Unless you're flying into this country, it's hard to keep appointments with people or landforms anywhere off the main road. The San Juan Expedition of 1878, the architects of Hole-in-the-Rock and the road leading to it are a good example of how such thinking can get you in trouble.

There were actually two expeditions to reach the exposed southwest flank of the new kingdom of Deseret. While those called to serve sold off their possessions and rendezvoused around Widstoe and Escalante, an advanced party struck out for the San Juan River along a circuitous southern route, past Jacob Lake near the north rim of the Grand Canyon, then east past the present town of Tuba City, deep in Navajo territory, and finally northeast to a spot just above the San Juan where they found enough prospective farmland in a place they called Montezuma Fort to begin a settlement. Unfortunately, water was so scarce on the journey and the Indians so hostile that the route was out of the question for the main party. Another way had to be found, and quickly because the advanced expedition didn't have enough supplies to last them through the winter, and if the wagon train's departure was delayed until spring or summer, it would be too late to plant crops for the coming year. There were two options: the Spanish Trail, blazed by New Mexican traders a half century or so earlier, which skirted the roughest terrain but wasn't suitable for wagons and took 450 miles to arrive at a destination less than half that distance as the crow flies, or an entirely new route through the wilderness and across the Colorado River.

The initial scouting reports concerning this second route were favorable. Charles Hall, one of Escalante's founders, had gone so far as to drag a single-axle wagon down through the notch in the sandstone escarpment which came to be known as Hole-in-the-Rock and ford the river and climb the other bank, and it appeared a route could be hewn through the rock on the far side. Add to this reconnaissance the expedition's youth—the average age being about eighteen—and it's faith, and Silas S. Smith, the expedition's leader, doesn't come across as quite so crazy in choosing the "shorter" route.

Soon after the wagon train set out, scouts returned with more realistic reports of stone ramparts, aphotic chasms and a more accurate description of Hole-in-the-Rock—a nearly vertical two-thousand-foot plunge to the Colorado. Platte D. Lyman, leader of the scouts and later de facto head of the entire expedition, would later describe the terrain as "the roughest white men ever undertook to pass over" and "the roughest country I ever saw a wagon go over" (Miller, 162). There was talk of turning back before winter set in, but Smith prayed the night of the scout's return and by morning had concluded that the expedition would continue on its present course.

The majority of the pioneers didn't actually make it to the starving members of the advanced party at Montezuma Fort, who were being harried by Indians, but they did come within eighteen miles. That last distance might have been the easiest leg of the journey but by the time they reached the present location of Bluff, Utah, four and a half months later than their best estimates, they and their remaining animals were at the end of their endurance. They looked around, saw rich bottomland that might yield a good crop and settled where they were.

Not a single human life was lost on the journey, although an older member expired about a month after their arrival, presumably from exhaustion. Little wonder. Again, we have Lyman's account of the wilderness they passed through, which was "almost entirely solid sand rock, high hills and mountains cut all to pieces by deep gulches which are in many places altogether impassable" (Miller, 163), and also the account of George W. Decker, who was fifteen when he joined the expedition: "(It was) the most rugged gorge, the most tempestuous river, the loneliest and most frightening country I have ever seen" (Miller, 202).

Silas S. Smith had parted company with the mission early on to procure funding and powder to blast through the rock, leaving Lyman, who'd argued against the route from the beginning, in command, and Lyman's charges picked and blasted Hole-in-the-Rock until it was wide enough to accommodate wagons. Lamont Crabtree, who chronicled their struggle in *The Incredible Mission*, estimates they removed nine hundred thousand pounds of sandstone from a single one-hundred-foot stretch of the trail (43).

The pioneers rode their roughlocked wagons down the forty-five degree slope with livestock and men yoked behind them as living ballast. They forded the partially frozen river on a 16' x 16' raft and climbed a defile on the far bank, crawled up Cottonwood Canyon and blasted more pathways for the wagons through solid rock—Little Hole-in-the-Rock, the Chute, and the Slick Rocks—then crossed an otherwise impenetrable canyon on a sand dam, since washed away, and hewed their way through a cedar forest, their animals all the while falling from precipices or collapsing in their tracks or being slaughtered for food. Winter set in early and the trailblazers built their road in blizzards and a scouting party become lost in a storm and its members nearly died.

Comb Ridge, the final impediment, is a rock wall nearly one thousand feet high and thirty miles long. The train ran south along its length, the pioneers hoping to find a way around it, but they had no such luck: it terminated at the San Juan River, which was running too fast and cold to ford. Exhausted, the missionaries continued on the only way they could, blasting a road into the ridge and whipping their weakened horses, mules and cattle with azotes to pull the wagons up the steep slope, sometimes on their knees. Many of their animals collapsed into convulsions and some died on the spot, and the trail was marked by "the dried blood and matted hair from the forelegs of the struggling teams" (Crabtree, 112). The San Juan Mission, you see, had a schedule to keep.

The Stealth Fighter isn't the end of the adventure. Back on Highway 12, the carburetor gives out and I have to coast and push the Heap and sometimes crank the dead engine off the warranteed starter over steep rises in the silent dead of night to get ten miles back to Escalante, where I find a friend the next morning in the form of a rock-hunting demolitions expert, who drives me around town to get parts. There's more radiator repairs on the Navajo Reservations and I get the Heap back home in one piece, but I'm late.

The upshot is, I don't try to keep a schedule when traveling the desert south of Escalante. I let someone know where I'm going and approximately how long I'll be gone, I take plenty of water and all the tools I might need, but I leave my watch in my pack and calculate time by the sun, and usually I make it to my destination in due time. But not always.

Hole in the Rock Redux

My second attempt to reach Hole-in-the-Rock hardly goes any better. I drop a full five-gallon gas can in the back of the Heap and fill the tank and the other can on the rear fender in Escalante. I keep the speed below seven miles per hour, but lose half a tank before reaching the Devil's Garden.

I pull off into the garden's parking lot and explore by foot. It's late October and cold enough that I have to wear a jacket. I start on the trail but I get drawn off to the yardang terrain, the arches and pedicels and ancient dune combs, cones and ripples and solution caves, and then I walk the dry creek bed and climb back up to a terrace with black concretions scattered over it. Sand is piled against the stone's edge and into wells at the bottom of rock funnels, and lizard tracks arc from shady junipers to black sage and disappear onto slickrock. The wind sweeps grass awns around and their tips inscribe runic figures in the sand which I try to interpret, but I don't know the language.

Dark clouds scuttle north and the colors fade with the sunlight. I boil some rice on the stove and pour heated chili over it. By the time I'm done eating, the sun is a pale pink oval behind gray scrim.

I'd planned to camp on Fifty Mile Bench again but the further I go, the more apparent it becomes that the gasoline situation is going to be tight. The Heap is averaging a pathetic seven miles per gallon and things will probably get worse as I near the road's southern end, which is hewn from solid rock. The problem, again, is washboard, which is a harmonic oscillation, a self-reinforcing pattern of rills built up by a thousand bouncing truck suspensions. Every time the speedometer creeps above seven miles per hour, the Heap's framerail shakes as if it's about to snap at the welds. A couple of times I find a smooth stretch of road and open it up, but as soon as I hit the washboard the succussion fishtails the Heap violently and I have to slow down across the speed barrier.

When I was listing the mistakes I made on my last journey down Hole-in-the-Rock Road, I might have put more emphasis on bringing the right equipment and making sure what I do bring works, and the Heap isn't working in this particular circumstance. So what happens when your transportation is completely unequal to the terrain? As the monument in the prophetically named Carcass Wash will inform you, on June 10, 1963, the driver of a truck carrying Boy Scouts from Salt Lake City and Provo in its bed and headed for Hole-in-the-Rock, where the boys planned to board boats and ride down the Colorado, killed his engine near the top of the dugway on which I'm now parked and mashed his brake pedal to the floor to stop the beast with no effect. He tried to negotiate the curves in reverse but the truck's speed overwhelmed its maneuverability and he dumped his precious, screaming cargo over an embankment, and then the truck rolled over them, killing thirteen and injuring twenty-six.

I give up on Hole-in-the-Rock. Tomorrow I can explore the narrows of Dry Fork, but the faint disc of sunlight has fallen to near the top of the scarpline and raindrops are beading on the windshield. On my map there's a side road leading to Batty Caves almost directly east of the narrows in Spooky and Peek-a-boo Gulches, so I go back and turn onto the road and start climbing toward the mountain. The road is gullied, steep and windy, and it goes on for a long way, over dry stream channels and deep sand beds, into the apron of waste rock at the cliff's base.

There's a turn off to the left, up a rock ramp, and it's level on top, a good place to camp. I give up on my quest and ride up, unfurl the flapping tarp in mild gusts and tie it to the Heap's passenger side and stake it down. A cold drizzle begins to fall. When I come around to the back of the Heap, I see a cave about one hundred feet away, behind some brush, so I pull the flashlight out and investigate.

The cave is forty feet deep, maybe twelve feet high, the walls even enough that they must have been blasted out with dynamite, and there's a shallow, twenty-foot long metal boat hull in it. There are no navigable bodies of water closer than Lake Powell, past Hole-in-the-Rock, so I wonder what the boatmaker's plans were. Then I wonder if what I'm looking at really is a hull. It sure looks like one, with its metal ribs and a sharp end like a bow.

A few yards down, a weathered, wooden screen door that creaks on its hinges closes off the second cave. I step inside, shine my flashlight around, over two bed frames, a table, a bench. Wood stakes in the wall support shelves of black shalestone. The cavern is about thirty feet deep and its camp ceiling is ten feet high. The floor is smooth concrete.

The third cave has a wide barn door and a workbench inside. I figure it must have been a tool room and garage. The caves are about fifteen degrees warmer than outside. Suddenly, I have new plans.

The rain's tempo picks up. I quickly transfer my junk to the cave, which is remarkably clean. After dinner, it's time to relax on the front porch and watch the darkness seep across the land and the beaded lightning strobe-freeze the muddy rivulets washing over the gulch's edge. The thunder splits the gurgle of running water and echoes off fifty miles of Cretaceous cliffs, and below me, the gully overflows with rainwash.

It's almost cold enough to snow. I return to the cave and settle in, and when I turn out the light, I hear mice scurrying about and trying to escape through the screen. It's so warm, I can sleep on top of my bag, with just a blanket over me, but I don't go to sleep for a while because I'm laughing so hard.

Later, I discover Batty Caves' origins. They were blasted out by a couple of prospectors, brothers by the names of Bill and Cliff Lichtenhahn, collectors and purveyors of petrified wood, jasper, uranium and whatever else they could lay their hands on, back in the early sixties. The third cave held a machine shop. The object in the first cave really is a boat hull which they planned to float in Lake Powell (Woolsey, 172).

Next day the sun is shining and I smell the moisture and pungent tamarisk and cottonwood. I find the spot I'd planned to camp under a foot of water, and discover that the Heap has been invaded. I slept in the mice's abode and they escaped and took over my vehicle, helping themselves to my corn chips, instant rice, and bagels.

I cache my things behind a boulder above the second cave and drive down to Dry Fork, past a rusted brown wreck of an old car half-sunk in the earth. Again, I seem to have the place all to myself.

I stumble around for a while looking for the entrance to Peek-a-boo slot, hiking down a draw and up a sand dune and then I find the crack in the rock and march into it, and pretty soon I've got the camera and tripod in front of me and the water bottle in my trailing hand. There's enough room for me, turned sideways, and that's it. An overweight person would become jammed and other hikers would have to climb over him until he lost enough weight to squeeze through or died of cold or hunger or thirst or was popped loose and torn limb from limb by the next flash flood.

My baseball cap won't fit between the walls when I turn my head, and I don't really need it. I leave it on an outcropping.

At certain points I have to exhale to get through. Above the cornices, the sky is a crooked line of blue spar. As the gulch weaves, the sun rises and sets across the five-foot horizon. The rock is rounded off, gouged, planed. There are small arches like pentices where water has impatiently broken its way through rather than going over obstructions. Where the walls open up into chambers, there are shadowed pockets and smooth lenticular outcroppings, like eyes and brows and giant maws covered with cauls, which coalesce into wraithlike countenances, faces of the damned and the lost.

I shout into the vault and the echo returns to me instantly and only once, compressed and distorted as the wall's form and imbricate texture, unfamiliar enough to seem like the effect of an esoteric branch of physics. It's as if the sound evaporates a few steps beyond me and some other disturbance dissipating an equal amount of energy returns from the other side of the invisible barrier.

In other places, the canyon is anechoic. The silence is compounded on itself and sound is isolated down to its essences: the squeak and scuff of my shoe soles on sandstone and my breathing.

I hop over the first few shallow pools I come across, then pull my shoes off and wade through the cold water of the deeper ones.

The canyon expands into an alcove where more familiar laws of physics briefly reassert themselves. The sun stays risen, sound travels and the horizon opens from a slit to a rough circle. There's life here, too—Mormon tea and monkey flower clinging to the rock.

I rest for a while in the sunlight and continue, anxious to get to the end of this canyon, not because I'm short on time but because there's something drawing me on. After a few more coves and tight squeezes, the path curves up through loose rock and the channel widens from four feet to maybe forty and the horizon falls away on the left to a sand bank and time and space ripple outward like a shock wave.

A side trail takes me back down to Dry Fork and then over to Spooky Canyon, which has a plunge pool at its mouth and a log ladder propped to the entrance on the far wall. That's not my style, especially when I have a camera with me, so I climb up a bluff with striations offset like one foot map hachures, to a point where I can look down into the slot canyon.

There's enough pools down there between the membranous walls to make travel difficult so I resolve to explore Spooky another day, and I retreat to the Heap, making a quick side trip to retrieve my hat. I pack up my belongings and pour a couple gallons of gas into the tank, vowing next time to bring enough fuel to make the Heap into a rolling bomb, and head north as the Straight Cliff's shadow slinks over the sandstone convolutions, toward the hidden river.

The Brand Inspector

Arnold Alvey is a short old bowlegged cowboy who was born and raised in Escalante. I meet him in May of 2003 at his newer white house which is next to a barn and a stable and a pioneer home he uses for storage. He's got red-rimmed eyes and not much white hair left on his head, and he's wearing overalls and he's forgotten about our meeting but he seems willing to make the time to talk. We go inside and he puts his glasses on and draws some of the local brands, shown here, beginning with his father's:

$$\mathbb{W} \quad \mathtt{t}$$

The following is the local brand of Gail Bailey:

$$\mathrm{rh}$$

A couple of the Listons' brands follow:

$$\mathcal{X} \quad \mathcal{A}$$

This is the brand of Mac LeFevre:

$$\underline{F}$$

And finally, this is the local brand of Ivan Lyman:

$$\lrcorner \mathrm{I}$$

Brands, he tells me, are read right-to-left, top-to-bottom and outside to inside. If the symbols are touching they're "connected" and if two symbols share the same line as part of the design, they're "combined." Thus Gary Haw's brand is W H Combined:

$$\mathrm{WH}$$

Other than numbers and letters, brands commonly contain slashes /, circles O, half-circles (, bars —, diamonds ♦, boxes [ ], triangles Δ, hearts ♥, and crosses +, but the vocabulary is pretty much inexhaustible. A chevron symbol ^ above a figure is a "rafter" and an upturned half-circle beneath a symbol makes it a "rocking" brand. For example, the Boulder Mountain Ranch's brand is the Rocking C:

$$\underset{\smile}{\mathrm{C}}$$

If the half-circle is above the symbol, it's "hanging":

Symbols with wings, like Sorenson's (next page), are "flying." Symbols with lines slanted down to the right are "walking":

$$\varsigma \quad \mathcal{M}$$

And if the lines are slanted down to the left, they're "dragging":

Symbols are generally identified as "reversed" (also "backward"), or as "lazy" if they're on their sides or "crazy" (also called "inverted") if upside down. Tilted symbols are "tumbling." Leland Haws brand would be Reverse L H Combined:

⅃H

The brands Alvey gives me clear up a few mysteries, but I've got about three dozen more brands he doesn't recognize because they're too old or they're out of his jurisdiction, which doesn't extend down into Kane County. Also, it becomes apparent to me pretty quickly that there were hundreds of brands throughout the history of Garfield County. And none of them really stood that much above the other until recently.

"Everyone made a living off ranching, everybody had a farm and they raised grain and hay and there were no *really* big outfits. Most of them ran 150 to 600 head: none of them owned two or three thousand," he says.

The ranchers called the north half of the Fifty, which runs north-south, the West End and the south half the East End. I don't know why and neither does Alvey. He gives me a rundown of who owned which parcels out on that rangeland and it includes him and otherwise it's a confusing mix of Pollocks, Alveys, Baileys, McKinnleys and finally, Griffins and Dell LeFevre.

"Joe Pollock, whose brand was 44, used to run cattle on the Fifty," he tells me. "And before him Philo Allen had all that range. Used to have the whole mountain but when the Taylor Grazing Act come in, they broke that up."

"That's remote country out there where you used to run cattle," I say.

"Two-day flight out there for a humming bird," he tells me, "You know if there's anything out in that country worth having, they ought to let a man have it. Even the lizards pack canteens out there."

"Yeah."

"It's just a long ways to no place. Not fit for God, man or the devil."

"Yeah, well—"

"I don't think they ought to allow the tourists out there 'tall unless they got decent supervision—," he says.

"If your car breaks down—"

"These people that died just last winter was just on the edge of it and they should never have been allowed to come into that country 'tall. I think they should have been blocked right there or there should have been some signs there that told them, 'Hey, folks, you'll get in trouble if you don't know what you're doing.'"

I try to get back to the brands. I ask him if there's any big operations now.

"Now we got this guy Sorenson who's come in and bought up a lot of the grazing land. I don't know if that's good or bad. Here's his brand, Flying V."

$$\text{V}$$

I ask him how the art of branding has changed in his lifetime.

"These guys nowadays need a stamp, and they get a bunch of blotched cattle. When you put a stamped brand on a critter and he moves a little bit, which they usually do, and you take it off and put it back on, you blot it. But with a running iron, like they used to use, you don't blot it. And you want your brand plain as possible, so anybody can read it."

"So you can tell when you're dealing with somebody experienced?" I ask him.

"Yeah, and it's gone downhill considerably. Same thing with earmarks which used to be done to perfection. It's changed two-hundred percent."

The War

Steve Gessig owns a sheep ranch on the edge of Escalante from which he has prosecuted the war for western land rights for the last decade or so, sometimes on his own, sometimes in concert with groups like the unfortunately named, now defunct "People for the U.S.A," but when he first came to Utah it was as an enemy of the grazing industry he's now a part of.

"There was a lot of monkey wrenching going on. I'd never really been around cattle or anything like that. When I moved here I was a vegetarian and I tried beef one day and that's all it took," he tells me, "I started raising cows and I raised cows until three years ago."

I'm talking with Steve and his girlfriend Toni Thayer, an environmentalist, on a November day in 2002, in Steve's living room, and he's wearing jeans and a T-shirt that says something derogatory about the U.N.—I can't quite read it. Steve's got his hair slicked back and he's got a gray goatee and he's probably put on a little weight since he left Berkeley, and in his laid-back, southern California tone, he relates how he made the transition from environmentalist to rancher.

"I got to know the local people and learned about local history and I was moved by it all. I saw what they went through and it changed my mind. These people weren't corporate ranchers and they weren't bad people and they weren't ruthless like they're made out to be; they were just families trying to make it."

Steve is currently involved in a dispute with Kane County over Hole-in-the-Rock Road. It was an R.S. 2477 road, which means that it was constructed prior to 1976, when the Federal Land Policy and Management

Sign north of Widstoe

Act (FLPMA) was enacted and so would have been grandfathered in as a grant to Kane County. However, a FLPMA clause called Title V would transfer Kane County's rights to the road over to the federal government.

"We're fighting that like crazy," says Gessig, "We have a lawsuit against the federal government that was done with the slush fund that Marty Stephens (then Utah's Speaker of the House) set up and that money is being used to take ten roads in Utah into court to prove they are R.S. 2477, but in the meantime Kane County has signed a Title V on one of those roads."

But Steve and Toni have had troubles closer to home. Steve is on the board of the smaller of Escalante's two water districts, whose source is Pine Creek, which runs through some state-trust lands Governor Leavitt sold off, and he's been fighting the BLM, the new owners, over rights to the water. We take a drive out to the flume Steve recently put in and walk down a dirt track.

"They put a 'No Vehicles' sign up here, in the road," says Gessig, " I tore it out."

We walk upstream from the flume and he points to a curve in the streambed where he'd planned to put in a small hydropower generator, a plan which was shot down by environmental appeals.

"For hydropower?" I ask. "Isn't that clean energy?"

Steve shrugs. He shows me where the stream runs underground through a pipeline.

"We were hurrying to get this done before the land reverted to federal ownership. We were putting the pipeline in and they flew a helicopter over us and they came down here with measuring tape and I had ended up going fifteen feet too far here."

Steve drives me around town and fills me in on other aspects of the war. He shows me what's included in his district's water rights and we stop at the general store for some groceries and Steve introduces me to Lenza Wilson, the mayor, who happens to be buying groceries, and I think there has to be a mistake, this is just a kid in jeans and a jeans jacket, looks like he's not old enough to buy beer. In fact, Lenza is thirty and he's in his second two-year term as mayor and he skipped a term, so he was first elected when he in his mid-twenties, and then he must have looked like he was thirteen. But when he opens his mouth, it's obvious Lenza didn't stumble into the job or get it because nobody else wanted it, although I hear the salary isn't commensurate with the responsibility. I ask him why one of the town's two lumber mills closed recently. Was it because of the environmental regulations? The spotted owl?

"It's a complex situation," he says, "The market is bad and it doesn't show much signs of improving, and

Steve Gessig at the flume

there's been a pronounced change in where you can cut, and on top of that, environmentalists are trying to block all the sales."

Why is the Southern Utah Wilderness Association trying to stop the new Wide Hollow Reservoir, which the farmers say they need to survive, from going in?

"First off, it's payback because Escalante has been on the forefront of the environmental battles and we've opposed SUWA at every turn. Second, some of them probably have some actual concern that the reservoir will lead to development. But in fact, the reason we're trying to put the reservoir in is to keep agriculture viable. We're trying to put it in because we like it here and we like it the way it is. If ranchers and farmers can't make a living here, they'll have to sell out, and then you will see development."

How many lawsuits, which environmentalists brought against the BLM or Forest Service, involved Escalante?

"That would be a massive number," he says, "Every timber sale that I can think of, for years, they have either appealed or filed a lawsuit. SUWA has been the most active group in that respect."

As we drive back to Steve's ranch, he tells me about the grazing situation, and he fills me in on the story of Mary Bullock, "Wild Cow Mary," a maverick rancher who ran cattle on Fifty Mile Mountain and basically thumbed her nose at the BLM when they asked her and her neighbor Quinn Griffin, repeatedly, to pull them off the drought-stricken range, and so the BLM finally had them taken away.

"The ranchers were told there would be no changes to grazing, and the next thing you know, every rancher had to do an environmental assessment on his rangeland and they had to tell the BLM where they put their salt licks, what roads they were driving, and so for the first time the cattlemen have a lot of restrictions on them."

Quinn Griffin, the rancher who was in the middle of the range conflicts soon after the monument was dedicated, is now mostly involved with local real estate and has also become the salaried head of the yet-to-be constructed Escalante Center, which will be a sort of research clearinghouse for the monument. Quinn is out of town now, down in New Mexico learning the intricacies of government grants, so I stop in and see his parents, Delane and Thais, at their house near downtown Escalante. Delane was born in the now vacated brick home across from the elementary school and spent practically his whole life in Escalante. Decades ago he and his dog "Spunk" guided Randall Henderson, author of *On Desert Trails*, and anthropologist Jesse Jennings to the top of the Kaiparowits Plateau in a quest for

"Moqui" cliff dwellings by way of the same Batty Canyon where I sought shelter from the storm. There they found Indian glyphs and a few shelters, deer tracks, one doe, "one rattlesnake, a few jackrabbits, rodents and lizards" (Henderson, 145).

The Griffins themselves came into the area around 1878 or '79 and raised cattle and sheep until World War II, when they sold the sheep operation because of a lack of shepherds.

"Me and two of my brothers bought a cattle outfit down on the Fifty in 1969," he tells me, "and we didn't get out until the monument came in. The BLM used the drought as an excuse to pull us off. We fed the cattle until all our feed was gone, and the hay, and there was no more grass on the pasture, and then we began to sell them."

"Did you get a good price?" I ask.

"No."

So what does he think of the monument?

"They wanted to designate it so that it would be protected, and it was already protected."

Delane gives me his version of current events, the conflict between his son and the BLM that resulted in Quinn's cattle being "net gunned" by helicopter off the Fifty, and the final chapter, where Quinn had to hire a helicopter and a marksman to finish off the rest of his cattle, which were costing him thousands of dollars in fines, and he gives me the full story of their neighbor, Wild Cow Mary. As he tells it, after the BLM had rounded up her cattle and some Griffin cattle which had been grazing the same range, "They were going to herd them through Kanab, but they knew the sheriff and the brand inspector would be waiting for them, so they went around another route and got the cattle to the auction in Salina, and when they got there, the auctioneer wouldn't sell them and the brand inspector there, he said, 'The evidence I have is that the cattle belong to Mary Bullock and the Griffins; the BLM can't show ownership and I won't have anything to do with them.'"

Then things got interesting. Mary and a crowd of local cattlemen selling their stock at the auction appropriated the cattle on the spot, loaded them in their own trailers and drove them back to her ranch.

I ask whether there are any young people going into the cattle business.

"No. In fact, there's very few locals left in the business. A guy named Sorenson has come in and bought out a lot of locals. Most of us use the cattle business not as a livelihood but as a way to keep the family together, so we can work together and have some place to call home. My wife was a custodian at the church and I was a summer employee for the Forest Service, working on the range crew from spring until winter."

Most of the ranchers in Escalante and Boulder, I have come to find out, worked for the BLM or Forest Service at one point in their lives.

"There's still a lot of good people in both places," Delane tells me, "but they had a lot of pressure, especially when Clinton and Babbitt were in office. Look how many monuments Clinton's made, and I don't think he's seen any of them. He might have flown over this one but he never was here, didn't even have the guts to come up here."

Delane is touching on a bitter and divisive issue: the creation of the Grand Staircase-Escalante National Monument. President Clinton set 1.7 million acres aside for the new monument from the edge of the Grand Canyon on September 18, 1996. Members of the environmental community and the media were there with him, and a few celebrities were on hand but no Utah representatives or senators. Representative Chris Cannon later spoke for the entire Utah delegation:

> The first time anyone in Utah, including my Democratic predecessor, ever heard about the possibility of such an action (establishing the monument) was in the pages of the Washington Post, a mere 11 days before the creation of the monument. During the week before September 18, Utah's congressional delegation and Governor were told repeatedly that "nothing was imminent." (Subcommittee on National Parks, 21)

That slight continues to cause animosity, but the declaration itself, the "land grab," as many in Utah put it, probably shouldn't have come as a surprise. Back in the mid-thirties Secretary of the Interior Harold Ickes proposed another Escalante Monument, this one 4.5 million acres, centered on the confluence of the Green and Colorado Rivers. The proposal was held up by Utah politicians as well as local stockmen and miners and then it was reduced to less than half its original planned size and finally finished off with the United States' entry into the Second World War (Richardson, 116).

While the proposal still had life, Governor Blood lived in the perpetual fear that "Some morning we may wake up and find that . . . the Escalante Monument has been created by Presidential Proclamation" (Richardson, 127).

Before such fears were confirmed a full fifty-six years later, however, monuments were created all over southern Utah and turned into national parks, and Capitol Reef, declared a monument in 1937 and a national park in 1961, was expanded to six times its original size by President Lyndon Johnson in 1969 (Frye, 1). As this was happening the boosters of the original monuments, the local mayors and representatives and county commissioners, grew silent, and the local stockmen grew more vehement in their opposition to the creation of new parks and monuments and wilderness areas and the expansion of such entities, but by then it was too late. Blame the environmentalists.

"I'll tell you what's wrong with the environmentalists," says Delane, "They don't know and they don't know that they don't know, and that's serious because they've got limited knowledge and they're not willing to listen. They're always complaining about the condition of the range, and what they think is that if you take the stock off the range, it will become a Garden of Eden, but it won't 'cause it's a desert. It can't look any better than it does when it rains. In the spring the grass grows up and matures and that's as good as it gets."

"They've cut back logging here," Thais says, "and it just makes you sick because the forests are dying from the pine beetles, and once they catch fire, there's no stopping it. One of our mills has been shut down and these kids are struggling along. A lot of pioneers sacrificed everything they had and even their lives when they came out here, and now it's settled, and now we're told 'we want this land for *our* children.' Everything is for *their* children."

There's a picture of a line shack on the wall and it looks familiar. I get up to take a look at it and it turns out to be a small house, neat, well-proportioned, nestled in a slickrock cove. I've seen other photographs of that house in a book somewhere, but I can't quite place it. There's a news clip beneath the photograph.

"When did it burn down?" I ask.

"About 1996," says Delane. "It was the last one they burned. The Christensons had one burnt before that and somebody else had a cabin and trailer burnt on the same day. That cabin in the picture changed hands a few times. It was a homestead in Cedar Wash and they numbered the logs and tore it down and rebuilt it in Soda Gulch. There's some red clay hills out there and they gathered that up and plastered it in between the logs. My mother was born in that house."

"Makes you wonder who you're up against," I say.

"We know who we're up against," says Thais.

It's time for me to go. "What's your brand?" I ask Delane.

"We haven't got any cattle."

"What was your brand?" I ask, and he draws:

"We didn't have to do anything this summer," he says. "Don't have any cattle and we ran out of water so we didn't have to run the sprinklers. It

Bus near Escalante High School, by John Schaefer. Schaefer, a teacher at the school, distributed cameras to students so they could take photos for a project known as Children's Media Workshop.

was quite a vacation. We survive because we're old enough to draw social security."

"That big check really helps us out," his wife says, though I detect sarcasm. "You go all these years and keep putting heifers back into the herd, and in the meantime you're buying, and then all of a sudden it's all gone. And that's why we were rebuilding the herd, because that's what we were going to retire on."

"Then you two aren't millionaire corporate ranchers, I take it."

They stare at me.

"Do you miss that life?" I ask.

"Some people like to ride in a brand new Cadillac," says Delane, "and I feel the same enjoyment on a real good horse. They talk about tourism helping us out here and I can't see where tourism, no matter how many come through here, is going to benefit me. Somebody suggested I build a bed and breakfast"—and here he looks incredulous—"*a bed and breakfast*. Where would I get that kind of money? We're not living here because we're rich; we're living here to get away from the city and raise our kids up where they're free to go any direction they want, and they love the outdoors and when they go to college and get married, then they have to go somewhere else."

Kim Keefe is the soft-spoken secretary-treasurer of the New Escalante Irrigation Company and McKay Bailey is a big, retired local rancher with half a finger missing from his right hand and one finger crooked as a cottonwood branch on his left, and the day after I meet with the Griffins, the two have agreed to take me out to the proposed site of the new reservoir which the town has been trying to get approved for ten years. I meet them in the morning at Kim's tiny office in the middle of town, and we make small talk about Patrick Diehl and Tori Woodard, whose organization, the Escalante Wilderness Project (EWP), has joined with the Sierra Club and SUWA in appealing to the Interior Department's Internal Bureau of Land Appeals (IBLA) the BLM's decision to go ahead with the new reservoir. McKay and Kim don't have a very high opinion of the pair, and neither do most other people in town. Kim tells me, "Diehl is a strange person. He won't listen to anything anybody else has to say." And McKay says, "I met him once at the general store and I told him 'this town ain't big enough for the two of us. I'm leaving.'"

Kim worked for the Forest Service for twenty years and understood coming into the job what was involved in getting a project like the Wide Hollow Reservoir approved, but lately the obstacles have grown. Environmentalists are holding up final approval by raising issues that were addressed in the environmental assessments, but such concerns over the impacts to the land and the wildlife can be recast again and again in modified forms in each successive

Kim Keefe and McKay Bailey at the site of the proposed Wide Hollow Reservoir

Photo of Steve Gessig's property by Brittany, a fourth grader from the Children's Media Workshop.

appeal, and each time the irrigation company has to spend more money to clarify matters and restate their case to bureaucrats who are new to the situation.

The proposed reservoir site was initially outside the wilderness boundaries the Southern Utah Wilderness Alliance was recommending to Congress, and SUWA expanded those boundaries to include it. Diehl said the reservoir would siphon too much water from the Escalante River, though the districts' water rights entitle it to every drop the new reservoir would hold. SUWA is appealing the latest approval from the BLM on the grounds that the BLM has not proven that the proposed reservoir wouldn't severely damage the ecology of North and Birch Creeks.

"The environmentalists are also using the Southwestern willow flycatcher to hold things up, and a few other wildlife species, because Wide Hollow is a potential habitat site," says Kim, "and I think they want to get us on the riparian areas. What bothers us is the litigation we're going to face when the IBLA finally approves the project. NEPA is the problem. It was

I took this picture because it is a lot like our lives. You can always look at where you've been, while at the same time look ahead to where we can go if we work hard enough. Lucas

Photo by Lucas Schulkoski, from the Children's Media Workshop.

originally designed to mitigate impacts on the environment and it's turned into a nightmare of paperwork and legal battles."

The willow flycatcher, by the way, is a six-inch-long light-green and white passerine bird and dweller of thickets on the banks of streams. It joined the Mexican spotted owl, the Kanab ambersnail, the Utah prairie dog and the Kodachrome bladderpod as an officially endangered species in 1995. It's numbers may or may not be dwindling because of an insidious pest: the brown-headed cowbird, itself a declining species, which lays its eggs in the nests of other birds like the willow flycatcher and lets them raise its young. The cowbird used to feed on insects kicked up by bison, but now they follow cattle, and that has greatly increased their range.

Other objections to the reservoir focus on the BLM's supposed failure to address alternatives with less impact to the environment.

"The [existing] reservoir has been silting in since it was built," says Keefe, "and every conceivable alternative to solve that problem has been studied over the last twenty years. Dredging was one of the things we considered but it would have been very expensive and we would have to haul the dredged material somewhere else, and it would have required a lot of water to carry out, and it wouldn't solve the problem in the long run. We could also have raised the dam, but it would have flooded Escalante State Park, and the state put the existing dam on their 'high hazard list'; it's not safe, and we'd have to rehabilitate it, which would cost too much and leave us with the original problem."

According to the district's literature, a study by the state found that the present dam "was not capable of passing Probable Maximum Flood (PMF) without overtopping." Further studies by a private firm indicated that it "did not satisfy Utah State Engineer Criteria for seismic stability."

This is of interest to me because dams have a habit of breaking in these parts. One of the most spectacular failures occurred at Spectacle Lake above Salt Gulch back on May 29, 1938. Irene King-Ence records:

> Mary Moosman called me. "The reservoir dam has broken!" she said excitedly. "I can see a very big stream of water coming off the top of the mountain. Let everyone know.". . . We hurried to the pickup and drove over to Boulder, stopping on the Salt Gulch side of Boulder Creek. I said, "Just to be safe, we'll stop up here on the rocks." . . . Arthur Alvey was talking about the bridge. He pointed to the bolts, about two inches thick, and said, "I don't think any flood will move this bridge." . . . I took the girls up to the truck, wondering if it would be all day. I looked up the creek, then started screaming as I'd never screamed before in my life. I was petrified. I could suddenly see the front of the water coming, the trees and everything it was taking in front of it. There was a wall of debris fifty feet high. As it came, everything went over. . . . We all watched as the water hit the bridge below. It flew into the air like so many match sticks flipped away. Then the roar hit. We couldn't hear anything. (King-Ence 270-271)

Rehabilitating the present Wide Hollow dam to the point where it would be safe would cost three million dollars.

We get into McKay's '79 Ford pickup with his two faithful mutts, Fred and Barney, in the bed and ride out to the old earth dam below Escalante State Park, where dinosaur bones and conifers lapidified into agate have emerged from the bentonitic mudstones. From above, the dam *looks* sturdy enough. I expect to see a puddle on the other side, but it looks about half full, and that's half of half. When the dam was built in the late fifties, it held twenty-four hundred acre-feet of water and now it holds twelve hundred, and that drops every year.

"The reservoir fills up in the late fall and winter," says Keefe, "and then the rest of our allotment flows down river. Last year the reservoir was empty by June 28, and water didn't flow for another forty-four days. When that happens, people start using the town's spring-fed culinary system to water their lawns and their gardens, and this strains our culinary supply until we have to start rationing in order to reserve enough water to meet city fire codes."

We drive up the canyon, through ranchlands and fields of alfalfa. I ask Kim what kind of harvest they had this year.

"Normally farmers can get three or four crops of alfalfa, and this year they were able to get about one and a half."

I ask her why environmentalists were trying so hard to stop the dam.

"They don't want any reservoirs or any kind of construction on public land," she says. "The Glen Canyon branch of the Sierra Club has been fighting to drain Lake Powell. So they do what they need to do to get this reservoir stopped. They appeal it; they criticize the document. And it will never end until we have to abandon the project because it's too expensive. It sounds terrible but that's what they're doing, delaying it and delaying it until it costs us so much money we can't go on."

Already, the cost of the originally planned reservoir has risen over $3 million to $10.7 million, not counting the money the water conservancy district has had to spend justifying the project, and to stay within their budget they've reduced the reservoir's size from sixty-one hundred to thirty-five hundred acre-feet.

"How long is it going to take for the IBLA to return a decision?" I ask.

"It takes one and a half years to two years for an appeal to even get to the IBLA," says Kim, "and we can't wait that long. This drought has been pretty rough on the farmers and the reservoir really affects them. Opponents of the project have no sympathy for them either. They want to know why they are farming in the desert anyway. The farmers don't want people to feel sorry for them; they just want to continue farming what they farm best in this type of country, which is alfalfa."

I mention something Wallace Stegner had written about water being the economic substrate of the West. It's an old cliché but it's absolutely true: whoever controls the water controls the West.

"You haven't got much if you haven't got water," McKay agrees. "That's a fact."

We come up on an arroyo at the mouth of the hollow, the dam site, and McKay parks and we have a look around. The plan is to employ a rock slope as part of the dam structure. The earth beneath the arroyo would have to be excavated until they reached bedrock. I try to imagine where the waterline would be and what the reservoir would look like. Even by western standards, the reservoir won't be that large, 227 acres, but the hollow before me, the sagebrush plain and the arroyos cut into it and the low hills will be sunk.

"Real pretty country you've got here," I say.

"Yeah," McKay drawls. "As soon as we learn how to eat these rocks, we'll be set."

The Infamous Louise Liston

Louise Liston and her husband sold their BLM and Forest Service permits and now they raise quarter horses with roping blood lines on their ranch. Their brand is:

R̩

Louise was a Garfield County commissioner back in the eighties and nineties, and she was closely involved in a number of local battles over roads and wilderness, which culminated in President Clinton's designation of the land around Escalante as a national monument. I met her at her family's ranch house on the outskirts of town after I went out to see the dam site, and she agreed to talk to me even though she had a cold and a bad cough. She sat on the couch against her big front window and I sat across from her and she was backlit; I couldn't see her expressions unless I squinted. When she'd answered the door, though, I'd met a middle-aged woman with bright eyes and a half-smile on her lips, and I don't think that smile ever leaves her face except for brief moments because I can always hear it in her voice. It's not a mask, a politician's smirk; it's a genuine smile that involves her whole demeanor. It's the way she does business; she could keep the same dreamy tone of voice, the same pleasant smile while telling you that you're dead wrong and she's going to do everything in her power to stop you in your tracks.

Louise's voice is also tinged with a weariness which is only partly due to a cold, but as she speaks, she rapidly rallies, and she leans forward for emphasis, and then she falls back again because really, there's wasn't much she could do about the situation even when she was in office. I start off by telling her I think it will be at least ten years before the Interior Board of Land Appeals and the courts have finished reviewing the Sierra Club and SUWA's objections to the Wide Hollow Reservoir and construction can begin.

"Escalante's ranchers and farmers won't be here in ten years," she tells me, "It'll be another Escalante. We can't survive that long. We've had a lot of liquidation this year because of the drought, and you can't begin to pay your assessment for your water taxes on one crop of hay."

Louise reiterates the problems the town has faced on the reservoir, how environmental groups like SUWA wanted the BLM to conduct a "full-blown" environmental impact statement after three environmental assessments and then there would be more appeals to the IBLA and lawsuits, so I revise my estimate up a bit.

"It would take a hundred years," I say.

"It's really frustrating and it's such a simple project that could save a whole town and valley, keep open space, because when the ranchers sell out it's going to become tourist-oriented like Moab, though maybe not as big because we don't have as much water.

"I was involved in the Andalex Coal project in the monument and they have some mines over in Emery and Carbon Counties and they said, 'those mines are short-lived.' And what are we going to do when those mines are gone? We have in the monument the largest field of low-sulfur, non-polluting coal in the nation, maybe the whole world, and it's gone because of that proclamation and it would have been our salvation."

She goes on about the double-edged sword of tourism for a while but it's all summed up, showing the prevailing attitude as well, in the statement she gave before Congress on April 29, 1997:

> Our young people in rural areas feel that the freedoms guaranteed them by the Constitution are being violated more and more by Federal restrictions, regulations and designations. . . . Over 98 percent of my county is State and federally owned. With a meager 1.3 percent of the county's land base left to generate taxes from a population of 4,000, we are caring for over 3 million visitors. . . . we will handle their waste, provide law enforcement services, emergency services, search-and-rescue, try their criminal cases in our Courts, and maintain safe roads for them to travel on to recreate on the nation's public lands, all on a very limited budget that is further eroded away by the loss of taxes generated by stable industries that no longer exist.
>
> We in the West are tired of having our destiny decided by greedy preservationists and a Congress sympathetic to their cries of wolf. We take offense when accused of abusing the land and destroying its beauty, when, indeed, we have been such caring stewards that the land is now beautiful enough to be declared a "national treasure." (Subcommittee on National Parks,151-154)

I ask her about the fight to pave part of the Burr Trail.

"We actually received a court decision which said the Burr Trail belonged to us and we walked outside and our attorney said to SUWA's director, 'well, we won that one' and she said 'Delay is our victory and we'll delay you all the way.' In one way or another delay is their victory. That's what they're doing with the reservoir, the delay tactic. In the last four years the cost of the reservoir has gone up over two million dollars because of all the delays and appeals from environmentalists so we have to do everything over and over, and finally you just give up because you don't have the money to fight it and you don't see an end to it."

I come back to the reservoir. There's been a break in the town's main water line and the town's water supply has been shut off. School was cancelled. Louise points to the row of bottles and jugs on the counter she filled before the supply was stopped.

"We have to shut down the whole town," she says. "You know we love this western flavor, and rural towns depend on the land for a living, and if you take away the land, you're going to lose that flavor and the open space is going to fill up with growth and development. It's inevitable. It happens all over, and that's what we want to prevent. That's the reason for the reservoir, so we can preserve the agricultural lifestyle, the farming and ranching and cowboys and the western flavor that people come here to experience in the first place."

Louise has said some unkind things about the politicians in Washington in the past. "Did you ever meet Al Gore or Bruce Babbitt?" I ask. She leans forward into the house's light and she's beaming and she starts laughing.

"There was a hearing and I was testifying and Babbitt came in and someone said, 'Why don't you go up and introduce yourself?' And I said, 'Oh, I don't think that would be a good idea,' and he said 'Oh, go on,' and I thought 'O.K., maybe he needs to know who I am because I know he's heard a lot about me.' So I went up to him and said, 'Secretary Babbitt, I thought maybe I'd introduce myself. I'm Commissioner Louise Liston,' and he said, '*Ah*, the famous Louise Liston!' And I said, 'Probably the infamous Louise Liston to you!'"

The Environmentalists

That night I'm on the porch of the person who calls himself "the most hated man in Escalante." The man who answers the door is taller than me and I'm six feet; he's in his fifties, balding, but what hair he has is encomic and long in back and unkempt. He's wearing jeans and tennis shoes and a kind of striped shirt that's been out of style since the sixties. He's a big man, not heavy, but he has a large frame, a square jaw. He's intimidating, a cross between Henry Fonda and—he'd dislike this visual comparison but it's true—Clint Eastwood. This is Patrick Diehl, environmentalist and doctor of comparative literature.

He invites me into the living room, which is taken up by chairs and a desk, a rack full of cassette tapes, maybe one hundred of them or more, and a piano, and he introduces me to his partner of the last seventeen years, Tori Woodard, who wears thick-framed glasses and parts her long straight hair down the middle. Tori was raised on a cattle ranch in Colorado and moved to southern California at some point and met Patrick through an anti-nuclear weapons organization at Berkeley. Patrick Diehl was born in Texas and raised in Tennessee and he also spent some time on a cattle ranch in his childhood. He received his bachelor's degree from Harvard, got a fellowship to study in Paris, got a full career fellowship and his Ph.D. at U.C. Berkeley and took a second bachelor's degree at Oxford as a Marshall scholar. He's written two books, *Dante's Rime* (Princeton University Press) and *The Medieval Religious Lyric* (University of California Press). He was an acting assistant professor at Berkeley, taught there for about eight years and didn't get tenure and then he "went straight into the anti-nuclear movement."

They met in '82 and their relationship became serious in '85, and then Tori developed multiple chemical sensitivity, a type of environmental illness, a chronic, elevated immune response to low levels of perfumes, pesticides, detergents and other inorganic, and sometimes even organic, compounds. She didn't necessarily get MCS from the smog in southern California or from exposure to any particular toxic chemical, as often happens, but it was *something* in the urban environment, and they had to get out of that part of the world, to the high desert where particulate levels were much lower. They settled on Escalante because it's fifty-seven hundred feet high and because, as Tori says, "Patrick loves this area."

Tori keeps an electric air filter going at her feet throughout the interview. They've just come back from a trip down Davis Canyon and they didn't see one jackrabbit on the way, not one coyote, "and the place," Tori tells me, "should be crawling with coyotes."

Patrick is the vice-chairperson of the Sierra Club's Glen Canyon Group, whose primary goal is to drain Lake Powell, and Tori is the chairperson of the GCG's nuclear waste and conservation divisions. They and three other people also make up the five board members of the non-profit Escalante Wilderness Project, and as far as I can tell, its board members are its only members. This group of five people has been partly responsible for bringing a number of projects in and around Escalante to a complete halt through lawsuits and appeals to the Interior Department's Board of Appeals based on discrepancies in the BLM's environmental impact statements and environmental assessments, and one of those projects is the Wide Hollow Reservoir. One of the aims of the EWP is to end grazing on public lands.

"The viewpoint the people in town have is the Mormons moved in here, they built the roads, created the town and made their living off grazing sheep and cattle and now they're being told they can't continue that lifestyle—," I start.

"They're not making a living off that, though," says Patrick, "The statistics show that agricultural income is a minus figure."

"I'd like to address grazing," says Tori. "I grew up on a ranch, so when I moved here I wasn't particularly down on grazing. Patrick had a more critical view of grazing. In fact, when we first moved here I helped bring the Grand Canyon Trust here to meet with ranchers, and they met with them, cash in hand, to keep the land from being developed. So that's how I felt. And the local people seemed to think that was probably a communist plot. There had to be something really fishy with handing over any rights to your land. They didn't like that and they ended up not liking me. And that's when I started to change my view. As far as the question of grazing cows on public land, I don't think we should have any cows on public land. They overgrazed initially and they all know that. They ran way too many sheep here and they started grazing cows, and they [the BLM] cut [grazing] down and cut it down, and I feel like, yeah, you could probably support a few, like enough to feed the people, but not enough to export. Yeah, it wouldn't hurt you to have whatever it would take, maybe twenty-five cows running around to feed this place, but not more. They ignore all the scientific literature. Grazing is no longer viable; it's just not possible, and I feel like no one's to blame for what happened because they didn't know."

"How long," I ask them, "will it take the range to recover from the damage?"

"Never," says Patrick, "We're talking about centuries, with a lot of investment. The riparian zones would recover to some extent, but when you've got thirty-five foot deep arroyos, you're talking about a long time scale. We're talking about four or five feet of soil. If you look at the uplands, the shrubs are on little pedestals, and that's because the soil has been taken out around them. The diversity decreases. The bunchgrasses get extra attention by the cows. They've been eaten down to the roots. The damage is permanent enough; I certainly don't expect to see much improvement in my lifetime. Sometimes, where there's water, though, where cattle have been excluded, recovery can happen in five years."

This is one of the reasons they oppose the Wide Hollow Reservoir. A lot of water runs past the present reservoir, and Patrick and Tori believe that deforestation of the surrounding slopes by ranchers and the timber industry is mostly to blame. Less ground cover translates into more water moving faster downstream. Microbiotic crust, Tori says, "soaks the moisture right up. You can watch it," and this soil has been severely trampled by cows.

We talk about the old roads in the monument and the national parks. I try to introduce the idea of freedom of travel into the conversation but the Doctor, a member of the ACLU, will have none of it. "The constitution doesn't say anything about freedom of travel," he says, and our discussion moves along the lines of what's legal, and at one point Tori indicates she doesn't have much of a problem with allowing people to use the old roads in the monument.

"But that would allow people to just go wherever they want," says the Doctor, and he asks my opinion about the point of the controversy, about why the county and state are trying to claim so many cattle trails and deer trails and old four-wheel drive roads as "highways" or "roads."

"Well, part of it is to hold up the process of creating wilderness."

"Exactly," Patrick says, "and the courts don't look kindly on that sort of thing, using a pretext like that to stop another process."

The conversation turns to Highway 12. I tell them about a trip I took with Wade Barney, who does maintenance on Highway 12, about the Hog-back between Escalante and Boulder and the only way to widen it being to dig down fifteen feet. There are few fatalities, we all agree, for such a narrow and apparently dangerous road.

"I like it that way," Tori tells me. "I don't want it any wider. It's one of those nice old narrow highways that twists and winds; you're close to nature; you can interact with it. I'm an environmentalist that loves this highway. I want them to keep it nice and smooth, no pot holes, lots of money for them to keep it in good shape, just like it is. They're going to get a lot of money now that it's an All-American Road. What are they going to do with all the money?"

"Put in sidings," I venture. I don't really know.

"We'd like to see more educational signs along the Highway 12 corridor," says Patrick. "Maybe people will get some more information, maybe slow down a little and get to spend some time in Escalante and Boulder."

We talk about mining. Tori objects to me using the term "locked up" when referring to the extractable resources surrounding Escalante.

"Ten to fifteen percent of the monument is covered by mining claims," says Patrick.

"But nobody can stake any new mining claims," I reply.

"No."

Andalex sold its claim on the coal beneath the Kaiparowits Plateau for about fourteen million dollars after the monument's creation, Tori reminds me.

The Doctor says that Ruby's Inn, next to Bryce Canyon, is now the single largest employer in Garfield County, outside of the federal government. I tell them I think most of the cowboys here probably don't want to wait on tables or work in convenience stores or clean toilets for a living and the Doctor has a ready answer: "They'll have their wives and girlfriends do that for them," his point being that small-scale ranching in the West, right now, is so unprofitable that many of the local families look at it more as a hobby or lifestyle than an occupation. Often the wife has to make ends meet working a service job or two in town.

Patrick and Tori moved here about the time the monument engulfed Escalante but the two were welcomed nonetheless and some of the ranchers even helped them unload their furniture from the moving van. Patrick, who has had some acting experience and who is a classically trained musician, got involved with the church choir and the local drama club. Then they wrote an editorial that was critical of the proposed Wide Hollow Reservoir in the *Salt Lake Tribune,* and the Sierra Club picked up on it and got a court injunction to halt construction until further environmental studies could be completed, and that nixed a deal between the New Escalante Water District and the National Guard, which was loaning them a few hundred men and some equipment to help with the initial construction. According to Patrick and Tori, the deal wasn't legal to begin with, but regardless, the water district lost several hundred thousand dollars and the two were warned they'd "better get their Kevlar vests."

Not long after Patrick and Tori initiated the process which shut down construction of the new reservoir, somebody opened the water valve in their backyard and thirty-two thousand gallons of water spilled out, ruining the excavation for a studio Patrick and his son were going to build.

"You know," I told them, laughing, "that's actually pretty clever. And it shows some restraint."

But Patrick and Tori don't think it was funny, and neither did the water board, which accused them of opening the valve themselves as a "publicity stunt" and fined them $1,150. They fought the fine and lost—according to Tori, the judge "sneered" at them—and then they appealed that ruling and won. The suit and the appeal cost them a great deal more than the fine, but Diehl says "it was a matter of principle."

It took them a long time and a lot of hassles to get their water hooked back up. Meantime, somebody broke into their house while they were away and trashed it and somebody smashed their car's windshield. Somebody called Tori in the middle of the night and told her "I wouldn't sleep too sound if I was you."

Bob Walton of Salt Lake City is a representative of the Utah Wilderness Coalition and a friend of theirs. At a BLM hearing in the high school, according to Patrick, a cowboy grabbed bumper stickers and pamphlets off the table Bob had set up and out of his hands and shredded them with a bowie knife. More cowboys gathered around him and threatened Bob's life—one of them said "We ought to kill you," according to Walton—and Tori and Patrick had to help escort him away.

Diehl was handcuffed during an anti-wilderness gathering where one speaker, a bishop in the LDS church, likened the battle with environmentalism to a "religious war." Later, he was told the handcuffs were for his own protection.

Throughout all of this their only friend was Sheriff Monte Luker who, most people agree, later lost his job for standing up for them and protecting them.

The Doctor was involved for years with the "Escalante Center," a planned local interpretive center and a staging point for geological, archaeological, ecological and paleontological studies in the monument. Louise Liston's son-in-law, Quinn Griffin, the guy who had to shoot some of his own cattle last season because he couldn't get them off the Fifty, took over the directorship of the center.

"That must be kind of galling," I say.

"It's been very interesting," says Patrick, "It actually got co-opted. It started out state-driven. The Escalante Center was supposed to be an art center, science center, museum, visitors center, something for everyone—they allocated ten million dollars—and it's evolved into something that's not the original concept. I'm on the board of the Escalante Canyons Center for Arts and Humanities and we were a partner in the center originally and our group was thrown out of the partnership because I was on the board. 'Thou shalt not suffer an environmentalist to be part of your organization.' That was quite a dramatic moment. They expelled our representatives and two months later they had it back together minus our organization."

"Was it rational for you to move here?" I ask them.

"Are you asking if it was safe?" says Tori.

"Both."

"We came here for my health. It's a high desert, and Patrick loves this place. And the garden out back is starting to produce. Why don't they (the people of Escalante) leave?"

"They are leaving."

Patrick nods, "Escalante has a long history of that, young people leaving town."

That doesn't surprise Tori. "Their basic philosophy is to go out and multiply and subdue the earth," she says.

They give me examples of taciturn locals treating visitors rudely and a list of the worst offenders. I can add from personal experience that if you look like an environmentalist in Escalante, you will probably be mistreated.

"I'd like to put a rumor to rest," I tell Patrick. "I've been told that you had a hiking accident out in the monument and the people of Escalante had to rescue you."

"I went over a cliff in Phipps Wash in '97 and broke my pelvis in two places and my left forearm, the ulna. I lay there for thirty hours, and Tori tried to convince the search and rescue commander to just go down the route that I went down. She knew where I was. If they'd done that they would have found me real fast. They had a plane out there and I saw it go by four times. I was in the shadows and I wasn't very mobile with my pelvis broken in two places, so I couldn't make myself visible. I'm lying there, the plane is flying by and you know, I was wondering 'why don't they come down to the rock above me?'"

"The BLM guys couldn't go against what the commander of the search and rescue said," Tori tells us, "so we all got together down by the Escalante River to see if they'd found Patrick and nobody had so the commander of the thing went home."

As it turns out, the search and rescue commander, had been up all of the previous night, and there was some sort of miscommunication between him and Tori. When he called off the search, the BLM members kept going on their own, following Tori's advice this time, and they found Diehl a quarter-mile down the trail.

"What were you thinking for those thirty hours?" I ask.

"He was doing pain management," says Tori.

"I figured Tori would get people to the right place eventually," says the Doctor. "That's what I was thinking."

"You didn't have any religious experiences?"

"Oh good Lord no."

"They normally wait twenty-four hours after a call has been made to begin the search," says Tori, "but Monte Luker, our friend the sheriff, decided he was going to initiate the search that day. He believed there was something wrong, and there was a storm coming."

"I was lying right there with a cliff above me," Diehl tells me, "and I was right where a couple slopes came together, so that afternoon, as I was waiting to be rescued, I was trying to move myself out of the bottom of this gully, and I'd managed to move about a foot up through soft sand at the cost of extreme pain, because I could smell the rain coming and it was going to come right over that cliff. I'd already been out there a day and exposure was a real problem. So anyway, and I don't want to be nasty about it, but I don't see myself as having been rescued by the people of Escalante. I was rescued by some BLM employees who finally were able to do their jobs when they ceased being ordered around by somebody who'd jumped to conclusions about where to look."

Later, Patrick and Tori set up an information booth and handed out literature on the environmental consequences of grazing next to the steps of the BLM's Interagency Center. The BLM wanted them outside a certain radius from the front door and suggested they put their stand next to a maintenance shed at the far end of the parking lot. Tori was cited for placing the booth too close to the front door and then Patrick was cited and hauled away.

"I started a hunger strike in Purgatory Jail, over by St. George, and they freaked," says Diehl. "The press was all over it. I couldn't believe how much attention this thing got. You know, just a little minor civil disobedience."

Says Tori, "They let him go right away. [BLM law enforcement officer] Larry Vensel said to Patrick, 'This is how you're thanking me for rescuing you.' Larry rescued him and Patrick said, 'I would have done the same for you.'"

"If they (the locals) *had* rescued you, would you have felt differently?" I ask.

The Doctor has to think about that for a moment. "Not really," he finally says. "I would do the same thing for any human being in my position. In fact, I tried to be on the search and rescue team so I could do the same for other people, but . . . ahhrrgg."

The long and short of it is that they didn't want him on the search and rescue team.

I hint at another rumor as I leave; that although they had helped bring the construction of the Wide Hollow Reservoir to a stop because they thought it might lead to developments other than alfalfa fields, the two were in fact planning their own fifty-home development somewhere on the edge of Escalante. At the end of a conversation about Patrick's run for Utah's Second Congressional District on the Green Party ticket (he got 1.3 percent of the vote), I allude to the rumor in a sideways manner: "One thing I think you and me and the people of Escalante could agree on," I say, "is that we don't want Escalante to be developed."

They don't bite. I tell them I think all the locals want is to be left alone, and Diehl says, "That's not going to happen." They encourage me to move down to Escalante so the town could have at least three points of view.

The Timber Baron

Imagine the look on a guy sitting on a thousand-pound bull that's just stomped its last rider to death and you will see the look on Stephen Steed's face. His teeth clench in a nervous smile, his eyebrows arch, his head tilts down a bit and he looks past me once in a while to where the sky would be, like he wants to see some patch of sunlight before they open the rodeo pen doors.

Stephen Steed is manager of the Skyline Forest Resources sawmill at the edge of Escalante, but just barely. A few months back, the operation looked doomed: it was hemorrhaging money and the owners were going to shut it down and they'd already started laying the workers off. But Stephen and his brothers begged, borrowed and finagled enough cash and credit to buy the owners out, and here he is, in his own office where the sounds of the yard are still clear, sitting on that bull that's ready to stick a horn in his gut.

I've seen that look before. I saw it on local cowboy Dell LeFevre's face when I spoke to him on his ranch, but only for a moment because he actually did ride bulls in his younger days and he's the sort of nut who'll wager his own money and up the stakes when he gets on a bull like that and leave the rest to God. And I see it on the face of my father, CEO of a wire-rope mill in Pennsylvania, every time I ask him how business is going. There are a lot of entrepreneurs and executives in the manufacturing sector of this country who are putting in sixteen-hour days and feeling lucky—not good but *lucky*—if their operations break even. I don't pity them: they're adrenaline junkies and they got on the bull themselves, but I don't envy them either because their work beats them to pieces even if they do go the full eight seconds.

Stephen doesn't have much time to talk and he gives me the abbreviated version of the mill's history: His family has been in the logging business for four generations. His father built Escalante's other sawmill in 1958 and it burned in 1975, two years after his father died, and they rebuilt it and it was bought by Allied Forest Products and then Kaibab Forest Industries, which closed it to keep their operation in Panguitch going, but that mill died too and so did another one in Fredonia, just south of Kanab, and about four hundred people lost high-paying jobs around here in the early and mid-nineties. About that time Stephen and some partners got a few loans and grants together and bought this mill, which used to compete with his father's, and brought it back from the grave and gathered some equipment from the other mills at discount prices and hired a few people who'd been laid off and went back into business processing salvage timber for the Forest Service. The mill was bought by Bighorn Lumber out of Laramie, Wyoming, which kept him on as manager but also made a business decision to shut the mill down again in 2001, and that's when he and his brothers bought the mill back.

Salt Lake City's *Eyewitness News* (July 24, 2002) covered the mill's rebirth. Here's a few lines.

John Hollenhorst: Stephen Steed pretty much presided over the funeral of the plant last winter. The sawmill was losing money. Shutting down. Fifty people out of work. Now, in a summer surprise, they're all going back to work.

Stephen Steed: Yes, hah, hah. I am surprised.

JH:　The brothers may be surprised the deal came together, but some workers aren't.

Mark Lison, sawmill mechanic: They're really down to earth, and what they say they're
    gonna do, they do.
JH: And they did.
ML: And they did! Hah, hah hah.

Since then they've purchased a micro mill to process specialty products
and they've concentrated on niche markets to pay the bills: vigas, beams for
Navajo hogans, rails, shakes, pet-litter shavings, landscaping mulch.

"What's responsible for the slump in the timber industry?" I ask.

"Lower labor costs and less regulation in other countries, a strong dollar.
You can ship finished wood in from Europe, Canada, Australia and South
America cheaper than you can buy it here," he says, and then he gets that
nervous smile and he watches me like he's thinking I'm going to jump over
the desk and try to throttle him over what he says next: "And Eric, the environmental movement has played a role as well, and NEPA. There have
been excesses in the past we're not proud of. There's been overgrazing,
nobody denies that, and there are roads in places we don't need roads. If
we weren't willing to learn from our mistakes and change our ways maybe
we shouldn't be here, but we love this place and if we didn't we wouldn't
be here."

As it turns out, the Mexican spotted owl also inhabits the forests around
Escalante, as do many other endangered species, and that means the BLM
and the Forest Service have to complete huge environmental assessments
before a single sapling can be cut. The logging Steed's contractors are doing
on Griffin Top required nine file boxes of paperwork, and while the government processes its EAs and EISs, some nearby forests are being decimated
by spruce beetles.

"Have you seen Cedar Mountain?" he asks. "The trees are dead. We
could have stopped the spruce beetle infestation at its inception but now it's
an epidemic, and *now* the Forest Service wants to cut down all the infected
trees on that mountain. It will be thirty or forty years before commercial
harvesting can begin again."

That's bad planning or bad luck, but the timber industry got some perversely good luck lately when the West caught fire. In 2000, fires burned
about 8.5 million acres of forests in the U.S., an area bigger than Maryland,
much of which had been set off limits to loggers by environmental lawsuits.
Whether the fires could have been prevented by logging is still up to debate,
but many western politicians made that assumption and the Interior Department began to let out more thinning contracts.

"The Kaibab Fire," says Steed, "was 450,000 acres. *Now* we've got a con-
tract to cut diseased trees down there."

We're joined by Steed's imposing top machinist, Wally Veater, the man who keeps the mill's saws sharp, who commutes all the way from Panguitch on the other side of the Paunsaugunt Plateau. He agrees with his boss on what caused the mill there to close, and he tells me about an environmental group called Friends of the Dixie who lived in and around Dixie National Forest, who saw it as their mission to protect the Dixie from logging and other abuses.

"Now they are surrounded by dead spruce," says Wally, "and nobody wants to buy their houses because they can't get fire insurance, hah, hah."

"Up in Brian Head, you used to have to get a permit to cut a tree on your own property, and then their trees were infected with spruce beetles. Now, if you find a tree that's infected, you'll be fined if you *don't* cut it down."

Skyline Forest Resources only employs about sixty workers but that still makes it the largest employer in Escalante, and these aren't service industry jobs. Steed also keeps a lot of logging contractors working.

"We contribute about seven million dollars to Garfield County's economy," he says. "I know a guy who lost his job at the mill, and he and his wife went to work for Ruby's Inn, and the two of them together don't make as much as he was earning alone at the mill."

What does the future hold for Skyline Forest Resources? Stephen sees the economics and public opinion coming around.

"Things will cycle," he says. "Right now people like Patrick Diehl and Tori Woodard have control, but the environmentalists aren't just trying to keep the locals out of the forests and parks, they're trying to keep the public out, and people will begin to realize that."

Does he believe Patrick and Tori are going to give up?

"Escalante will be here long after they're gone," he says, and the mention of these two jogs his memory, "Have you seen what they were planning?" he asks.

I don't know why, but Stephen's got their newsletter on his desktop. It's titled "Resources for the Chemically Injured" and below it says "Proposal to Build a Housing Community for People with MCS."

I skim through it.

> Escalante House is a nonprofit, non-religious organization with three guiding principles: conservation, creativity and compassion. . . . We are currently negotiating with the State of Utah to locate MCS housing on 325 acres of land owned by the State three miles south of Escalante, Utah . . . Garfield County requires six acres for every home site. That means there could be up to 54 home sites on the proposed site. . . .

And so on:

. . . camping area, low-income apartments . . . medical clinic . . . cafeteria, offices . . . small auditorium . . . natural food store . . . studios . . . workshops.

"Well," I say.

Veater offers me a tour of the mill. In the middle of the floor stands the sash gang saw, and it is one malefic-looking piece of machinery. The blades of the sash cycle faster than the eye can follow, ripping planks into straight lines and sawdust to the accompaniment of a clamant nasal buzz and a scrannel machine screech, and when I get closer, I hear a high-voltage hum relayed from the Page power plant via Garkane Power and I feel the floor boards vibrating as that bandog tugs on its mounts and tries to break free.

Walking somebody from Friends of the Dixie in here would be like walking a vegan into a slaughterhouse, I think.

The gang saw is in the middle of the operation. When the boles arrive at the log yard, they're sorted into classes according to type and quality and bucked to a particular length. Then they're debarked, loaded on a log deck and drawn onto the carriage by an endless lumber chain at the sawyer's command.

Wally leads me into the sawyer's booth and closes the door, cutting off the noise, and I am instantly at home. In fact, I want the sawyer's job. He sits, while everybody else in the mill stands, in a closet-sized space dark as a video arcade, with a switch-studded joystick in each hand and pedals beneath his feet, before a window, leaning over the headsaw and a panel lit like a car dash, with gauges and meters and more switches and buttons, with his attention focused on the log on the rolling carriage and the red laser guide rippling over its raw, blonde surface. The guy running the show now doesn't even look up to see who we are, just tips and spins the joysticks as fast as they'll roll, but when Wally asks him to explain the process, there's no urgency in the sawyer's reply. He could be talking to us over a cup of coffee with his full attention on us, just as I was once able to chat with my friends while my hands shoved and twisted and flapped the controls of a video game, trying to save my virtual life.

Frames called "knees" press against the log, and attached grappling irons, or "dogs," snub it to the carriage. The computer scans the log with a red laser beam and uses an algorithm to calculate the optimal cut and the sawyer fine tunes the selection or overrides it based on grain and knots and the general shape of the log and his experience and then aligns the carriage to set up the cut, and then cables fed through idler pulleys to keep the motion constant draw the carriage and the log, riding on wheels known as "trucks," through the band saw and back through it again on the return stroke, and then the sawyer may set up another cut on the same face or release the dogs and manipulate the claws and bars of the set-works to gig the log for another angle. A large ponderosa like the one loaded up now can be reduced to workable cants in about a minute. This is the heart of the mill and it's where the operation bottlenecks, so the sawyer has to know his job.

The curved outside slabs go to a horizontal resaw where another sawyer salvages what he can from them, and the inside cants go to graders who evaluate them for tightness, appearance, and defects such as burns, knots, gentle "sweeps" in the grain or abrupt "crooks" and advance them to a trimmer who planes and edges them down to their final dimensions and then a sorter who sends them down a "sort chute" into one of twelve piles. The thick center cant, meanwhile, arrives at the graders' tables by way of the gang saw. The scraps from all these processes are shipped to an outfit in Circleville, which tosses them into a tub grinder and makes pulp or mulch or wood chips out of them.

We pay a visit to Veater's workshop, where half-a dozen men are kept constantly busy machine grinding the blades and working them by hand, checking their hook and pitch, welding cracks and shaping them and swaging them in preparation for use. Each blade takes about one and a half hours to grind and the blades run on the drum four hours at a time. When properly maintained, an eight-hundred-dollar blade will last about nine months.

Long ago, lumber mills used to rely primarily on circular saws, but the larger operations all use band saws now because they have a thinner kerf and waste less product. The double-cut continuous saw blades, the ones Wally works on, are thirty-two feet long and have a kerf of 150 thousandths of an inch.

Wally points out the micro mill they've set up in the yard for processing the smaller jobs they're anticipating. Right now that mill, which is about the size and shape of a ship container, is locked up, just as the thinning contracts are locked up by environmental appeals. Then Veater turns me loose to explore the yard on my own, and I wander past the kiln, where almost all the lumber has to be dried these days to kill off the beetles, and the stacks of finished lumber, past a John Deere 744E log loader parked on the side of the lot, which looks like a regular front loader on steroids, with two giant, worn teeth on its lower jaw.

From outside, from a short distance, the mill appears as big shacks and utility sheds and pipes, vats, bins, hoppers, roller chains, cables, a few massive Caterpillars and flatbeds ready to roll with the finished product, and piles of sawdust. Everywhere in the yard and for a radius of at least a mile when the wind is blowing, you can smell sawdust.

Steed's brand is:

$$S_S$$

Red Breaks

My plans fall to pieces that first night on Sheffield Road. I wanted to walk down Phipps Wash, where Doctor Diehl almost died, and see the arch and the natural bridge where it joins the Escalante River. Maybe I would even hike up to Bowington Arch on the far side. I wanted to explore Harris Canyon, where Charles Hall rerouted southbound pioneers a few years after he helped put through the route to Hole-in-the-Rock, and there were a couple of sandslides I wanted to take a look at further down where his route intersected the Escalante River and there was a chimney somewhere off the road I wanted to see, the only thing that remained of Sam Sheffield's cabin, but I don't do or see any of these things, and I blame the rocks for that.

I'm part-way down the road, past the old corral, the stone beehives and idol's heads when the sun begins to set so I pull off to a white rock outcropping, and the Heap crawls far enough down it for me to be hidden from the road, down to the rim and a stack of rocks blocking the wind from an old fire pit. I park on the other side, perpendicular to the breeze, to form a wind shadow and then gather up deadwood and start the fire. And then I sit on the edge, with the disjointed orange sunlight refracted into planes by contrails ebbing into white pulses, and study the prairie known as Big Spencer Flat that begins almost at my feet and the red billows and mesas out near the Escalante River and the three spectral-blue peaks of the Henrys and the black cap of Navajo Mountain and the rock wedges out at Red Breaks, and I think, *Those rocks at Red Breaks are what I've been looking for all along, I've got to go there.*

Next day I take a side trip in low four-wheel-drive off to the west on a sand-trap road, to a sharp-tipped nameless red inselberg. It's a "class 4" climb to the top, according to Steve Allen (100), and I've got places to be, so I only hike up a hundred feet or so, and I make notes on the slickrock, study the seams that develop independent of the bedding planes and split it like linear faults and the resulting "critical partings" delineating the dangerous concavities where the Navajo Sandstone domes curve down into a vertical plane and then jut back out into a nearly horizontal footslope, and other thin fractures that funnel water to the brush that takes root in them to pry them apart.

Sheer, unsupported sandstone cliff faces could be five thousand feet high if they weren't weakened by fractures (Terzaghi, 251-270), but all of them are, to one degree or another. Cracks propagate linearly as "fracture mirrors" from microscopic semi-circular flaws or radiate out in successive circular hackles. The fractures may initially be imparted by tectonic action; valley floors with their overburden of rock removed tend to bulge upward. They may also result from weaker, underlying shales giving way unevenly, which tends to cause "rotational" block failures. In any case, weathering loosens the calcite bonds in the slickrock along minute cracks, water pours in and freezes and plant roots dig down and loosen things further. Domes exfoliate rock in sheets and cliffs spall off blocks which tilt outward until their centers of gravity cross the hinge at the base and they topple or rotate loose. In some parts of the world, if the block is large enough, it may ride the loose rock slope beneath it intact for up to seven miles (Watson, 522-548).

Sandstone faces organize themselves into arched alcoves and blind windows because these are the most stable forms for supporting overhanging loads. A single slab failure will initiate the process by redistributing stress lines from the new keystone laterally onto the adjacent rock; the resulting horizontal compression serves to hold that rock in place. Where thrust lines pass through the stone, it's kept wedged in place; otherwise when it loosens, it's free to fall.

Straight sandstone walls form bays and amphitheaters through a similar mechanism. Convex walls are simply more resistant to lateral stress than straight escarpments.

The "elephant skin," or "hadrosaur skin," as I call it, the polygonal cracking, is a surface phenomenon; it extends only a foot or two into the rock.

Around here, wind and sheetwash strip the rock away one grain at a time. Hence, no talus fans at the bottom of the slopes.

The road turns to washboard, then potholes, and then it's just two tracks in sand. I have to spin the tires to get through and I brake hard enough to almost get the Heap sideways just before the sand transitions to rock because the wonderful frictional gradient between rubber and slickrock will sometimes snap a spinning axle like a pencil.

The last part of the road is a sandstone shelf. I walk in a wide circle to make sure the road doesn't pick up again anywhere and then I pour some peanuts into my pocket and fill the water bottle and walk into the slickrock anomy near Red Breaks with no plan in mind but exploring.

Right off, before I've reached the breaks, I find iron bands in the sandstone with concretions birthing from them like sterile rock eggs: double concretions and UFO saucers, shapeless blobs, bifurcated brains and yo-yos and sombreros. Soon after, I come to ziggurat buttes with cross-bedding like

Hackles in sandstone near half-dome

rope coils and past them the white rock fades out and leaves the red sandstone that gives the breaks its name. I find a survey marker pounded into
stone in 1937; it says "Fine for removal $250."

I climb into the breaks, cross by a cairn, though there's no trail here I
know of and certainly none I could follow, climb around the side on a narrow bench and out to a successive weirdness of massive, dune-bedded white
domes, the faces of which are landscapes in and of themselves, and I climb
one of these domes to its brown caprock, a flat of manzanita, thistle and
juniper with another, smaller bench on top of it, which I also climb. Coming
over the edge, the wind almost pushes me off but I lean into it and, squint-
ing, I can see the whole length of Fifty Mile Mountain, the Henry Mountains, Navajo Mountain, breaks in the wall to the east where I can see the
red Circle Cliffs, another far-off Navajo dome which is actually a half-dome,
a white, ice-cream scoop dome, maybe a fossil meander from the ancient
Escalante, now thrust into the sky, and up north there's the infinite black
edge of the Aquarius Plateau.

Not a straight line in sight, not the domes or the streams or the junipers
or even the undersides of the cumulus clouds above the Aquarius, which are
curved to its surface, not the sky nor time nor the rock which erodes into
bows, only the lines in my journal, which I can't follow because even when I
sit, the wind blows me sideways.

It's taken me most of the day to get here. I walk down from that wind-blasted peak to find another way back but I come to an amphitheater with smooth concave walls and I can't help rolling a few circular stones off the top. The results are spectacular; when I toss the rocks down spinning, they pick up speed and shoot out the bottom, maybe two hundred feet below, like lethal projectiles, skimming over the floor at a hundred miles-plus per hour, skipping off obstacles like trees and boulders and launching through the void for two heartbeats while they pick up *more* speed, until these indurated cap-rocks detonate like fireworks against a cliff-line at the far edge of the flat.

This phenomenon requires scientific study, so in the time I should be finding my way down, I'm tossing different-sized rocks off the rim. My eventual goal is to get the rocks through gaps in the cliff at the far corner of the stone plain below me, into the narrows beyond it, sort-of like knocking a pinball past bumpers at the machine's upper end. I have to strain my back to get a few specimens moving and the larger ones tend to disintegrate as they go and they come out of the slalom like shotgun blasts with a few fragments headed in the right direction but with so much kinetic energy sapped by breaking free and getting up to speed that none of them makes it to the edge. Rocks the size and shape of a discus hold their integrity well, but I have to go further and further out from the edge to find them and finally I worry more about their flatness than how circular they are, which turns out to be a wise move because they shape themselves as they tumble. Near the cliff line they hum like a tire spun off a semi-tractor trailer. Round stones also perform well, which surprises me because they're too solid to be chipped away into a more perfectly circular shape.

I catch myself grimacing as I watch these bullets ricochet and go airborne for a hundred feet and splatter into red sprays at the end of the course.

I also experiment with different launching points. At one location—the black hole, I call it—rocks stop dead against some hidden obstacle at the base of the wall, which might be sand because a soft thump is often the last noise I hear from them. Another spot imparts a super-high velocity but there's no break in the cliff in that direction and no ramps beforehand to help stones clear it. An hour in and I find the sweet spot that puts the rock in a terminal, high-speed, high-jumping trajectory for the gaps. A disc finally shatters off a boulder near the end of the course and a few fragments spin past the crags, over a sand trap and into the abyss. A few minutes later I get a hand-sized rock to do the same thing without losing more than a few pebbles off its mass. The experiment is a success, and with the sun half sunk through Fifty Mile Mountain, it's time to get back to the Heap.

In the morning, I drive Sheffield Road to where it quits at a drill pipe. Again I walk out in a circle from the deadend to see if there's a connecting road, onto yellow-banded slickrock and into blanket sand where I do find deer tracks but not much else. By midmorning I'm on my way back to Highway 12, listening to AC/DC's "Back in Black," which is inappropriate music for this environment and makes me drive too fast. I take another side road and it leads me to another abandoned pipe. Hendrix sings about a room full of mirrors and Robert Plant says "It's been a long time," and then, as I turn onto the highway, headed for Escalante, where the dam will surely fail when the heavy rains finally come, I feel the heartbeats of titans that walked the earth before the gods in my sternum, and the harmonica wails from all corners of the sky and I feel the levee about to break.

Half-Dome

A few days ago, a woman froze to death not far west of here, up on the Kaiparowits Plateau, on Death Ridge, and here I am sweating in a T-shirt as I drive down Harris Wash.

My plan is to drive the length of the wash, cross the Escalante and drive up Silver Falls Creek to Moody Canyon Road. I know there's no way that's going to happen because part of the route is in the Glen Canyon Recreation Area and it's fenced off, and the locals tell me the old road is washed out, but that's the plan.

And it quickly goes awry. The road to the trailhead at Harris Wash continues on the other side—though none of my guidebooks show it and it's not on the 1:100,000 scale USGS maps either. It *is* in the Utah Wilderness Coalition's compendium of potential wilderness areas, *Wilderness at the Edge*, oddly enough, and looks like it was penciled in.

It's a good road so I decide to follow it rather than drive down the wash. It skirts a low cliff line and swings up towards Red Breaks and detours around an arroyo that's eaten its banks back twenty feet—the original road now goes off the edge of the wash—and I have to throw the Heap in low four-wheel-drive and plow through a few sand dunes that have drifted over the route to get to the plain south of a giant white slug of Navajo Sandstone. It takes me a minute to realize where I'm at; the base of the half-dome peak I'd seen in the distance the day before.

Now the day is completely shot. I have to climb to that half-dome, that abandoned meander in the sky, if that's what it really is. I park the Heap, take off across the plain, zigzag up the face, past white arabesques in red rock and pizza-crust rock and swirling incoherences which are the shape of the wind and red stone oozing up from pores and dozens of potholes which are hidden until I'm almost on top of them, sunk like shafts fifteen feet or more into the sandstone, at the bottom of which I half expect to find some explorer's bones.

What looked like a solid outcropping of Navajo Sandstone is actually incised by three valleys—one, visible from the road, draining south from a mouth halfway up the side, the two flanking it draining north. Near the top, on the west side, I find a sill, a critical parting far above the piedmont, and follow it around to the head of the first valley which has a broad mouth and joins with the third valley further downstream, but upstream quickly thins into a V and then a tight narrows, the floor of which is over a hundred feet below me and hidden from view by the curve of the wall. There's a thin lintel of red sandstone, a future arch, above the slot, which becomes just a fissure as it curves up to the head. Nearby, there's a four foot tall spire, an altar to this temple.

How can we blame those who would worship nature in an environment such as this? The temples are ready-made in this country and Mormon churches pale in comparison. The only question I have as I stand near the altar is which deity does this temple honor? I get the feeling that it's the spirit of running water, in whatever name it goes by, that is invoked here, specifically the streams that can develop such temples over millions of years from mere cracks in the sandstone.

I climb up a redrock chute and cross the red beam, the caprock of sandstone so friable I can crumble fragments of it in my hands, and follow the sinuous ridge that joins all three valleys, to the top of the south-facing draw, which is broader than the first but ends in another sheer wall and I keep hiking out to another red altar, ten feet tall, to the abandoned meander wall that faces me, or rather faces the sky behind me. There's a line of square openings high up in that edifice, like pueblo windows, and its base is a shaly purple rock in which, with binoculars, I discern a tiny doorway, or perhaps just two fallen slabs that give that appearance.

Below me is a hidden, sublime sand valley flat formed from walls turned down in ideal geometric curves. There's rabbitbrush, manzanita and Russian olive growing in the sand and the cracks, and some grass and juniper and pinyon, and there's a water pocket in a shaded alcove. Perhaps a Fremont Indian grew crops here eight hundred years ago and climbed to this altar each day to pray to the god that made that meander and that then scoured and disintegrated the rock plain around it until it became the channel of the river of wind that pours through these last peaks. If I were a Fremont Indian, I would certainly try to make a go of it here, damming that alcove with a low masonry wall and constructing catchwaters in the valley to feed my fields, and I would build a small pueblo or cliff-dwelling at some defensible point and put a granary beneath the meander, symbol of my god, and make offerings to it at the altar, and when the rains came, I would dance in the liquid veils which must pour in from every nick on the rim of this small kingdom.

I feel compelled to tip my cap at the altar, a sign not of humility, I hope, but of recognition and respect for the entity or the deity or force that resides behind the ancient face, the immortal spirit whose true name has not been spoken by the wind since it built up this dune. And having paid my respects, I now feel safe to approach. I walk up some amoeboid red steps of sandstone on the thin ridge and slide along a thin kerf to the head of the third wash, and around it and across the steep slope on the far side, hugging the wall and testing the rock face because if I slip I will accelerate down the steepening convex face and into the canyon, with my head bouncing off the narrowing walls far below until my body becomes jammed between them like a cork driven into a bottle.

A thirteen-foot drop from a shearing weathering rind is the last obstacle to the flat stone pediment beneath the wall. Inching down it I realize again that this is precisely the sort of thing I promised my wife I wouldn't do. But the crescent plain is worth the effort and danger. The two slabs beneath the wall were put there intentionally, chinked in place with mud probably a thousand years ago. I check the interior for corn cobs and search the area but find no artifacts save for a cairn, four black slab rocks piled three feet high. I also find bizarre geofact concretions: a hinged flange, a column with layered cross-sections like tree rings, a bottle with a curved neck, a jar, a hollow tube, a mandrake root. Up on the wall I find natural, faint, wavy ghost etchings, one with its arms raised up in supplication or warning, one leaning into shock waves. Where the patinad rock has crumbled the stone beneath is pink like new skin.

Hiking back down the checkerboard slope, I come across potholes that bear an uncanny resemblance to the two dimensional illustrations of gravity wells or black holes you might find in a physics textbook, and I wonder when I will find one that's a portal, that goes right through the rock to the next world.

Next day I follow the road out to its end, a drill pipe

Edge of the Escalante River Gorge

with some English and some Greek words torched into it: 660 FSL 1980 FWL, 11-4-71, Amoco Prod. Co. U.S.A. Amoco "G" #1. After an extensive survey, I determine that the trail does not continue from the pipe in any direction, which is disappointing because a few miles back, where the road came down through a stone draw, I found wagon ruts. In fact, I'd been expecting to find those ruts the whole trip because the low rock shelves abutting the road had been picked back from it, which wouldn't have helped drillers at all, but would have saved the pioneers a lot of effort.

I'm supposed to be searching out old pioneer roads and I'm not; instead I'm stumbling on them. But I don't know where the original pioneer road runs, where it turns off, how it reaches the river gorge, where the connecting road is, and after a few hours of searching, I'm no closer to finding out.

On the assumption that the old road here connects to the sandslides the pioneers used to access the Escalante River, I park the Heap again and hike due east, making for the gorge, which turns out to be about three times further away than it appeared, and then I hike the rim northward, which turns out to be the wrong direction. But a strange thing happens. I head side canyons and hike up to shale shelves and old banks covered by water-polished stones now six hundred feet above the river, down to draws filled with volcanic boulders from the Aquarius Plateau, out to the edge of the gorge, which I follow for miles, but the sun remains motionless, and so do my watch's hands. Time stays still while I struggle upstream.

I come to a spot where the river meanders right up against an overhanging wall five hundred feet high and, further on, an overlook of an abandoned meander, a billion-ton boulder in the middle of the stream. Three ducks swoop and dive up the gorge, and one breaks off as if on a dare, rockets through the old channel jigging like a jet fighter, rejoins the other two and they skim the walls until they're out of sight. Further on, a side canyon's walls spiral out from the Escalante gorge like a snail shell on its side. The canyon's mouth is ten feet wide; you could hold off an army here, and there are a few overhangs under which to build a shelter, but I see no signs of Fremont habitation from the rim, only footprints.

Walking back across the prairie to the Heap takes twice as long as walking out. Mostly I'm crossing low dunes and sand sheets held in place by sagebrush and some ring grass and Mormon tea. Sometimes the sand has been striped away by the wind and I will walk over the bare top of a delitescent dome which will rise someday as half-dome has risen. I find my own footprints once in a while but I lose them when I cut across my own meanders and I find coyote prints on a dune face that have been so elongated that I initially mistake them for human tracks.

Axle used as a fence anchor in Harris Wash

Mare's tails drift over the still sun. A private plane, maybe a Cessna, drones by just above the sandstone peaks. I get back to the Heap and record how time has alternately sped up and slowed down the last few days, how each strata of rock carries its own temporal properties, how landmarks move, how the quickest route is never a straight line, how there are no straight lines, how you'll never find something when you're looking for it here.

When I start the Heap up and begin the journey back, the sun resumes its western drift. It's time now to explore Harris Wash as far as I can drive it, and I ride up the stream as it cuts deep into the sandstone. Sting is singing "Demolition Man" but soon I can barely hear it above the engine roar reverberating off the bluffs.

I *like* the Heap loud, by the way. I *like* a throaty snarl from the exhaust. I clamped a cherry bomb to the end of the pipe because I *like* to set off car alarms in parking garages. But after a half-hour of this, I get annoyed myself. I shut the Heap off and an overpressure of silence rushes in to fill the vacuum. The stream burbles just loud enough to cover the tinnitis in my left ear and the cottonwoods creak and sift the light breeze. The sun is in the trees but I still have a little time and I get out of the Heap and walk upstream a half-mile or so, take some photographs of the cottonwoods against the red rock, and stop in midstream and listen for a while.

As I head for Hole-in-the-Rock Road, Sting sings "One world is enough for all of us."

"Oh shut up," I tell him.

Fence Canyon

When I came through Escalante a couple days earlier, I forgot to fill the six-gallon water can and that's normally not a problem but I've been making a lot of coffee lately and now, in the parking area above Fence Canyon, I only have a few drops left. Going back is out of the question: I'd waste half a day.

"Difficulty: Strenuous," says Rudi Lambrechtse of the hike I'm about to embark on in his guidebook on the Escalante region. "Length (one way): 3.5 miles" (131).

Three-point-five *steep* miles, with no water. I pack the stove and the mess kit and walk down the steepest grade, feeling nauseous already because I didn't drink much the night before.

The faster I get down, the sooner I drink, I think, and I hurry and get lost, take the wrong branch of the canyon and end up following a wash through a slickrock tunnel, down into dry, wave-bedded slickrock chambers to a three-hundred foot drop-off. There's some murky water in nearby potholes and the thirst receptors in the back of my throat are beginning to register strongly but I backtrack instead, past a block of sandstone that's pulled back from the wall just enough to form a narrow arch, back to the ridgeline, which I follow down until I find the usual signs that cows once grazed here, which is reassuring because cows don't do much climbing.

Across the canyon from me, huge honeycomb grottos have been weathered into the wall, some of them connected to each other by tunnels further back in the rock. I scan these with my binoculars but see no cliff dwellings, no granaries, nothing, and these hollows look like they are highly defensible.

Were the Fremont insane? I wonder.

Soon I can see the trail I should have been on all along below me and I find a debris train I can slide down and footprints at the base, so I know I'm not alone in descending the wrong canyon. At the bottom, I have to thrash through a thick tamarisk grove to get to the trail, but the rest is comparatively easy.

Lambrechtse's book has a picturesque line camp on the bench near the end of the side canyon, with some antlers tacked to the front and what appears to be a ladder on the cliff face next to it, but the line-camp was torched by arsonists back in April of 1990 according to writer Steve Allen. Now there's just some charcoal on a concrete foundation and a small corral, some petroglyphs of rectangular-bodied antelope or bighorn sheep, some Moqui steps and a few cowboy names: Perry Liston, A. Crespin, and what I believe is Dell LeFevre's brand:

$$7X$$

And there are a few others:

$$=L \quad J\rceil \quad + \quad \overline{A} \quad 6R$$

I hear hikers coming up the trail and crossing the Escalante. I introduce myself to them: three men, a couple of women and a dog, "Chester," who actually trotted up and inspected me before the others got there to make sure I was all right. They all camped on the banks of the river last night. One of the young women points to the clear stream from Fence Canyon mixing into the Escalante's vomitous pea-green water.

"That's the last place you're going to find fresh water," she says.

I ask them if they saw the other petroglyph panel nearby and they all give me blank looks, and then they look skeptical. I tell them it should have been hard to miss, but apparently they walked right by it.

"Was it in any of the guidebooks?" one of them asks.

"No," I say, "Reece Stein told me about it. You know, the newscaster on Channel 2."

Now they look very skeptical, and I'm wondering if I'll have to do some serious searching to find it. I tell them about the petroglyphs up on the bench and they show me the best place to cross the river.

Crossing the river wasn't on the itinerary, but it's a hot day and I'm up for it. The Escalante is waist high and fast flowing, so I have to face into it, and it's still ice cold, so my feet go numb before I'm halfway across. On the other side I scoop some water up and put it on the stove and explore out to each edge of the sandbar. It would be handy if I could find a route up to the top of the bench but I can't, and the river winds back against the cliff, in several places it looks like, which means several crossings where I don't know how deep the river is going to be.

The water takes ten minutes to boil and I keep it going for another ten minutes to be safe and then I boil another pot. All in all, by the time I've boiled half a liter and let the river cool it, I've wasted a full hour, but when the water hits my throat it seems worth it.

I trudge down the trail, cross the river four times and I'm at the panel of wavy lines and block-bodied anthropomorphs, bear tracks walking up the cliff, herds of antelope and bighorn, hunters and aliens, caped figures,

Anthropomorph petroglyphs near Fence Canyon

and a baby held by its hair, a waving eyeball, a couple of fighting Irishmen probably etched by pioneers or bored cowboys, a sun and a shooting star, a trapezoid Fremont with a feathered headdress in his regalia of necklaces and epaulets, a two-headed sheep, a coyote, a stippled figure and newer etchings: Hall, March 21, 1881; William Osborn, 1894; Roe and Ray Barney, 1946; E. Allen 1881; Jas Liston, Feb. 3 '08, and these:

☿ W̄O 7D ⊠ ℛ

Beneath the cowboyglyphs and the more recent petroglyphs, at the back of time, there's a corn stalk and an ear of corn and there are hovering horned-figure surprints so faint I have to stare at the wall for a minute for them to materialize.

Why did the Fremont peck their art in these walls? Why do cowboys and tourists and hunters carve their names in the rock and in the aspen trunks on the Aquarius Plateau? Why do graffiti artists keep tagging my mother's garage in Salt Lake City?

I walk upstream and spot more old glyphs, look for artifacts and find a stairway carved into the side of the wall leading up one story to a bench and a sloping pasture. It would satisfy me to walk out to the house-sized headstones at the east end of the prairie to see if there are any more petroglyphs at their bases but the sun is almost behind the cliffs and I've got a pint of water left. I cross the river four times again, in the shadows now, climb up a Moqui ladder someone has built near the last crossing, to a landing which pinches out after half-a-mile, hike back, climb down, cross again and hike

Sun and circle petroglyph

up the canyon in the evening light.

This time I follow the trail up the switchbacks to the bench, to the rock face. I can see the cairns even in darkness. The last steep grade is murderous, seems to go on for hours, makes me light-headed. I take a step and rest and step and rest until the stars come out, and I raise my bottle now and again and a couple drops fall to my tongue.

Later that night I'm speeding toward Escalante, coughing, laughing. I'm almost sick enough to pull over sometimes but I don't because there's water ahead.

"Good old Heap," I say, "parts fall off it but it keeps going."

Ghost Rock

Chimney Rock is a monolith out on a plain east of Hole-in-the-Rock Road, another monument to an ancient white rock wilderness that was spirited away by rain splash and sheet wash a million or so years ago. What protected it while the rest of the mesa was washed out, nobody seems to know, but it's visible for miles as a sort of beacon for travelers in this remote wasteplain and every pioneer and tourist and every cowpoke who came this way left his name on it.

This morning, I'm reading the inscriptions on the base of Chimney Rock. I'm looking for local names and I find them: LaMont Griffin, November 20, 1939; Ray Griffin, November, 1914; Don Griffin, December 1, 1945; Kenneth Griffin, Horace H. Hall, December 16, 1912; D. L. Spencer, Andrew Spencer, February 7, 1914; V. I. Spencer, 1939; Vic Alvey, Edson Alvey, 1965; Thomas Alvey, January 3, 1925; Reece Shirts, Denton Schow, Ken Schow, E. E. Wooley, March 7, 1908; W. L. Wooley, Reese J. Roundy, March 8, 1903; Lenza Wilson, 1925; Rex Allen, Lavon Allen, Bud and Wanda Woolsey, Lozell Heaps, May 21, 1934; Elden Allen, Dale Lyman, April 1955.

I also find the brands of sheep herders and cattlemen who ranged here when nobody else was much interested in this backcountry, and some of them are still running cattle out here, though I don't see any cows today:

Ⅱ   V̇   V̄   Ⱶ   E\   Ⱥ   Ꞃ   Ⱶ   Ⱨᗷ

Some of those ranchers, no doubt, were involved in plans, decades ago, to put a road through Coyote Gulch just east of here, and not just a bladed wash-bottom road but an honest-to-God, blasted-through-any-obstacle paved highway that would have passed by Hamblin Arch, Coyote Natural Bridge and Stevens Arch and would have continued east across Capitol Reef and up to Bullfrog Basin.

Edward Abbey, writing about the proposed road in *Slickrock*, said "The conservationists and wilderness advocates contend that funds for economic development in southeast Utah should be spent on the improvement of already-existing roads in the area, many of which are yet unpaved" (55). When the proposed road through here was abandoned, however, and Garfield County followed the advice of those "conservationist and wilderness advocates" and tried to pave the Burr Trail further north, environmentalists sued the Department of the Interior and the county and everybody else involved in the paving to bring it to a halt, and they are still suing today.

I've been down that ghost highway. The night before last I studied maps of it by moonlight while I laid in my sleeping bag and the next morning I walked down to a slickrock plain and over to Crack-in-the-Wall, which is just what the name implies; a crescent of rock separated from the sandstone rim of Coyote Gulch, about a foot and a half wide. It leads to a sand hill above an abandoned meander with a massive red fin in the middle of it leaning over the trail, with Stevens Arch immediately visible to the east, a wall with a great hole punched through it by an angry old god.

I followed the ghost highway down the sand slope to the stream at the bottom of Coyote Gulch and walked upstream a few miles to Cliff Arch, which looks like an elephant skull and trunk. Beneath the high Wingate cliffs, the sand and talus angle down to a bench above the river, which is immediately cut back so the water washes over the rims of stone and maidenhair in freestanding waterfalls. It was cool down there and there were muddy grottos and deep pockets of rock filled with reeds bent downstream and cold emerald plunge pools. I found scattered bits of old charcoal and pottery shards.

That ghost road would have been a wonder of the world, but Coyote Gulch is already a quiet wonder and would have been diminished by it.

Nobody talks about the highway now, and so it has joined a sort of imaginary topography. There are phantom national monuments here and

Coyote Gulch Wall

phantom wilderness areas and a phantom green river and a spectral canyon beneath Lake Powell. Upstream on the Escalante River is a phantom dam that was never built and there is another one in the Grand Canyon, and there are a ghost city just below the Kaiparowits and more ghosts of dreams and grand schemes than seems possible for such an empty land.

Potholes

The landscape around Bellemont, Arizona, where I once lived, is covered with dead cinder cones and I've always wanted to spend a night in one of them, ensconced in a closed world, a womb, only the earth and the heavens and me.

This fall morning I wake up in a pothole. It's not a large one; it's roughly eight feet long, maybe three and a half feet deep, but it blocks out the whole world except for the sky. I studied the stars last night through binoculars and followed the lights of jets, listening for the growl that came down when they were two-thirds of the way across my field of vision.

Yesterday I explored Dance Hall Rock where the pioneers of the San Juan Mission, with their wagons circled at Forty Mile Camp, spent their evenings

Rockscape behind Dance Hall Rock

while scouts tried to find a way to the river. The sign at the head of the road read "Spirits were high before news of what lies ahead arrived," and I wondered why. They could have seen the slickrock confusion they were fated for from where I was standing.

I watched for cowboyglyphs and local names again on Dance Hall Rock and I found them: Heaps, Woolsey, Jepson, Alvey, and these:

C7 ㄥP

Somebody has inscribed "Jesus is God" on the floor.

My guidebook said it was worth exploring behind the Hall, so I walked around it and then I walked off this world, into one of Edward Abbey's "science-fiction" landscapes of lumps, bumps, billows, banded rock at odds with itself, fossil seifs, disharmonic folds, red mound monsters and narrows and potholes. Potholes most of all—a garden of wallows, bowls, pits and basins of any size and any shape imaginable or not. The first one I came to had scooped out the side of a parabolic rock dune so its edge became a rounded enclosing wall and inside there was an apostrophe-shaped courtyard, a small lake, a cottonwood tree on the bank, a sward of grass never touched by cows. Nearby there was a thirty-foot-wide wormhole augered straight down about twenty feet with a grass glen at the bottom and cottonwoods just cresting the rim. Further on there was a hole overhung by its walls, maybe forty-five feet long and fifteen feet deep and no way to climb out and only some rabbitbrush on a pile of sand at one end for a trapped man or animal to subsist on.

Some potholes had their own ecosystems: grasslands and cottonwood groves, and some contained lakes and island oases. Some were Z-shaped, some round, some bunched so thick they were blending into each other, and there were a few massive ovoid amphitheaters with groves or passageways at one end where the water finally broke through.

I found a Zen garden, a rock flat where cobblestones in pockets had been arranged *just so* by water evaporating between the low dunes, the sand and rock proportioned by some cosmic constant, and came to a cross-hatched yellow and white cone at the garden's far end and I sat there and contemplated it, and I contemplated that place, the schizophrenic slickrock molded into shapes beyond the normal vocabulary of landscapes, and I decided that since the water pools and digs down and evaporates, since it doesn't flow anywhere except into holes, the pothole garden is morphological kin to plains gouged out by glaciers, because neither of them have the coherent drainage patterns we generally rely on for classification.

As for the formation itself, what do you call a massive mound of solid serpiginous rock risen out of some basal mental recess? You could call it a bornhardt or inselberg, but these don't communicate the deep emotional resonance of such places, or the logic bent ninety degrees, or the rock octopus tentacles I witnessed at its edges, slinking back into the sagebrush plain. Where are the names for such things?

In the evening, I drove further down the road and climbed Sooner Rocks, another pothole garden, but with the crucial difference that where the piedmont of the rocks behind the Hall sloped gently into the ground, here the transition was a two-hundred foot cliff-line. Narrows simply drop into oblivion and if you slipped from the top of a dome, you'd have the ride of your life.

The deeper potholes usually contained water but very little vegetation. They were shafts, wells, human traps. One was thirty feet deep and only a third as wide.

I stayed in the Sooner Rocks' interior for the most part. I climbed down to the nexus of three great sandstone bubbles, with a stagnant pool in it and some thistle nearby and a passageway leading out to the edge, and I climbed a ledge to where it ended just close enough to a steep rock face for me to reach out and pull myself across the drop-off with my fingers.

That's the way Sooner Rocks are: just a bit larger than the human scale, hence just a bit dangerous.

From the top, in twilight, I spotted a bleb of rock towards the road shaped like a walrus nose and I saw a giant doughnut-shaped, Mars-red sandstone lobe north of me, eaten away from the inside. I climbed down to the base and hiked up a short rock wash; two planes of sandstone meeting at a V so tight it pinched my feet and I had to stem through.

Then I looked around for a pothole and found this one. I was actually looking for something deeper and wider but the darkness forced the decision. I threw my flashlight in first to see how a lit pothole would appear from a distance, and it looked like you would expect, like a subterranean dweller had turned on a night light. Then I threw in a couple books, unrolled my sleeping bag and read for a while as cutworms tried to escape up the side, and then I turned off the light and all meaning was reduced to what I could see from the narrow horizons of my cocoon; stars and nebulae, the Milky Way, the clouds, a crescent moon, an occasional airplane.

I can recommend sleeping in a pothole to anyone, unless it's raining, but even then a tarp over the opening would make a good shelter. You get out of the wind. Your personal effects don't roll away from you. The cutworms will keep you company.

The End

Soda Gulch, "the Sodie" as some locals call it, is just down the road from Sooner Rocks. There's not much to see on the west side, just an echo chamber rock corral, the foundation of the Griffins' burnt line camp and an old trailer that's replaced it. But the Sodie was the last recorded place Everett Ruess was seen.

Ruess met two sheepherders here, Clayton Porter and Addlin Lay, on November 9, 1934, and spent a couple days grilling them about the surrounding country, what was worth seeing and how to get there. The information came in handy for him, got him into Davis Canyon, though he told the sheepherders he was headed for Hole-in-the-Rock.

Three months after he left Escalante, Everett's parents received his uncollected mail from Marble Canyon, Arizona, near present-day Page, Ruess's supposed next destination. In early March, a search party found his two burros alive, though there's some controversy about their condition, in a brush corral in Davis Canyon, near the only point where it's possible to trail animals down there. His footprints were all over the canyon—he'd obviously done a great deal of exploring—and there was garbage scattered about where he'd camped and the searchers found "NEMO 1934" inscribed in some ruins near the arch local cowboys called the Moqui Window, but that's about all they found of Everett. His "outfit"—his bedroll and painting kit, camera, food, journal, and cooking pans—was also missing.

Further searches turned up more size-nine footprints leading to the base of Fifty Mile Mountain, which the party also thoroughly explored, and another "NEMO 1934" inscription beneath a pictograph panel in Davis Gulch, and that, by most accounts, was the end of the trail.

The mystery of Ruess's disappearance has kept a number of amateur sleuths up at night and there are an equal number of implausible theories out there, among them that Everett abandoned his burros and crossed the Colorado River and washed clean his ties to his family and civilization at large in the process and took a wife on the Navajo Reservation, where he lived the rest of his days, and also that instead he kept walking and ended up in Mexico, and also that Emery Kolb, famed explorer of the Grand Canyon, might have killed him when Everett refused his sexual advances (one of Mark A. Taylor's hypotheses—though there's good evidence both men liked women).

Baring the above, we're left with three possibilities: that he died in a natural accident, that he was murdered, or that he killed himself. The last one seems far-fetched to me but Gary James Bergera tries to make a case for it in his article, "The Murderous Pain of Living," with quotes from Everett's letters, journals and unpublished short stories. Bergera makes Ruess out to be a manic depressive, and he makes the usual connection between "Nemo," Latin for "no one," as per the inscriptions in Davis Gulch, and Everett's last letter, where he referred to the wilderness around the Colorado River as a place where "no one lives." The theory sounds plausible if you start from the premise that "a terrible melancholy permeates almost every line" of Ruess's writing (49), but I believe most readers see a guileless, angry young man, an earnest youth who's maybe read too many books.

What's more, Everett wrote prolifically through the last four years of his short life, 175,000 words according to Bergera (50), so there's plenty of material that could be lifted out of context to make him look melancholy or exuberant or cruel, loving, hateful, sensitive, insensitive, brash, shy, pretty much whatever the researcher chooses.

One aspect of Ruess's personality nobody argues about is his recklessness. Ruess liked taking chances, traveling alone, living on nothing and not knowing where his next meal was coming from, riding the rails, hitchhiking, climbing cliffs to Indian ruins. There's a strong possibility he got in over his head on some adventure. Everett could have fallen to his death somewhere outside the gulch, or he might have drowned in the Colorado River, as his parents once believed. As Taylor himself suggests, maybe he made the same mistake Abbey and Taylor did, jumping down into a hanging canyon from which there was no escape.

So why would his outfit be missing? Possibly someone absconded with it after Ruess died, but *A Vagabond for Beauty* author W. L. Rusho discounts this theory on the testimony of McKay Bailey's father, Gail, a member of the initial search party, who "denied that he or anyone else could have removed the outfit before the main group of searchers found the camp site" (204). Bergera has Ruess transporting his outfit by burro to a remote locale and hiding it, returning the burro(s) to the corral, returning again to his outfit or finding a "wild, lonely spot" (67), some place nobody would ever think to look, and killing himself. If he'd moved the outfit and brought the burro(s) back in preparation for an extended sojourn into some rocky corner of the Escalante country that didn't have any feed for his animals and then died by accident, however, his body and equipment might have been easier to find, but otherwise the results would have been nearly the same as if he'd deliberately killed himself.

The most popular theory is that somebody murdered Everett and took his outfit. It might have been the cattle rustlers who were known to operate at the remote borders of the Escalante drainage, or maybe it was a Navajo outlaw named Jack Crank. Crank was rumored to have killed a white man in the vicinity where Ruess vanished and he was rumored to have confessed to the crime, but no formal charges were ever brought against him, and his alleged confession puts him in the same league as one of the rustlers who also *supposedly* claimed to have killed Everett. Rusho notes, "Against this theory is the fact that no searcher reported seeing any footprints other than Everett's in Davis Gulch" (222). But what if the rustlers or Crank had come across Ruess outside the gulch? What if he'd moved his outfit nearer Hole-in-the-Rock Road and led his burro(s) back to the brush corral and met his murderer(s) when he came back?

Rusho further notes, "In the summer of 1957, an archaeologist working on the Glen Canyon Archaeological Survey (prior to the filling of Lake Powell) came across the remains of camping equipment—possibly Everett's—in a canyon tributary (Reflection Canyon) of the Colorado River southwest of Hole-in-the-Rock" (210). These consisted of a "rusty cup, spoon, fork, kettles and pans, and a large canteen" and a box of razors manufactured in Los Angeles. Ruess's mother "could not be sure, but she doubted that they belonged to Everett" (211), leaving the possibility that they *did* belong to him, leaving the most remote possibility that he died after marveling over the faith and willpower of the people who'd built that notch-in-the-cliff road he must have traveled down to the river.

Hole-in-the-Rock Road has been rough since I passed into Kane County but past the Sodie it gets worse. The bedrock is exposed and I'm riding over wagon ruts in sandstone. Ahead of me, the stippling of Navajo Mountain's blue slopes is beginning to resolve into trees and brush and I'm stunned by the scale of it up close; it's as if a huge blue and white aerolite had half-buried itself into the plateau.

There's a turnoff about five miles before Hole-in-the-Rock where you can park your street car and hike/mountain bike in. A twenty-something couple, Julie Woodke and Scott McKim, as I will come to find out, park their red economy car and unload their bikes as the Heap lurches fearlessly up and over the sandstone waves and domes in four-wheel drive. It gets me to Hole-in-the-Rock about five minutes before them and I occupy my time reading my guidebooks and the trail register.

"Saw space ships," reads one entry. "So did we!" reads another. "Toto," says a third, "we are not in Kansas anymore!"

Hole-in-the-Rock was just a slot down to the river when the pioneers discovered it, and it's still a slot, though it leads to Lake Powell now. The grade was forty-five degrees in places back then and it's worse now because the agger the Mormons used to fill in the drop-offs is washed out. A modern, fuel-injected Jeep might have been able to make it down the original incline but an older Jeep like mine would probably have conked out in a few places where the carburetor was tilted too far from level to feed gas to the intake. Then again, the engine's primary function going *down* the road would have been compressional braking, something the pioneers weren't familiar with. They accomplished the same results by chaining the wagon's back wheels to the box and having a team of men hold it back with ropes or by tying trees to the ropes. "On occasion," says David E. Miller, "a horse or mule was hitched behind to pull back, but this proved to be rather rough treatment for the animal as he was usually thrown to the ground and dragged down the steep bumpy grade" (111).

Scott and Julie arrive and we introduce ourselves and decide to go down to the lake together. However, they quickly get ahead of me because I'm too busy reading the walls, which are like half-mile long message boards. The normal local names are present: Alvey, Steed, Wooley, Schow, Wilson, Moore, Jepson, Hall. Gene Griffin seems to have recorded his every visit to Hole-in-the-Rock. Fayette Alvey wrote "The first car to the Hole" on May 23, 1941.

I find the following cowboyglyphs.

$$\text{Ɇ} \quad \text{J}^+ \quad \text{7N} \quad \text{Ɵ} \quad \text{Ⱨ} \quad \text{Ⱳ} \quad \text{E/} \quad \triangle$$

$$\text{Ɉ} \quad \text{⊠} \quad \text{Ɵ} \quad \text{Ⱨ} \quad \text{7U} \quad \text{J2} \quad \text{Ⱦ}$$

A trading post operated briefly at the base of Hole-in-the-Rock twenty years after its construction and the steps we come across halfway down were built by the operators. A great deal of rock has collapsed into the slot and at one point we have to crawl beneath a ten-ton boulder to get through. Where the hole opens up, the path winds to the north side onto a narrow flange of slickrock which the pioneers called Uncle Ben's Dugway after the man who'd come up with the idea of chiseling out a corner wide enough for the wagons' inside wheels and then extending the road out from the steep face with planks and rip-rap supported by oak stakes driven into boreholes. The boreholes are still there.

Scott and Julie are swimming in a bice embayment of Lake Powell by the time I get down; though they're not naked, it's clear Katie Lee's days are over. I dunk my head in the lake, which is cool but not cold and follow the road down twenty feet with my eyes into the light green water. The lake's hue grinds against the orange cliffs like mismatched gears, and the hundred-foot high, bleached-white "bathtub ring" on the red walls around us is the clearest visible demonstration of the drought I've yet come across.

"I've never been on a boat on Lake Powell," I tell Julie and Scott, "but my dream, long ago, was to live on a houseboat here and explore it. This lake has more shoreline than the coast of California."

We consider trying to catch a ride on one of the powerboats that idle up the canyon but they don't come up to shore. We have some lunch, and I inform Scott and Julie they're seeing more of the road than is usually visible. They are both studying hydrology at Colorado State and they came down here for spring break. Scott, I discover, has a keen interest in Everett Ruess and he wants to see Davis Gulch. We decide to meet at its head the next morning and explore it. In the meantime, however, they don't know where they should camp.

"Where can't you camp?" I ask, "Just pull off the road where nobody can see you. That's where you camp."

"It was our understanding we could only camp in designated camp-grounds," says Scott.

"Do you see any cops here?"

I convince them they should camp at Cave Point, a few miles back, and they do, and I park the Heap on an old road that comes off Hole-in-the-Rock Road near Davis Gulch and hike a mile towards that gulch in the evening. I climb up a high ridge of "sandrock"—what the locals used to call it—have a quick look around, watch as the distant, clouded Aquarius Plateau and the heads of the Henry Mountains shambling north all fade to black and a domed peak behind the Henrys, the most distant thing I can see, glows with an orange forge light and then dims out of existence and the crags and weird-drock bluffs of the beautiful red wreck of earth on the river's far side burn out with the dying light.

I feel strongly that those bluffs were what Everett Ruess was aiming for when he met his destiny.

Scott and Julie at Hole-in-the-Rock

When I walk back, the stock pond where I parked the Heap has moved northward and I'm lost. In the faint light, the sand haycocks and waterpockets all look the same, just domes and shallows out to the base of Fifty Mile Mountain.

"Mais, c'est fantastique!" I say. The landmarks appear the same as they did at the quarter-mile-long flat where I parked the Heap but that flat is nowhere to be found. I trek north and finally drop into it, though I don't recognize it until I see the Heap half-hidden behind a dome, and even as I approach it, it vanishes and then peeks out from behind another dome and then another.

"I'm not leading this expedition," I tell Scott and Julie early the next morning.

They're not impressed by my story. They have a compass and youthful enthusiasm, and they convince me to write down the descriptions of the hike in my notebook and we set out. I take a bearing on the cliff line behind us, Fifty Mile Point, with a tiny arch on top, which would probably look about the same if we were miles off course.

We cross the side canyon perpendicular to Davis Gulch, which is much further down the "trail" than we expected, and I convince Julie that she and Scott should hike down into the narrows, since she's never been in a slot canyon before. I stay above and follow their progress and shout reassuring words like "It looks like it gets deeper ahead," and "I don't see any way out," and "Maybe you should turn back now" until I lose contact with them, but I walk back a half-mile and we meet up again near the top of the narrows.

"There was a drop-off," says Scott, "And I thought there might be more up ahead, so we came back."

Never go alone, I think. When you take friends with you, sometimes you get exposed to this kind of rational thinking.

We continue. The cattle trail doesn't materialize so we just keep the gulch in view. Once in a while we come across a cairn and occasionally we can follow it to another, but for the most part we're operating on faith.

Water-filled potholes have green blobs in them the size and shape of carrot-sticks cut in half. On closer inspection they turn out to be cutworms bloated up a thousand times their original size. We find an arch sloped from an old dune to the rock plain—only a foot tall and four feet wide but it qualifies—and I name it "Scott and Julie Arch."

Lambrechtse says to watch for a "vertical cleft" in the flat mesa top across the canyon (165). Scott makes noises about how far we've already hiked and that leads to a discussion about the water situation, the late hour and the generally unreliable nature of guidebooks, but I convince the two

I can see that cleft, which I really think I can, not too far ahead. It turns out I'm right, though there aren't as many cairns around to confirm our location as we were led to believe there would be and there's still no obvious cattle trail. The slickrock flows across the overhung walls and into the gulch and after lunch we follow it, lose the trail and find it and crawl the last hundred feet down a thin rock spur that slants to near verticality at the base.

We all wonder how you could get cows down that last section, or horses or burros, for that matter, without actually pushing them. What was the attrition rate?

Right away we come across some Indian art, though it's not the negative pictographs I was expecting, and it's too abstract for us to make heads or tails of: lines, contours, depictions of weather fronts. From these we hike upstream towards the narrows and Bement Arch, a.k.a. Nemo Arch, with Scott up ahead setting a grueling pace, and Julie, who has never complained, growing weaker with each step, and me in last place watching for alcoves with ruins in them and more art. I spot a few likely candidates for cliff dwellings but we don't have the time to explore them. Patrick Diehl and Tori Woodard weren't kidding, I note, when they told me I'd need at least two days to explore this canyon.

Black-stained walls tower and enfold. I see why few locals hold much stock in the theory Everett fell to his death down here. There are three sets of Moqui steps to the rim but the first party apparently searched carefully beneath them, and beneath all the alcove ruins. Otherwise, there aren't too many places to climb.

On the other hand, the gorge is filled from one side to the other with sand dunes, sand hills and sandruns, and a few months passed between Ruess's disappearance and the searchers' arrival. It's possible a slide could have buried his body in the meantime.

One other thing becomes clear as we hike upcanyon through the tamarisk and willows: it's been years since cattle grazed here. This is the first time I've seen the foliage so thick on the creek bottom, and Scott compares the grassy slopes to a golf course, which is ironic because golf had its beginnings on Scottish rangelands.

I'd been pestering the BLM to show me some examples of overgrazed range and I'd been seeing them all along, every time I hiked up some hidden canyon with some soil in it and running water. Davis Gulch, I realize, is the first creek bottom I've seen that's anywhere close to its pristine state, and even this place is only recovering. With no cattle trampling down the stream banks and eating and trampling the vegetation holding the soil in place, the banks are narrowing, except where beavers have ponded the flow with their dams. Where it runs, the water is so clear I'm tempted to take a drink. Sedges and young cottonwoods are reclaiming the hillsides.

There are frogs on the muddy banks. An owl swoops over us from a notch in the rock, the first one Scott and Julie and I have seen in this corner of the West.

Davis Canyon switches back a half-dozen times and we don't seem to be any closer to the arch, which I assure Scott and Julie is "huge—you can't miss it." Scott waits up and reminds me of the long walk ahead of us, the steep hike out of the canyon and I convince him we should keep going for another two bends in the canyon and he takes off to scout the terrain like a long-distance runner and twenty minutes and three bends later, we hear him shouting his discovery ahead.

Nemo Arch is a sandstone slab propped against a wall; a vaulted arch, and it doesn't reach down to the floor of the gulch as I'd expected so we have to climb up to it. We drink the last of our water at the base and hike into the boulder field beneath it and pose for photographs and we search a little for a "NEMO" inscription which I mistakenly believe is nearby and walk into a deep cut-back in the cliff at the same level as the arch, where I expect to and *do* find a standing Fremont or Anasazi wall and the fallen remains of a good-sized pueblo, and then we start back for the cattle trail, with Scott setting a maniacal pace because we're running out of daylight.

Julie and I quickly fall behind. If I was fifteen years younger I still couldn't have kept up. I do know from previous experience that we wouldn't have much trouble making it back in twilight or darkness, and I do know I'm nowhere near my own limits if I take it easy, but I can't convince Scott to slow down. I'm worried about Julie, who doesn't have much experience at this sort of thing. I tell her to let me know if she starts to feel lightheaded or sick and I tell her not to push herself *at all*. I've already mentioned that we can drink from the stream if we have to.

"Perhaps we shouldn't have been so ambitious," I admit to Julie, "This is a ten-mile hike. It's my fault."

"Oh come on," she croaks, "I'm having a great time."

Scott, who is carrying Julie's pack, waits for us at the base of the sandstone column that's supposed to be a cattle trail and as soon as he sees we're all-right, scurries up and out of sight. I want to kill him. Julie scoots up on her hands and knees and I just slog. Again, Scott waits at the top until we arrive and then he takes off. Julie falls to the rock and pantomimes squeezing a device next to her mouth, and then she points at Scott.

"Scott!" I shout, "I think you've got Julie's asthma medication in your pack!"

Soon enough after Julie takes a hit on the inhaler, the color returns to her face and we continue on, together. We decide we should get to know each other better, exchange medical information and other vital facts, but soon we're philosophizing.

"What's the most important problem facing our society?" asks Scott.

"I don't know," I say, "I mostly worry about making next month's rent."

"Well, yes," says Scott, nonplussed, "but I think it's our environment."

Scott and Julie want to find a cheap way to desalinize ocean water. Julie wants to save the Great Lakes before pollution turns them into sludge. She further reveals that reservoirs are ugly to her. She likes to see rivers and streams flowing free.

"Don't say that in town," I tell her, "You'll get shot."

Julie also tells me she would like to see some examples of cryptogamic soil.

"You just walked through some," I tell her.

She is horrified and promises to do something wonderful for the environment to make up for this transgression.

Again, Scott gets out ahead, and I know what he's thinking. His eyesight is keen, he can probably see the cars from where we are, miles away, he knows we're going to intercept the road about a mile north of them, so he wants get to them before we do and drive the car up to meet us. And why not? Julie is breathing all right and Scott looks like he could hike another twenty miles and not even be winded. Soon he's a speck on the rock.

We dunk our heads in the waterpockets and trudge. We find the paths of least resistance. Julie has to rest for a few minutes to get her breath back and I try to convince her to slow her pace even more. I've got a flashlight and I don't care if we get back at two in the morning.

Fifty Mile Point looms over us. I'm convinced we've come to the last grade before the road, but Julie is tired and her back is beginning to bother her and she's not convinced of anything, so I go delirious, decide I have to save us both and run up to the top of the slope while Julie loses her footing and slides down a slickrock face towards a drop-off and arrests her fall just inches short of it. I lay on the shelf with my lungs heaving in massive sucking spasms and then I go back down and find her and lead her up to the sagebrush bench and Hole-in-the-Rock Road, and soon we hear the whine of the red car's engine approaching.

It all works out.

We drink deeply and drive back to Escalante at night and stop at a service station to refill the water bottles. I call my wife Sarah in Salt Lake City and find out I'd set the date on my watch wrong and it's the fourteenth, not the thirteenth. I've missed my brother-in-law's wedding and everybody hates me, but they'll be glad to hear I'm alive. My mother and my wife contacted the sheriff's department and they're going to initiate a search in the morning, but I make another call and put a stop to that real quick. The same twenty-four hour waiting period that almost got Doctor Diehl killed saved a lot of good people from wasting their time finding me.

Julie and Scott want to buy me dinner for dragging them all over the far end of the desert, but I don't think there's anything open this late. They've got to be at Bryce the next morning and I've got places to be as well, so we say our goodbyes and go our separate ways, and I append my rules about traveling in this desert again:

Expect to be late. You won't be disappointed.

The Lower Road

East of Escalante, Highway 12 rides along the edge of Alvey Wash and turns northeast onto sage- and juniper- and pinyon-covered Big Flat, where Hole-in-the-Rock Road takes off like a shot for that notch on the far side of the Escalante drainage, and it covers the flat more or less in two straight lines: northeast and then almost due east to the Head-of-the-Rocks. This was the easiest section of the lower Escalante-Boulder Road for the Civilian Conservation Corps to build, but the difficulties multiplied on the flat's east end where the world drops away and the road cuts abruptly to the right and south and signs drop the speed limit to thirty and warn of an eight percent grade and then a big yellow sign like an internet pop-up blocks out the fantastic scenery—the incised tableland where Phipp's Wash, The Gulch, Death Hollow and Horse Canyon wend their devious ways to the Escalante, and the Circle Cliffs beyond them and then Capitol Reef and the Henry Mountains, and, far away, that last peak beneath the Henrys, the Abajo Mountains. But you should focus more on the sign than the tableau of red, white and black earth, breaks, flats and mountains at this point or you and your passengers will take a headlong plunge over the white edge of Big Flat and find a new short-cut to Phipp's Pasture.

You can gawk at the scenery less than a mile down the road, where there's a turnout that was initially built for slower traffic—you have to cut across the oncoming lane in an instant and you'll have to do the same at the Boynton Overlook—and when you've had your fill of scenery (I never have), you come down the Head-of-the-Rocks switchbacks cut into the ubiquitous Navajo Sandstone to the sandy pasture where the road straightens its back again for a few miles before taking another ninety-degree right turn at the Overlook, where the red domes of Wingate Sandstone begin to predominate, and then plunging down and curving around the Kiva Koffeehouse, built by Brad Boman, the man who invented "Bomanite" concrete, who moved here from

The edge of Big Flat

Carmel, California, in the seventies, down to the fuzz-crowned cottonwoods and the shaded Escalante River where the Fremont built their dwellings and chipped and painted their idols on the stone.

Then the road climbs again through Calf Creek Canyon, beneath red ledgerock and overhangs, past the turn-off to Calf Creek Campground and up a fourteen percent grade to a dugway and into the Navajo Sandstone again, to the top of Haymaker Bench, where the sandstone is nearly completely covered with black volcanic boulders carried down from the Aquarius Plateau by glaciers a little over one hundred thousand years ago, and then out onto the Hogback where the earth falls away into Calf Creek on the west and Dry Hollow on the east and you're clinging to a narrow, winding two-lane road bowed down to each edge with no guardrail on either side. Here again, you might want to stop and enjoy the scenery—first glimpses of the green pastures of Lower Boulder, the black arc of the Aquarius, the bent, backwasted white ruiniform insanity where Death Hollow cuts into the Escalante Anticline on the west, and similar crazyrock canyons on the east—and soon there are some pull-outs to accommodate you. Otherwise, there's not much room to park.

Twelve touches down again on New Home Bench and within a couple miles a road peels off to the west, bound for Salt Gulch and Hell's Backbone. Then the highway curls up around Dry Hollow and Boulder Creek which run parallel to each other, jogs right, curves left and drops into Boulder.

Highway 12 is the ridge and the ravine, the canyon floor and the mesa top.

"I doubted Truman Lyman when he told me this was an old road, and now you're doubting me," says Doctor Jerry Roundy as we pick our way down a slope that's covered with landslide debris, towards Dry Hollow. "You're thinking how much things can change in one-hundred years, and they do."

Jerry and his wife are the last Roundys left in Escalante. There used to be several Roundy families; it was a big name in these parts, right up there with the Heaps, Griffins, Halls, Barneys, Twitchells, Allens, Schows, Shurtzes, Listons, Kings, Spencers, Woolseys and Alveys, but now the Roundys are practically extinct here. Jerry wanted to stay on the family ranch but his father, Wallace Napoleon Roundy, a forest ranger who'd gone to Washington and worked on the Taylor Grazing Act, convinced him to get out of town and see the world and get an education, because the government was cutting grazing back on the open range even then, so he joined the navy and then went on a mission for the Mormon Church and then got a masters degree from Brigham Young University in political science and history, and later earned a Ph.D. in western American history at the same institution, and he taught for the LDS Church for thirty-three years and then moved back to town near where he'd grown up and wrote *the* book on its history: *Advised Them to Call the Place Escalante*. After his first wife, Colleen passed away, Jerry married Sheree, who had also grown up in Escalante and whose great grandmother, Mary Alice Barker Shurtz, was the first European-American to set foot in the Escalante Valley.

Jerry is a half-foot shorter than me, just like most people his age who grew up in this part of the country (Arnold Alvey, Wallace Ott and Larry Davis are all "short" from my point of view and Jerry and Alvey are also bowlegged, like me). He's got a flat boxer's nose, though it looks inherited rather than acquired, and a white head of hair. He and I are locating all the roads which preceded Highway 12 between Escalante and Boulder, the ones he's already been over a dozen times, and there are quite a few. The first ones were the Indian trails the Mormon militia and Thompson and some earlier prospectors followed on their way east through here, and then there were other Indian trails across Death Hollow, but the wagon trails mostly came through approximately where Highway 12 is now. *Approximately.* The first "road" cut across present-day Highway 12 from north to south on Big Flat and swung out past another totem known as Chimney Rock, still visible from the highway, to the south end of Head-of-the-Rocks, where it skirted a Navajo Sandstone fin and dropped into Phipps Wash some distance from its head and then emptied out into the Escalante, where the "road" ended. In 1895, Amasa and Roseannah Lyman and their children and horses and a pig became the first to take a wagon down this route and then on to Boulder, but they had to disassemble the wagon at the base of Haymaker Bench and haul it up in pieces, and reassemble it for the rest of the rough trip over the bench and down into Boulder Creek and out to Boulder itself. It took them five days to get from one town to the next, whereas I've made the journey in the Heap in thirty minutes flat.

As Jerry says in his book, "Amasa's successful journey from Escalante to Boulder inspired the settlers in Boulder to construct a road from Boulder to the Haymaker ranch on the Escalante River. . . . This became known as the Boulder Road and served as the main wagon road between Escalante and Boulder for many years" (140).

Around the turn-of-the-century the pioneers engineered the Second Road which dropped off a dugway just north of the present Head-of-the-Rocks Overlook and crossed the modern highway and went almost straight down into Phipps Pasture, and crossed it west of Highway 12 and then switched back east to the Boynton Overlook and followed a ledge down to the Escalante River. Then, in the mid-twenties, according to Doctor Roundy, the third road, the Cream Cellar Road, was carved in switchbacks out of the north end of Head-of-the-Rocks. It's route was something of a mirror image of the modern highway and it got its name from the cellar at the top of the Head-of-the-Rocks where cream brought up by mule from Boulder was stored until trucks could haul it off to Holt's Osiris Creamery. Turn north off Highway 12 just before it drops off Big Flat and walk over the hill and you can see the remains of the cellar and the road cuts down to the pasture. Walk north from the Head-of-the-Rocks pull-off about three hundred yards and you'll find the remains of the dugway from the Second Road coming down to the highway from the hill with the radio relay on it. Walk west from the road the BLM has closed south of the pull-off, at the top of the switchbacks, and you'll find Chimney Rock, where the original road passed on its way to Little Spencer Flat; all the roads came through this area.

They also came through what's now known as the Boynton Overlook. While you're at the overlook reading one account of how Washington Phipps shot and killed his one-time partner John Boynton, the cuts for the Second Road and the Cream Cellar Road, which join together about a quarter-mile back, will be directly behind and above you. Walk back up Highway 12 a quarter-mile and you'll see the cut for the Cream Cellar Road curving around a red fin north of the present road, making for Head-of-the-Rocks along the slope above the Escalante River. It's still in good shape, makes a nice trail with views comparable to those of the new highway, and if you were to shove the rocks off it, you could probably drive a Jeep up it.

Jerry also shows me around Escalante: the chimney and the cellar and the swimming pool and maintenance shed and the warped boards in a field which are the remains of CCC Camp FS-42. He lived just down the block

from here when he was a boy and the workers, many of whom had never been outside New York and Chicago and the other eastern cities where they'd grown up, would pay him a nickel to ride his mare.

"I was rolling in money," he says.

Sheree's mother used to teach reading and writing to the men; some had joined the CCC unable to even sign their own names. One night Jerry's father allowed some of the CCC boys to sleep in beds that had been moved out on their lawn—a common practice in the summer months—and in the morning, Jerry's mother fed them stacks of pancakes and eggs and bacon.

"Word spread," says Jerry, "And then we had all these CCC guys sleeping at our place."

In his book, Roundy says those boys who slept out in the open, "couldn't believe there were so many stars in the sky" (195).

After I've had the tour, after Jerry has shown me all the old alignments of all the old roads and told me where I could find Thompson's Turnover, where Willis Thompson flipped and wrecked his wagon when he took a curve too fast and left it where it lay, and Peters' Whip-up, where James Peters failed to persuade his balking horse team to pull his wagon up a grade, and the Lollipop Tree in Phipp's Pasture, which still has a lollipop shape, where the Second Road changed course and headed for Boynton Overlook, and the McInelly twist, the switchbacks James McInelly put in near the Hogback in 1915, after he's shown me the old CCC camp and the house he grew up in, we part ways and I head back to Calf Creek Campground to put one more piece of this road into perspective. I've already hiked up to Lower Calf Creek Falls, the high, clear ribbon unraveling into mist and rainbows a few miles upcanyon from the campground, and I've studied the petroglyphs on the walls but there's one I missed high on the cliffs, the most important one, the dark figure. No trail goes to it so you have to make your own way, and I do: I climb off the worn trail and scramble up red ledges while a few tourists look on disapprovingly, to a Navajo Sandstone wall where the dark figure awaits. He has no arms or legs or eyes and his body is a black wedge and he has horns like a bull. I have seen him before, seen him in some dream, met him on some ethereal plane. I know this demonic visage, though I don't know his name. His two horns are the oppositions of things: up/down, good/evil, male/female, right and left, pointing to each other. This idol is the heart of Highway 12.

The Upper Road

FS 153 is Hell's Backbone Road, usually impassible in winter, but it's been another dry year and the road hasn't been closed off. I come up from the Escalan-

te side, pass by a few empty logging trucks that must belong to contractors working for Steed, skate through a few patches of snow at the onset, which make me wonder how it is further up. To the right, the Escalante Monocline is a long white shield wall with a hole in it where that meek little trickle of Pine Creek bashes through five hundred feet of solid Navajo Sandstone to run along the roadside. To the left are the scaly Black Hills and Skull Spring and Lost Creek, bad portents, all.

FS 154 branches off for the plateau top, Posey Lake and Cyclone Lake, the Awapa Plateau, and Bicknell, eventually, but I keep right and find more snow, stretches of snow hundreds of yards long, especially where the trees have shaded the road from the southern sun, so I take it

Chimney from the CCC
camp near Escalante

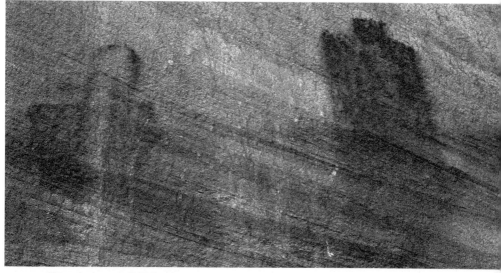

Ghost figures at Calf Creek

slow, put on slow music, some Brahms, a collection called "Songs Ring out to the Heavens," which is appropriate because my side-view mirror has been knocked back so I can keep my eye on the drift clouds, so I can watch the sky.

Pretty soon I'm in a forest of ponderosa and limber pine, firs, scrub oak, rabbitbrush on the roadside, and yellow signs warning me to keep my eyes on the road. The sandstone is gone and black and red andesites and trachytes and black clinkers have taken its place. Boulder Mountain is a "pseudo-mountain," which means it was carved out of the landscape, left standing by "circumdenudation," as Dutton put it, rather than pushed up by tectonic forces or built up by volcanic eruptions. The volcanic cap, one to two thousand feet thick, is why the Aquarius Plateau is still here.

And when the cap is removed, the unprotected Navajo Sandstone is downwasted like a deep wound. Death Hollow came into being from the desire of Mamie Creek's Right Fork to get even with the surrounding terrain, four thousand feet beneath the Mountain, as quickly as possible.

Hell's Backbone Road gets its name from the knife-edge ridge that runs above Sand Creek. A CCC crew from Camp FS-18 at Blue Spring Ridge set up a spike camp near Hell's Backbone to build a bridge across the narrowest section. At one point in the construction it was necessary to move a compressor over to the other side of the gorge. As Jerry Roundy puts it,

perhaps the most daring feat was performed by local man, Loral "Sixty" McInelly. Loral was not a CCC enrollee but a local LEM (Local Experienced

Man) who had been hired because of his bulldozer driving skills. . . . When the compressor arrived, the main stringers were in place but the decking had not yet been completed. The stringers were two huge saw logs that grew close to the place where the bridge was to be built and had been felled in place almost across the span. They were winched into place and the tops were hewed flat. . . . Upon closer examination of the situation, it was discovered that the tracks of the Caterpillar tractor and the wheels of the compressor fit the stringers. . . . In order to protect the driver in case of a mishap, a cable was strung overhead between two huge pine trees from which a rope and a shoulder harness was suspended and secured to the driver. Then at least if the Caterpillar had gone over the side, the driver would have been left dangling safely (?) in mid-air. . . . Loral was an excellent "cat-skinner" and cautiously made his way across the chasm with the compressor as everyone held their breath. As the cat pulled onto the other side, a huge cheer went up from the on-lookers. (186-187)

They finished the job in five and one-half weeks with no mishaps.

I always have to toss a few stones off the bridge when I come through here, hike out to the edge to see into the deep cuts, peer down at the bottom of oblivion.

Past the ridge there's snow on the road for miles, so I put it in four-wheel-drive, crawl down switchbacks in tracks too wide for the Heap so it gets slung all over the road until the snow cover breaks. I spot a few old overgrown haul roads back in the woods and come to an aspen stand where every local has in-scribed his name and some of the dendroglyphs are so old and distorted by tree growth

The idol of Highway 12

that they've become illegible runes. From the aspens, the road drops steeply to the isolated ranches in Salt Gulch and to fields of sagebrush and rabbitbrush again, and dead pines turned to rust, and the road runs back out to Highway 12.

Death Hollow

According to Jerry Roundy, the trail through Death Hollow never was the official Boulder Mail Trail. Some letters may have come over it but you couldn't really haul anything substantial over what he calls the Death Hollow Trail because there wasn't enough room; it was too steep and narrow. This trail was the express route from Escalante to Boulder, a straight line from one town to the next, over and under hills and dales, cliffs, washes, whatever was in the way, and it was sixteen miles where even the modern road runs thirty and it was five hours by horseback where the original route was five days by wagon.

I've brought along way too much equipment for this adventure and I'll come to know my pack as "the beast" over the next sixteen miles. I start off at noon from the turnoff to Hell's Backbone, next to the Boulder Airport which is a dirt runway by an airplane fuselage mashed nose-first into the ground with a windsock on a pole bolted to it and "Boulder Airport and UFO Landing Site" scrawled on the side. The first part of the trail drops into the head of Sand Creek and I already have to rest after two miles, set my pack down against a rock and find a shaded, bare spot of ground amidst the rabbitbrush and cottonwoods, tamarisk, Indian paintbrush and limber pine and listen to the creek's purl for a while. I wonder at that point whether I should turn back and lighten the load. I've got a gallon jug and a 1.5 liter bottle of water, which proves to be just enough for the journey; a heavy, self-inflating sleeping pad which won't deflate anymore because embers from campfires have burned holes in it; a sleeping bag that must weigh ten pounds; a change of clothes; a couple cans of tuna; some chips; and miscellany like a fire grate and guidebooks and other items that probably add about fifteen pounds of weight. I bought the external-frame backpack, a Kelty which must be at least twenty-five years old, at Deseret Industries, a thrift store, for five dollars. Suppose I were to use pine boughs in place of the pad and replace the sleeping bag with a blanket and build and feed a big fire to stay warm through the night? Suppose I try to do all sixteen miles in one stretch tomorrow without a heavy pack? But I decide to continue, hoping my body will adjust as I go.

The trail hooks up with the Forest Service telephone line that was strung along trees between Boulder and Escalante in 1910 and the trail stays with the line down to Escalante. Lose your way and you can pick up the route again by following the line, which is good because the trail is often nothing more than a row of cairns.

Death Hollow

I meet isolated groups of backpackers coming the other way, the wrong way as far as I'm concerned: uphill. Two of them are in their sixties, having a hard time of it but they're managing, which puts me to shame. I rest often during that afternoon but make ten miles with this monster on my back. The views on the top of the trail are wide open to the dim and distant Henry Peaks and Navajo Mountain and there's a pleasant breeze winding through the ponderosa and over the manzanita flats that keeps the gnats off me. I come to the Slickrock Saddle and gaze into the abyss, the chasm that's still dark with the sun nearly overhead, and I hike down the blasted-out dugways, down the switchbacks where cattleman John King slipped on ice one night and dangled for a moment or two over Death Hollow by the bridle of his braced horse, to the river bed and I rest for a while in the cool shadows.

Like most photographers in southern Utah, I've become fascinated with desert varnish, long vertical black and red streaks on the rock walls, oxidations and mineral precipitations, minerals fixed to the surface through organic action. These patterns are like absorption and emission lines; it's as if some distant star had transmitted and filtered its light, the inimitable record of its size and age, directly onto the walls of this canyon.

And this canyon, Death Hollow, has the most impressive streaks of desert varnish I've seen anywhere, and not just impressive for their size but the variety of their sizes, shapes and hues: puce and mauve and a shimmering red ocher just the color of blood. Hematite and hemoglobin have the same Greek root, and that's because our blood gets its color from the same element which precipitates from the sandstone walls, iron. Every red blood cell has four iron atoms to bind four oxygen molecules and blood turns a rust brown as it coagulates because it *is* literally rusting, oxidizing, as it dries.

I use a lot of film getting pictures of those walls and I find myself wandering down past the turnoff point and I pay for it when I slip on a stone in midstream and dunk my pack into the water. My clothes are saturated and the sleeping bag gets wet but my camera stays dry in the butt-pack and so do my books, which are on top of the backpack. I also jam my right thumb into a rock as I'm flailing around, so fairly soon I can't use it.

Back I go to the trail, through ferns and horsetails that resonate a Paleozoic presence, and up the side of Death Hollow until I can view the weirdness downstream, the whaleskin walls and white fins squeezed up to monolithic heights, like the temples of Zion National Park, which is the next spot west where the Navajo Sandstone appears after it dives into the earth at the Escalante Monocline.

When I pause near the top of the hollow I'm instantly set on by gnats and the attack inspires me to invent the *gnat count*, the number of gnats in a given volume in any particular environment, which could be tacked onto the end of the weather report like a pollen count.

Up on top, a zephyr throws the gnats off and sets the frame of my pack humming like a flute. Dark clouds roll over the sun and the light leeches away and I come down from a flat into the sand wash of Mamie Creek where I will spend the night. My guidebooks call Death Hollow a "moderate" hike, but my shoulders are about to separate and I wouldn't notice if they did because my upper body has gone numb with shock. Want to know how a packhorse felt about the pioneer experience? Strap on a fifty or seventy pound pack and hike over the Death Hollow Trail.

I collect some firewood with one hand and lay out the sleeping bag, which is dry inside where my intermediate bag with its cotton/polyester blend cover would be dripping wet, so I have to add water resistance to the list of benefits you get with synthetics. It's May and it's not likely to get too cold tonight but pretty soon I've got an inferno burning next to me anyway, and I rest and cook my dinner on the grate and peruse my guidebooks by the firelight, which is ironic because this is how they read.

What is more traditional than a campfire? Yet the arrival at that perfect campsite can be ruined by the numerous fire rings already there. When you hike in the spring and the fall, the need for warmth can easily be provided for by extra clothing and a good supper. The reality that a campfire is not a necessity

Desert varnish, Death Hollow

is a difficult ethic to convey. Hopefully the reason you are here is because this area offers unique wilderness experiences. On a more practical level, evaluate the time spent gathering firewood, digging a pit, burning your dinner, etc., compared to spending that time reading, listening and observing. Due to the damage associated with campfires, the National Park Service is considering establishment of "stoves only" zones in fragile or heavily used parts of the canyon system. (Lambrechtse, 12)

And there's more:

> *Fires:* Campfires can no longer be tolerated in the wilderness setting. They do an immense amount of damage to the land. Not only are the blackened rocks of a fire ring ugly, the charcoal and ash residues seem to last forever. Fire rings demarcate campsites and tend to draw people to them. This promotes over-use. Use a light-weight stove for cooking and a candle lantern as a gathering beacon for nighttime socializing (Allen, 18).

I pile some more logs on the fire—I've got an ample supply, enough to last all night—and record some thoughts here.

First off, perhaps fires *are* a necessity. Hang over a stove fire and your clothes will smell of butane or propane. Smell is the original and most primal of the five senses; the receptors in our noses are wired directly to the emotional centers of our brains and the smell of burning ponderosa or cedar stirs something quite pleasing in those deep-down nexuses of our lizard minds. Also, campfires get the gnats off you *right now*.

Second, if your wilderness experience is ruined by an old campfire ring or any other single artifact of man, you may need professional help. There is a high probability you will not be the first person to go anywhere on this earth, and you may just have to acknowledge that fact.

Third, I can read while my dinner is cooking and not burn it. This comes with practice. Further along in one guidebook:

> The meticulous practice of "leave-no-trace" camping technique can help spare the land; but this is no longer enough. We must now become our brother's keeper. . . . Insensitive hikers can no longer be tolerated. It is our obligation to help educate those who do not know and to chastise those who do know but do not care (Allen, 14).

When I skim through the introductions, they are full of "musts" and "don'ts." I believe that if you want the wilderness to remain in an absolutely pristine condition you don't write a guidebook about it.

A friend of mine, an environmentalist, once confided to me that it was impossible to "leave no trace" unless you stayed entirely out of the wilderness. Are you going to scratch your tracks out as you go? Reset the twigs you snapped as you struggled through the brush? Carry the rocks you dislodged coming down a switchback to their former position and try to orient them as they were before? My motto is "don't make too much of a mess," and I know it doesn't have the same cachet as "leave no trace" but it works. I burn my garbage in the fire and pack out anything unsightly like black plastic that's been left alive. I'll use an old fire ring before I construct my own and an old campsite before I clear a new one, and I won't make a fire ring unless the wind is high and the timber is dry and I don't want to start a conflagration, and if conditions are absolutely right for a forest or range fire, I won't build a fire at all.

Having recorded these opinions, I am now free to enjoy the night and the solitude and dwell on other things and let the fire die down to a simple blaze and sleep right beneath the telephone wire until morning, when I must harness myself again to the beast. The next day I'll continue my trek with my swollen thumb and the pack seeming to weigh a great deal less, up the slope of Mamie Creek, over the slickrock sulci past Antone Flat, down a wash by the big white "E" on the side of the Escalante Monocline and into Escalante itself. The hardest part, as I'd been warned by a few fellow hikers back in

Death Hollow, will be to find a ride back up to the turnoff to Hell's Backbone, but tomorrow I will finally get together with a couple from Ann Arbor, Michigan, headed for the Burr Trail, trying to see all of the Southwest in a week, and they'll get me close enough to where I can walk back to the Heap.

Tonight I'm comfortable and warm and only separated from the earth by an inch of foam padding and a few layers of plastic and as my mind tips into the night, even those barriers vanish.

chapter four

Photo opposite: Approaching Boulder from the west, Aquarius Plateau in distance

—The Eastern Rim, the Eastern
Spokes and the Hub—

Boulder,
the Burr Trail,
the Aquarius Plateau
and Beyond

Cliff Dwellers

Larry Davis is in the Heap's passenger seat, gripping the dashboard bar while we swerve over the Hogback headed toward Escalante, and he's describing for me the wrecks he's seen on this road in the thirty-two years he's lived in Boulder.

"A guy went over about right here," says Davis, "fell about four hundred feet, climbed back up. His alcohol level was about 1.9 when they tested it, probably about 2.4 when he went over. Broke the fifth vertebrae in his neck, couldn't hold his head up. He should have been dead or at least paralyzed. He fought the paramedics the whole time."

Further on, where the road curves sharply to the right:

"A guy driving a dump truck, doing construction . . . this other guy says he passed him on this curve doing about seventy. He hit the wall here head-on, crushed his cab down to about two feet."

And a little further, above Calf Creek:

"A motorcyclist hit the cement barrier here and went over."

I examine the drop, keeping one eye on the road. The rider must have been pitched a hundred feet through the air, must have fallen at least as far. There's no way he could have lived. The Heap wobbles a little as we come around.

"Don't worry," I say, "I won't get you killed."

"If you do, my wife will kill *you*," says Davis.

Davis, the retired director of Anasazi State Park in Boulder, is shorter than me, and he's got two prosthetic knees, but when we get to the point where Highway 12 crosses the Escalante River, he takes the lead scrambling up the sandstone slope. We reach a shelf of rock and hike back to a wall of Fremont petroglyphs; a wedge figure with wavy lines radiating from its forehead, and bighorn sheep.

Sheep are the most commonly depicted big game animal in Fremont petroglyphs, he tells me. Second to deer, they were also the most important big game animal in their diet.

"Here's a funny figure," says Davis. "It's almost like he's upside down—Interesting [panel] here. Don't know if it symbolizes a tree or it could be a dragonfly. And then it looks like an antenna or something on top. I don't know what it is."

There are lines chiseled in the rock around one of the sheep where someone has tried to wedge it out.

"I can't lose sleep over it," Davis says of the vandalism, but he still seems irked.

Further on, he points me to a recess high in the rock, beneath which 120 positive, white Fremont handprints are arranged in four rows. The climb is steep and I use my binoculars to get a closer view, but I can't tell if they belong to more than one individual. I wonder if I could discern fingerprints, or how large the artist's or artists' hands would be compared to mine.

We move up to a dwelling site underneath an overhang. I would never have recognized it as such, but Larry points out the raised foundation, the cisterns in the floor, the groves in the wall where the Fremont sharpened their spear points. There's a pinyon log nearby that Davis believes is connected to the site. It would be "fun," he tells me, to analyze a core sample from it to come up with an approximate date for the site's occupation. Davis also shows me hammer stones, egg-shaped rocks with distinctive radial fractures which developed from being knocked against the sandstone several hundred years ago.

The site has been picked over, dug up, looted. Larry's pragmatism, his congeniality, seem to fade. He tells me, "This is as much a part of our cultural heritage as anything else. We need to teach respect and we didn't. I reviewed a history text a few years ago and it had a whole chapter on the political climate in Spain prior to the voyage of Columbus but only a paragraph or two about what Columbus found here—the people—but after that it was just about European history and they just ignored the Indians. You know, we look at Indians as less important and that's how we treat these things."

Across the canyon, there are kids rappelling off Boynton Overlook, down to the sand dune at the cliff base. Their shouting and laughter reverberates off the stone walls.

Davis tells me about a helicopter ride he took some years back. The pilot told him, "I'm going to take you to this ruin nobody's been in. And we just hovered in front of this overhang. Nice little ruin and the doorway was still sealed. And it's so sheer that you couldn't come in from below, and it overhangs so far you couldn't rope in from the top. So it's just there. And it's kind of neat. . . .

"And then, twenty-five years ago a friend of mine had a flying service over in Canyonlands. His name was Dick Smith. He flew me into an area, told me 'I'm going to show you some ruins nobody's been in before, Larry.' Flew me right past these ruins in the cliff and I'll bet you fifty percent of them still had the doorway sealed. We were going to go see if we could work our way into that canyon and a year or so later, he was killed in a plane crash."

"You know, the vandals now are using helicopters, so they can get into any place. Earl Shumway over in Blanding, he's probably the king of vandals. He served time in federal prison and he said, 'I carry a .44 magnum. The next person that catches me isn't going to leave in the same position he found me in.'"

Here's an article about Shumway from *High Country News*, September 4, 1995.

> A Pothunter is nailed at last
> By Shea Anderson
>
> Earl Shumway, the notorious pillager of Anasazi burial sites in Utah, has been convicted of looting. Shumway had built a record of illegal pillaging of historic sites since 1984, bragging that he was untouchable (HCN, 12/26/94).
>
> When asked by the *Salt Lake Tribune* to describe Shumway, Utah state archeologist Dave Madsen was brief: "Pothunter. Looter. Or just scumbag. You probably can't print any of the other words I'd use."
>
> Shumway barely escaped a conviction in 1986 by testifying against his friend Buddy Black in the high-profile Basket Case, in which the two looters excavated a collection of Anasazi baskets. That strategy kept him free for a while—Shumway got away with probation. Now, a Moab helicopter pilot has testified in federal court that Shumway offered him thousands of dollars worth of Anasazi baskets to pinpoint certain sites from the air, including one within Canyonlands National Park.
>
> But pilot Michael Miller said he realized Shumway wasn't going to split the proceeds from artifact sales with him, much less pay for any of the helicopter's gas. Law enforcement officials expect Shumway's Nov. 13 sentencing to be stiff: he was convicted of four violations of the Archaeological Resources Act. Shumway's offenses could net him up to 15 years in prison.

According to Davis, the helicopter pilot brought his mechanic along with them and it was he who finally turned the two in, after Shumway unwrapped a child's body from an Anasazi grave and "chucked" it. Shumway got five years and now he's free again.

"They make so much money," Davis tells me, "There's a collection . . . they call it the 'Shumway Collection.' They wanted to sell it to the state one time so myself and another guy went over to appraise it and we had to go to three different houses and the family rooms would be covered with pots. None of the utilitarian pottery. I asked this guy what's in the boxes along the wall and he said that's the crudware, the corrugated stuff. The other stuff was all black-on-white, red-on-orange, black-on-red, some of the most wonderful pots, something like 320 pieces in there. We, of course, recommended that the state not buy them because all you're doing is subsidizing an illegal activity. I asked him where'd that stuff come from and he says, 'came from patent property.' A lot of times they'd go out and stake a mineral claim on an archaeological site and then go in and dig it. It's still illegal."

"I've said it a lot of times, what they ought to do is stick the IRS on these guys. They sold that collection for seventy thousand dollars, to the Navajo Development Council. It's probably one of the best type collections of Anasazi pottery, there's a value to it, but there would have been more of a value if you could have seen where it came from, what the pots were associated with, what kind of site it was."

We hike out on a thin ledge to another panel of petroglyphs: horned, limbless anthropomorphs, dots and other abstract symbols and one hourglass-shaped hunter pointing a diminutive bow and arrow at a nearby mountain sheep. Yesterday's dark clouds with their virga trails, what Davis calls "teasers," moved on in the night and it's a clear, sunny day, and Larry takes in the view; the shallow "river," the scraggly cottonwoods on its banks, the cliffs on the far side. It would have been an ideal place to watch for game, but that aspect of the view doesn't interest him right now.

"Very peaceful here," he says.

Davis will be talking to you and he'll develop this shifty half-smile; he might reveal what he's thinking and he might keep it his own private joke. He's contemplative, deliberate, not a fast talker, and he'll drift out of a conversation into his own thoughts. I spoke with him in his house in Boulder the day before our hike and that smile crossed his lips as he described a trip over Highway 12 where it rose across the east side of the Aquarius Plateau.

"One of the real pretty times I remember on that mountain, and there's been a

Right and next two pages:
Petroglyphs near the
confluence of the Escalante
River and Calf Creek

lot of them, but I was coming over, it was late at night, it was in the winter-time and there was a lot of snow. The pine trees were covered. I was on the other side and I could look out toward the Henry Mountains. There was a full moon and the whole country was just silver, and there was an inversion and there were a lot of clouds down in that valley between the Henrys and me, and I just sat there, in my parked truck. It's just one of those moments."

As we walk back down to the river, I pass through a scattering of rocks and burnt sticks in the sand, nothing spectacular, but out of place. Davis confirms my suspicions.

"You're walking through a site," he tells me.

This meager collection of stones and sticks is what archaeologists call a "lithic scatter," and according to Davis, it describes the majority of sites in the national monument.

"Usually, when someone looks for a site, they're thinking of a granary or a structure of some kind, but most sites aren't like that."

Earlier, I asked for Davis's opinion on the migration of the Fremont's neighbors, the Ana-sazi, out of southern Utah and he attributed it to a combination of drought and friction between various Anasazi factions. There is a large and growing body of scientific evidence to back up Larry's belief in internecine conflict as a causative element in the withdrawal of puebloan Indians from much of the Four Corners in the thirteenth and fourteenth centuries, but such views have characteristically been met with hostility from the archaeological community. Jonathan Haas and Winifred Creamer are two of a handful of experts who aren't afraid to use "warfare" in the same sentence as "Anasazi," but

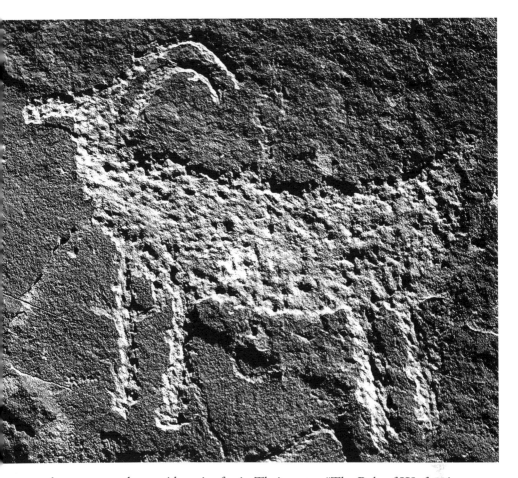

they appear to have paid a price for it. Their paper, "The Role of Warfare in the Pueblo III Period," begins:

> Because we have already succeeded in irritating most archaeologists in the Southwest with the seemingly preposterous idea that warfare played a central role in the Kayenta area during the Pueblo III period (Haas and Cremaer, 1993), we thought it would be interesting to take the idea even further. Basically we argue in this chapter that warfare was endemic throughout the northern Southwest in the thirteenth century, and that any explanations of settlement, political relations, and abandonment must incorporate warfare as a central causal variable (Haas, Creamer, 205).

And they cite a lot of analagous historical evidence to support their thesis: the historical puebloans tendency to retreat to higher ground when threatened; the conquistadores' eyewitness accounts of pueblos destroyed in the course of tribal warfare; the revolt of 1680, in which the puebloans rose up in unison and killed or exiled the Spanish priests who had enslaved them and tried to beat their religion out of them; and the vestigial war societies of the modern pueblos. They also cite the coalescing of smaller, more isolated communities into larger villages, as with the later aggregation of Mormon settlements during the Black Hawk War, and the siting of pueblos in the valleys around Long House Valley during the thirteenth century.

> These surrounding valleys were not abandoned, nor did they witness population declines. If anything the population in these valleys increased in the latter half of the thirteenth century. The reason these valleys looked abandoned is that the sites were almost all large pueblos of 50 to 200 rooms, perched up on top of inaccessible rocks and mesa tops. . . . You might look for shrines on these hilltops, but habitation did not seem likely. It got so that one of the best indicators of site location was when the survey crews were unable to find an access route to the top of a particular topographic feature. In each such case, a second effort revealed a skinny crack in the rock or steep trail up the cliff side, and a pueblo on top invariably dating to A.D. 1250 to 1300. (Haas, Creamer, 208)

There are enough skeletons in the Southwest with shattered skulls or arrowheads or even fossil shark's teeth in their ribcages and enough burnt pueblos to make continual low-level conflicts (such as ambushes and raiding) a possibility, maybe even a probability, and there doesn't seem to be any practical reason for the Anasazi to build their dwellings in such extremely remote locations as Haas and Creamer found in Long House Valley other than for defensive purposes. And it wouldn't have taken much to drive a neighboring community out of their territory; a few late-season raids on their fields, a few of their granaries looted, and they're facing starvation, and there's a lot of evidence of starvation during this period.

But if warfare was a formative element of Anasazi society, its effects are rather faint here, as was their presence eight hundred years ago when they had a settlement over in Boulder. The Escalante River was Fremont territory.

From the shoulder of Highway 12, with my binoculars, we examine a granary in a sandstone pocket a few hundred feet above us. The Fremont might have reached it through a narrow crack to the right of the alcove, but even thinking about that climb, the horrendous exposure, makes my palms sweat. There seems to be a Darwinian process occurring here. The Fremont may have built some of their structures in more easily-accessible locations, but those buildings probably succumbed to looters and vandals, both ancient and modern.

Petroglyph near Fence Canyon

Beyond the granary, the teenagers are still rappelling two hundred feet down from the overlook. We still hear their shouts. I suppose when they're all down they'll hike to the road to be picked up, or maybe there's a way back to the overlook from the cliff base.

Larry directs my attention back to the granary, the extreme overhang.

"A kid tried to rope down to that thing a few years back," he says, "and he died trying."

There are children splashing through the Escalante River below the bridge. We walk across the road and down a shady, sandy path to a clearing in the cottonwoods and he points out a jacal granary or dwelling in the cliffside thirty-five feet above the ground. A thirty-foot log forms part of its base, and I wonder what apparatus they used to get it up there. Even now, there appears to be no way to access the granary, other than a fairly technical climb. The Fremont were obviously an agile people. The clumsy probably died young. I mention this to him.

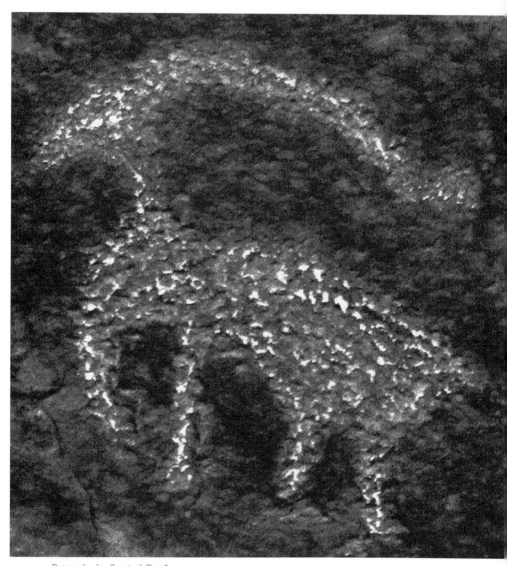

Petroglyph, Capitol Reef

"I visited this Hopi family once, lived right next to a cliff," he says, "couple hundred foot fall, and their children used to play near the edge and I asked their mother if it made her nervous. She said she'd never thought about it before I asked."

The Puebloans

This used to be the farm of Ephraim Coombs (rhymes with "dooms") and now it's a state park. In the visitor's center, there are exhibits of spear and arrow points, moccasins and snares and other relics, and there's a mock-up of an Anasazi dwelling with a ladder through the ceiling, which is symbolic to the modern Hopi of the *sipapu*, the entrance they used to get to this world from the one below, and there's pottery: Garfield black-on-white, Ivie Creek black-on-white, Black Mesa black-on-white, Middleton black-on-red and Citadel polychrome, which is the latest style you find here, because after that, the Anasazi left, and nobody knows why.

The Coombs site out back consists of foundations of an L-shaped pueblo and a U-shaped pueblo and a pit house and some more structures that haven't been excavated yet. According to Mike Nelson, the director, and Lisa Westwood, chief curator and an expert on human osteology, about sixty percent of the site was burned, but it wasn't all burned at once. When I asked these two what the Kayenta Anasazi were doing this far north, as far north as they ever came, they can't tell me, and they almost seem afraid to speculate. The Anasazi were trading with the Fremont, but the Coombs site didn't appear to be a trading outpost. It seems an entire Anasazi village or some other large group of people moved up here as an intact social unit, possibly as refugees from some kind of social strife in northern Arizona or as farmers looking for greener pastures, and they "bumped" the Fremont out of the way in the process. Nevertheless, there's no evidence of a prolonged conflict between the two cultures. Quite the opposite: the Anasazi built pit structures like the Fremont, and the Coombs site is unique in that they didn't create a kiva, just as the Fremont didn't dig kivas, and the Fremont adopted black-on-white pottery from the Anasazi.

Lisa shows me the pottery collection in the climate-controlled back room. She points out an example of the Fremont black-on-white and I study the motifs very closely; black widow markings, pawl-tooth edges and involutes, interlocking spirals.

"Interlocking spirals," I say. "What do you think that means?"

"Ceramics," says Lisa, "are like fine art. They're hard to interpret. It's hard to find a system that can positively categorize every style. It's like any discipline: there are lumpers and splitters."

Spirals interlock and unfold. Cultures trade and learn from each other and clash. Opposition rises up from the other end of the earth, beyond the boundaries of the People, as most native cultures identified themselves, or within the ranks of the People, or within the mind itself.

"Pottery," she says, "does not equal people."

"What's your favorite style?" I ask, and she answers without hesitation: "Miniatures."

She's got them lined up on one shelf: tiny, decorated ladles and bowls, jars and cups.

"They might be children's toys," she says, "Or they might have been used for ceremonies. Sometimes you find them in child burial sites."

I ask Mike and Lisa what forced the Anasazi retreat.

"The modern puebloans," says Mike, "call it the 'migration,' and nobody knows for sure."

"But you must have theories," I say. "Did they go to war? Coombs is out in the open, it's indefensible."

"There's been an overemphasis on the warfare issue," says Lisa. "There were severe droughts about the time they left. There was a change in rainfall patterns. The water sources were drying up. The Anasazi might have lost faith in their religious leaders."

There's little doubt they were living in a time of need. Lisa has studied the bones.

"We see a lot of enamel hypoplasia, interruptions in the growth of new layers in young teeth, in the Anasazi around 1150 to 1175, when they left," says Lisa, "and we can put that together with other lines of evidence of deficiency like stature and we know they were suffering from malnutrition."

Lisa thinks the Anasazi might have been motivated to move into cliff dwellings out of a necessity to cultivate every available inch of arable land, and others speculate that the Anasazi moved up there for aesthetic or religious purposes. The only thing that would get me to move up into a niche high on a cliff wall, however, and haul my food and water and everything I would need to live up there and raise my children on the brink of a drop-off, where every day we would have the opportunity to fall to our deaths, would be a marauding enemy.

I walk through the exhibits and I meditate on the patterns of pottery, the whorls and checkerboards, stripes, diamonds, the cross-hatching like you see in the sandstone around town and what I see is point and counterpoint.

The Cowboy

Dell LeFevre, whose brand is 7X, is a laconic old cowboy. He's almost curt sometimes. He's a busy man, doesn't like to sleep, doesn't like to waste time talking when he's got something to do, and as a rancher and commissioner for Garfield County, he's always got something to do. He likes to *get straight to the point.*

I learned this when I first met him at his two-story ranch house on the north end of Boulder, which had a dozen bicycles spread over the yard and cats prowling about and some of Dell's big-eyed East-Indian munchkin children staring out the windows at me. Dell isn't home when I get there and I speak to his wife Gladys for a while until he pulls up and climbs out of his pickup and gets in my face, this middle-aged, hook-nosed, leather-skinned man who probably outweighs me by thirty pounds of ropy muscle, whose sloppy cowboy hat makes him six inches taller than me, wanting to know who I was and what I want with his family and so on, until I convince him I am a writer and then it is "Who are you writing for? What's your angle? Who have you talked to?" Finally he settles down enough that I can put some questions to him, specifically about the Burr Trail. But Dell is in a hurry now, and once he's convinced himself I'm not a threat, he loads a few things on an ATV and hops on himself, with one of his tiny boys jumping on behind him and grabbing tight. All I get are a few sound bites:

About the Burr Trail controversy: "It's a war, it's not about the environment. It's about control, plain and simple. Who controls the land."

About the environmental movement: "They won. They got what they wanted. We took this place from the Indians, they're taking it from us and somebody will probably take it from them someday."

"They [developers] want to turn this place into a Vail, a Moab."

"There's no young ranchers anymore, no young farmers."

And then he paused for just one moment and looked over his spread and laughed and said, "I bought this place straight out for forty thousand dollars a few decades ago and I'm still paying for it."

Then he was off in a cloud of gray dust, into the midst of a four-year drought to try and save some of his cattle.

Next time we chat, I set up an appointment in the evening, and Dell sits me in his living room and he and his wife, but mostly Dell, answer my questions when they're not being distracted about homework or some emergency on the ranch by one of their adopted children. Dell tells me about his relationship with the Forest Service and the BLM.

"I try to keep a good working relationship. You have to work with the government; they're your landlord. You have to get along with them or they can make it rough on you. And it's hard sometimes. There's other ranchers who wouldn't work with them and their attitude was that it was just somebody putting regulations and regulations and regulations on them and they just fought back."

I ask him about the current and former BLM management. Kate Cannon used to be in charge of the monument and she wasn't very diplomatic, rubbed a lot of locals the wrong way, especially ranchers whose cattle she was impounding, and she was finally forced out. But Dell liked her.

"She'd spit in your eye. She stood up and told you where to go," he says. "Said she was going to impound the cattle on the Fifty and then she did it."

And the natural resources around Escalante and Boulder: would these towns ever have access to them?

"That will never happen. The coal deposit out there on the Kaiparowits is the largest known coal reserve in the world and it's clean-burning coal and Clinton buttoned all that up so we can get Asian coal. When I first got on the commission, we redrew all the monument's boundaries so we could get to the coal, but Bush hasn't got the—I shouldn't say this—the balls to change those boundaries. It's a small issue and Utah is a Republican state, so he's already got the votes locked up."

And the economics of the situation?

"Calves are selling for the same price now as when I got into the business in 1973," he says, pausing to let that sink in. "The United States is buying beef from Australia, Argentina, Canada, and that keeps the price of beef down because they can ship it here cheaper than we can raise it. To make it in the ranching business you need two dollars a pound and we can't get that. The economics are killing the ranchers more than all the government regulations." And more than environmentalists, he's said elsewhere, though he believes it all plays into the demise of ranching in southern Utah. This year the income for Dell's ranch will just break even with his operating expenses.

Dell grew up in these parts, in a shack with no running water and he wanted to be a cattleman from the time he was ten years old (Jay Haymond, "LeFevre," 1). He was dyslexic, but he says he "had a good memory on me" (2). He got into bull and bronc riding when he was young and "took some hits" but couldn't afford the lifestyle in the end.

"I didn't have the money to do it. That was a rich man's game back then. I'd have to work and get a little money and then I could go rodeo for a while and then I wasn't good enough to go where the money was at. There's a lot of cowboys out there. They finally got it up to where the top fifteen are making money, but back then it was just a sport."

"That's funny," I say, "You have to pay money to get on a bull and get the—"

"That's right, to get on a bull. You might get some money back but back then the entrance fee was fifteen, twenty, thirty—a big rodeo was fifty dollars, and a fifteen-dollar rodeo would have a seventy dollar purse for first place, and you're competing against fifteen to twenty people. And they paid three places or four, and fourth place, you were back to your entrance fee again. So by the time you drive down the road one hundred and fifty or two hundred miles to a rodeo, by the time you figure gas and the motel and your meals, it was a losing situation."

So he joined the army, and he and a Navajo friend went AWOL for a while from basic training so Dell could get busted up and win seven hundred dollars riding bulls in Reno, Nevada, and then he came back and was given fourteen days hard labor, breaking rocks with a sledge hammer, and stationed in Alaska on a security detail attached to a group of scientists monitoring the Russian nuclear tests, and they somehow ended up lost in Siberia at one point, for four or five days. Dell got pneumonia from the cold during this stint and surgeons had to remove the lower half of his left lung, and when he'd recovered from that, a Russian Eskimo prisoner who was handcuffed to him bailed out of an airborne helicopter and wrenched Dell's shoulder, which had already been damaged by bull riding, until the muscle and nerves were completely destroyed (Haymond, "LeFevre," 12).

Discharged from the service, Dell roughnecked with a drilling operation in Casper, Wyoming, and became a "pusher" or straw boss, and then he bought into the company and saved his pennies, moved back to Boulder and bought a ranch.

He also married his one true love, Gladys Lyman, daughter of cattleman Ivan Lyman, who once employed Dell, and a descendent of the Lymans who'd settled Boulder Valley. They spent fourteen childless years together while Dell drilled in New Mexico and Missouri, Wyoming, Michigan and Colorado and while Dell bought the ranch and began buying out smaller operations whenever he got the chance, and then they adopted a couple of Mexican boys, Sean and Keith, and an infant named Jonathan.

Dell became county commissioner and they put off adopting children for a few years, but then they got into it in a big way, flying down to Bolivia with a suitcase of cash and coming back with two children and then adopting kids in bulk, two or three at a time. They now have fourteen children, "And that," says Dell, "is it."

Dell's children probably won't have much of a future in Boulder unless they can adapt to the new economy of tourism and development.

"That's the way it's going to go," says LeFevre. "I won't say it's a good thing, but that's the way Boulder's going to go; it's going to turn into ranchettes. It's already gone. If you've got money that's a good thing, but you're taking it away from the working-class guy who can't afford a place in Boulder. It's going to become a Sedona, Arizona, a second-home place, because there's just no way you can make a living here, other than tourism."

"That's too bad," I say, "because I've worked in Sedona and Park City and you've got two classes of people, the wealthy and—"

"Seven dollars an hour."

I ask him how the atmosphere has changed.

"It used to be all ranching, it was a ranching community, everyone worked together and now there are hardly any ranchers left. And the new people are not bad people, they're just different, they don't have the ranching background and most of them don't care about ranching."

"That's also too bad," I say, "because I think that's why they moved to Boulder."

"Right. But when they come here, a lot of them want to change it like it was where they come from. They come here for the open space, and then they buy a lot and chop it up into little tiny pieces."

Back in the eighties, "eco-terrorists" shot twenty-six of Dell's cattle and burned two of his line shacks.

"About that time," he says, "I picked up this backpacker, a kid. Threw his backpack in the bed of the pickup. I had my little girl in the truck with me at the time. We rode along for a while and I told him about my cows getting shot and I started interrogating him about what he knew and he finally told me, 'I'm glad the cattle got shot. Maybe they should start shooting ranchers too.' So I pulled out my forty-five while I'm driving, and I cocked it and poked it in his rib cage—there was no bullet in the first chamber but he didn't know that—and I said, 'Mister, you just went over the line.' Man, his eyes got big.

"Now remember, my little girl was in the truck and about a week earlier I'd picked up another backpacker about the same place and my daughter had been along with me then as well, and after a minute or so with me holding the gun on this kid, my daughter asks, 'Dad, are you going to leave him in the same place you left the other guy?' And that's when he just flew out of that truck."

Dell is laughing so hard he has to catch his breath.

"He disappeared," he says. "I had to throw his backpack after him."

Not too long ago, Dell was approached by Grand Canyon Trust, which wanted to buy up his permits for rangeland along the Escalante River and retire them. The BLM had been cutting back the time of use so the banks were overgrown. "There used to be some pretty meadows down there," he says, "and the vegetation in the river grew up so bad, those willows and tamarisk, you couldn't get to the river."

Then Dell's horse tripped on a beaver hole down by the river and flipped over on him and pinned him for a day, and while he was under that horse, he thought, "what am I getting out of this, really?" and he decided to sell. He's gotten no end of flak from his fellow ranchers for that decision but he was still reelected county commissioner.

Dell worked with the Forest Service, still smarting from the huge fires all over the West, to get some of the woodlands on the Aquarius Plateau opened up for Stephen Steed's operation.

"The timber from the Arizona fires would have run every mill in the United States for one year," Dell tells me.

I ask him if he ever gets discouraged and he tells me about a friend of his, Buck Shaw, who was captured in the Vietnam War and held captive in tiny bamboo cage and fed nothing but rice for five years. Buck told him, "As long as I was breathing, there was hope."

"Why," I ask, "would somebody stay in the cattle business when the economics are so poor?"

"We're too dumb to get out. I don't know, but ranchers aren't staying in the business, they're selling out."

"Why do you stay in the business?"

"That's a tough one. I guess you marry the land. I don't know, a dream, maybe. We've all got to have a dream."

The Developer

I decide to pay an unscheduled visit to the development Mark Austin is building on Black Mesa, on the outskirts of Boulder.

Austin is an interesting character. He studied architecture at the University of Utah, my alma mater, and he moved away from Utah and moved back again and built the Boulder Mountain Lodge before Clinton's proclamation, and so he took a chance on Boulder, but the town didn't seem very willing to return the favor. Austin beat his head against a wall for years trying to secure the privilege of serving alcohol in his restaurant, and Boulder only relented when a couple of Buddhist women took over the restaurant and couched the problem to the town board in economic terms.

I call Austin's house and somebody tells me he's at the work site, and he gives me directions to meet him and those take me up the Burr Trail to a side road and up the mesa, past numerous "no trespassing" signs, to the frame of a house on a cut in the mesa where Austin is directing the construction. I park at the end of a line of enormous, shiny, new black and gray pickups and just walk up and shake hands with him.

Austin looks to be in his late forties or early fifties. He doesn't look like a developer. He's slim and a little sun worn and he wears a canvas jacket and jeans. He's looking at me in a skeptical manner and maybe he's wondering if he should throw me out. His contractors are trying to size me up as well, probably trying to decide if I'm an environmentalist. He tells me he can spare a few minutes, but only that, and I ask how he ended up here.

"Everybody would like to find a Shangri-La, and this was mine," he says. "Some friends of mine owned a ranch here and I liked it here so much I moved. This was the end of the road, at least until the seventies. There was talk about paving Highway 12 over the mountain and when it finally came to that, I fought it. It was a twelve-million-dollar invitation to the world. And I fought the paving of the Burr Trail. I regret we didn't prevail in preventing that destruction."

I ask him about the design concept of the community he's building.

"We bought this property in '96," he says. "It was going to be subdivided like the trailer park at the end of town."

I seem to remember passing it by, but I haven't been in there.

"We had our own vision and we went to the county to get it approved and they wanted the streets paved and they seemed to have the attitude of 'don't make us have to fight you,' but when they saw what we wanted to do, the aesthetics, the 'less-is-more' approach, they were blown away, and we helped the county put together a new method of development. We divided the land into ten- to twenty-acre parcels instead of one acre lots. We wanted to build affordable housing—"

"What do you mean by 'affordable'?" I break in, "How much does one of these units sell for?" There's a completed house down the hill and the Anasazi design, the custom brickwork, the heavy vigas, the tiled roofs all look pretty expensive to me.

Austin's answer: "I assume you're writing about the aesthetic aspects of the highway."

I know what he means. "I'm talking to environmentalists," I say, "and I'm talking to people on the other side."

This makes him angry and he points at me.

"You know, when they paved that road, I told them there was going to be development, and here it is. 'If you build it, they will come,' and it's not a question of if but how, and you're either going to have nice, quality development or it's going to be bad, and the ranchers don't understand that. What do you hear when you talk to the cowboys? They say, 'we don't want change.'"

Austin talks about how he helped get the Southern Utah Forest Products Organization together and how he helped change Forest Service policy so the parcels they were putting bids out on weren't so large as to exclude local operations, but I'm thinking about where he was pointing. Austin's obviously not a rude person and he wasn't really pointing at me as much as he was pointing at those cowboys in the valley—that's where his eyes were, anyway—but that gesture has given me pause, and I'm thinking that Patrick Diehl, Tori Woodard and I and much of the world all did come in and continue to come in on the same road he didn't want paved. Mark might just as well have said, "write a book about it, tell people about it, and they will come," or "build a road and people like you will come," or "how is what I'm doing that different from what you're doing, except that it's a lot more profitable?" And he would have a point.

I snap out of it. Austin is talking about the Dry Hollow Reservoir in Escalante.

"I thought it was a big mistake for SUWA to oppose that," he says. "I told them 'you are just fueling the fire.' I've lived in southern Utah for thirty years and I understand the situation really well and I try to avoid drawing lines in the sand. And what about the jobs I'm providing?"

"What about Dell LeFevre?" I ask. "Is he one of the cowboys who doesn't want change?"

He takes a few seconds to think that over. "No," he says, "Dell sold his permits on the Escalante to Grand Canyon Trust and he caught a lot of flack for that and I think it was because some of the locals were jealous and a lot of them were more interested in a fight than actually accomplishing something."

So be it. I see a similarity between him and Dell LeFevre, which is a willingness to try something unconventional when the usual approach doesn't work. And Austin makes a point of buying and hiring locally, so he certainly couldn't be accused of *harming* Boulder's economy, even if he wants to change it. And if *I* were a developer in southern Utah, the first thing I would do would be to join SUWA. In fact, I don't see why the residents of Escalante and Boulder don't join en masse; their input and their votes would more than offset any benefits SUWA would accrue from the paltry membership fees. What's more, the other members of SUWA would actually get to meet the people they're fighting, and they might just decide ranchers are human after all.

Getting back to Austin, though, I think Boulder's future, for good or ill, belongs to him—to him and people like Dell LeFevre. Some locals call LeFevre a "sell-out," but I doubt they do it to his face, and soon after he did sell his permits, the cattleman's association sued the BLM to halt the practice of retiring permits, and so the Grand Canyon Trust has stopped buying. I would call that pretty good timing on LeFevre's part.

I excuse myself and drive back down the road and I drive around the southern half of Boulder for a while, past the isolated farm and ranch houses, where horses and cattle graze in the fields out by the white sandstone domes with the red light of the low sun shining on them almost straight on, and then I come back to the middle of town and park the Heap and walk by the old farmhouses with sheep in their backyards and the rotted fences and the old gray barns, the leaning telephone poles, the orchards, the cottonwoods, the rabbitbrush crowding the roadside.

It is a perfect day, temperature in the high-sixties, no clouds, no wind, no traffic, so still I can hear people talking in their houses.

I drive towards Boulder Mountain, past Austin's Boulder Lodge, with its rusted roof and its rip-gut fence and its stucco walls, past a sign advising me to "use your forest resources wisely," to the development on the north end of town, where everybody has done his own thing, and it's pre-fab houses and log cabins, double-wides, red fireplugs, green and brown aluminum siding, chain-link fence, two-hundred-gallon propane tanks, bulky air conditioning units, shacks painted aquamarine, chained lots, none of it very tasteful. But I used to live in a trailer lot and I know the kind of residents who live here and they're mostly working-class people. Some of them are retired, some of them are on their way up, some have fallen down and some just like things the way they are. That last category would have included me when I lived

Petroglyph near Fence Canyon

Burr Trail at Boulder

in a trailer down in Arizona, and it would include me now because I admit, I would rather not see Boulder change. But it will.

The Burr Trail

> A: With the increase, we just kept getting more and more complaints. More and more, that we had to put a shed in Boulder to try to maintain that road.
>
> Q: What do you mean? What complaints?
>
> A: Tourists. They'd call you up.
>
> Q: Say, "What a nice dirt road you've got here"?
>
> A: Right.
>
> Q: "We've had a wonderful experience"?
>
> A: And "When are you going to grade the 'blank, blank' thing."
>
> Q: Isn't the appeal—maybe not the entire appeal, but isn't there a strong appeal for that road—the fact that it's a dirt road?
>
> A: No. That is absolutely asinine.
>
> (Deposition of H. Dell LeFevre, Sierra Club vs. Hodel, 20)

The conflict began in 1987 when the Sierra Club filed suit against the BLM, charging that the changes Garfield County wanted to make would constitute a trespass on federal land, that the county needed to get permission from the government before making such changes, that the "improvements" would impair the wilderness qualities of the adjacent lands and that the BLM hadn't fully studied such impacts. It took six years for the Sierra Club to lose on all counts and for the judge to decide that the county did hold title to the road, but the Sierra Club appealed the ruling while the Park Service sued the county in 1996 for bulldozing away a blind curve east of the Waterpocket Fold, near a spot known as the Post. This time the county was in trouble for not consulting the Park Service before beginning its repairs. The county felt it had absolutely no obligation to obtain permission from the Park Service, the BLM or any other government agency before upgrading or repairing a road it held title to.

Garfield County's argument, and the argument of every county to ownership of the roads in its boundaries, is based on the 1866 statute known as RS (Revised Statute) 2477, which states: "the right of way for the construction of highways across public lands not otherwise reserved for public purposes is hereby granted." The exact meaning of "construction" is still being contended, but "highways," at the time meant any throughway from a cattle trail to a major road. By "reserved for public purposes," the statute meant *already* reserved; when the government declared a monument or park, the counties retained ownership of their roads, and when there was a dispute between the federal government and an individual or a county over RS 2477 roads, the courts invariably deferred to state law in their decisions.

That was how things stood up until 1976 when the Federal Land Management and Policy Act (FLPMA, pronounced "flip-ma") was implemented. FLPMA repealed RS 2477 but recognized all preexisting RS 2477 grants. Environmentalists refer to these self-actuating grants as claims and contend that the counties bear the burden of proving their roads were constructed before 1976.

Under Interior Secretary Donald Hodel, practically any line in the dust could be considered a "highway." Bruce Babbitt nixed Hodel's criteria but was blocked by Congress from imposing his own standards, and now the definition is being fought over in court. Garfield County is still claiming river beds and cow trails as highways (but not necessarily roads) but SUWA's definition of a highway appears to be strictly modern, though the term was first employed back in the late nineteenth century, and they define a road as something that "looks like a 'road' to a hypothetical typical American" (SUWA, 14).

Why all the wrangling over roads and highways? Because highway grants could theoretically be developed into roads. An overgrown, century-old cow trail, for example, could *theoretically* be developed by the county into a six-lane highway under the present law. And SUWA and the Sierra Club are worried about how such roads, developing from practically nowhere, could affect potential wilderness areas. According to Section 4c of the Wilderness Act:

> Except as specifically provided for in this Act, and subject to existing private rights, there shall be no commercial enterprise and no permanent roads within any wilderness area designated by this Act and, except as necessary to meet minimum requirements for the administration of the area for the purpose of this Act (including measures required in emergencies involving the health and safety of persons within the area), there shall be no temporary road, no use of motor vehicles or motorboats, no landing of aircraft, no other form of mechanical transport, and no structure or installation within any such area. (Powell, 187)

If Garfield County didn't have title to the Burr Trail, it might not have title to any of its highways, and by extension, no other county in the United States and certainly in Utah, could securely claim title to the highways within its borders.

> Q: Were there trees taken out besides what was necessary for the road itself?
> A: Not if their plans was to change the road, no. But back then, you just pushed trees. We just loved to knock them down. Nothing better than a dead tree. Unless it was a dead hippie.
> Q: There aren't any of those anymore, are there? Either hippies or dead ones?
> A: I'm going to find one. Yes. I'm going to find a hard-core backpacker with his belly up, died of starvation on the Escalante River because the cows messed in the streams.
> (Deposition of H. Dell LeFevre, Sierra Club vs. Hodel, 64)

> A: I got too many cow numbers in my head to be worrying about what somebody wants to know about this Burr Trail. Especially the environmentalists. Or when they're going to sue me, or whatever you're going to do to me.
> Q: Did you give her (a woman from Garfield County Attorney Ron Thompson's office) any other information of value?
> A: No. What's value? How do you place value?
> Q: What else did you tell her?
> A: I don't even know if I told her she was good looking or not.
> Q: Do you want that on the record?
> A: Yes. I don't know her. I don't know. That's been three weeks ago. I mean it's kind of like asking you what you had for breakfast three weeks ago.
> Q: Maybe. Have you prior to today talked with anybody about your testimony today—what your testimony would be today about any of these matters?

A: No. . . . Hell, I'm over there where they don't care what you guys do. Listen, just let us build that road.
(Deposition of H. Dell LeFevre, Sierra Club vs. Hodel, 86-87)

So far, the county has succeeded in double chip-sealing the road from Boulder to the boundary of Capitol Reef.

Driving down the Burr Trail towards Capitol Reef, it's hard to believe you're in a war zone; there are no signs decrying the paving of the road, there are no protestors laying in front of bulldozers, no saboteurs pouring molasses into the crank-cases of bladers, no road construction equipment visible at all and in fact, very few humans visible in the off months, just a smooth and winding road, and a beautiful one at that.

On the first leg out of Boulder, the road skirts Durffey Mesa and cuts down a harrowing, hair-pin dugway. A few days before I drove through here a man tried to commit suicide by running his car at full speed off the Hogback near Boulder, and his airbag deployed and he survived with just scratches, and had he applied the same determination here, at the dugway, he probably would have succeeded in his primary aim. From the bottom of that dugway, you can park your car and follow The Gulch upstream or down, but the road enters Long Canyon, which is bordered on each side by high Wingate cliffs, so it's like a long red slot, and the Circle Cliffs beyond it are one of Dutton's centers of erosion; they're eaten back from the middle of an anticline where used to stand a Wingate dome. The cliffs, tilted towards where the apex isn't, and the plains, so vast they're simply known as the Flats, and the blue Henry Mountains just past the reef will draw the borders of the earth violently outward in every direction when you emerge from the red crevice of Long Canyon, and when the road drops you may feel you've been launched into the void, but the road is just making its way to the bottom of the Flats where the Wolverine Loop cuts south, and it will cross through White Canyon Flat, past the Studhorse Peaks, out past Wagon Box Mesa to Capitol Reef, where the Burr Trail, which now lends its name to the whole road, switchbacks down the face of the Waterpocket Fold.

Just out of Boulder, on an October night, I can turn off the Heap's lights and still see everything plain as an overcast day; the moon is that bright. I drive slowly, watching for deer, and pull onto a side road beneath a blue dome of sandstone. There are other domes up the road. It's cold and I build a fire and cook some chili on the grate, then let the fire die down and walk away from it, let my eyes adjust to the spectral light, and then I start climbing.

Night rock climbing, I think, *sport of geniuses.*

Long Canyon

The face is not so steep that if I lost my balance I would be in serious trouble, and the only times I do stumble are when I cross through shadows. When I reach the top I find there's a cliff behind the dome, maybe three-quarters of a mile away, and beneath it is a rock canyon flat littered with volcanic boulders about as wide as the Heap's tires, which drops off a steep incline to the east and narrows into a gulch that empties west of the dome. I walk into the canyon and back through the wash, shadowed by ponderosas, and back to my campground, and when I see the road again, I know that it is part of a ghost world.

In the morning, I hike down The Gulch towards the Escalante River. I have no intention of going the whole nine miles, but I want to get a feel for the canyon, and what I feel is a gnat attack. The little monsters envelop me whenever I stop to adjust my pack or get a drink or take a picture, so I stay on the move. There's a well-trod path along the creek and the brush isn't overgrown enough to be a bother, but the streambed grows monotonous after a few miles. I've been hiking the bottoms of canyons for months and

I'm tired of it and I want to get above the rim, and as I leave the trail and huff up the talus slope I realize that's what I've always wanted: to get on top of the walls so I can see where I'm headed and maybe choose my own course rather than have it dictated to me. No more meandering, no more wondering whether a side canyon is worth exploring, because now I can reconnoiter that canyon from above.

The problem with this approach is that you've got to head all those side-canyons, and just like Wallace Ott's jalopy, you end up doing a great deal of vertical traveling. But this time it's all right because I just want to get some idea of what I would be in for if I followed The Gulch all the way down to its confluence with the Escalante, and that turns out to be the massive, ancient, austere whitecap and table knoll terrain out by what the locals call the V, where Harris Wash meets the Escalante River. I am instantly drawn in that direction and I study the ridgeline for some shortcut and try to estimate the time it would take to get there, but with my present provisions, I would die out there unless I ate prickly pear cactus like Domínguez and Escalante or ambushed a backpacker and stole his gorp.

I study the map but it's no help; no old roads go out that way but the ones I've already followed through Big Spencer Flat. I start to search the terrain for a mining road, but I'm just fooling myself because it's not even a remote possibility. The only old roads which come through here follow the beds of the gulches, and they've been closed off.

So I turn back, and every step is weighted with remorse and every future step will also be so weighted to some degree until I get back to that canyon. I don't know why I find it so hard to turn my back on an opportunity to get myself exhausted and sunburned. I certainly don't do it because I like that kind of physical exertion, because I'll drive the Heap as close as I can to any particular destination before I start hiking. It's just that I have to know; I can't turn my back on the landscape when there might be an arch or a garden of pedestals or a stone form which has no name or Indian art or ruins right around the next corner. Call it greed if you want, this desire to see every bend of every canyon, every bridge and arch and slickrock dome—I'm guilty as charged.

I Die Laughing

Horse Canyon meets the Escalante two miles south of where The Gulch runs into it and you can drive to within three miles of this point, a fact the 1:100,000 map doesn't convey. One day I do just that—cut off the Wolverine Loop and drive south between the high Wingate walls with their salt-fretted hollows and long, vertical streaks of desert varnish and a few horizontal streaks, as if the rock had been turned ninety degrees after it was painted,

Desert varnish in Horse Canyon

craning my neck for petroglyphs, a pursuit that will drive any person crazy in time, but finding only cryptic technical messages uranium prospectors left for each other when they scoured this canyon in the sixties. The gas gauge reads a sliver above one quarter tank and there's no more gas in the can and I'm thinking *Bingo . . . Bingo*, like a helicopter pilot who has reached the point where he has to turn back, but I keep going until I get to the prefab-tin linecamp at the end of the road and I can walk in from there. I find many young cottonwoods that way and some spotted lizards and a few pale evening primroses along the path and also a variety of barbed wire that I haven't encountered before, with four barbs and four wraps around two tight-wound strands. For a while I kept an eye out for different brands of barbed wire in and around Highway 12, but I've been disappointed in this pursuit in that I've only come across two other types: the standard two wraps and two barbs tied around one strand and the older, flat, two-barbed kind, wrapped once around the strand.

Further downstream are gigantic amphitheaters of alveolar rock, which contain no Indian art, and beyond them, the sickly trickle of a stream I've been following empties into the Escalante, which is running waist-high, carrying cutworms to the Colorado, and which is choked with thistle, reeds, various weeds and tamarisk. Getting upstream to the mouth of The Gulch would be difficult without a machete or a shallow-draft power-boat. I do

Moody Canyon Road

manage to stomp through the brush to the splay of talus beneath the bluff, and from the top of the talus, I spot some seeps which must still be seeping because maidenhair ferns and monkey flowers and purple primroses have taken root in them and seem to be doing well. I also find dots pecked into the wall in the shape of a cricket bat, more cryptic messages, but I choose to believe these dots represent the number of times a Fremont Indian or a traveler from a more ancient tribe came this way.

You can walk up the mouth of Wolverine Canyon from Horse Canyon but I decide to come at it the other way. After a trip back to Boulder to fill up the Heap and get provisioned, I walk down that canyon from the head and come to a black forest. I've been finding petrified wood here and there at the edge of the Circle Cliffs, in the Chinle Formation. Up in Horse Canyon there are big, Jeep-crippling chunks of it right in the road, and it looks like some joker went after it in the hills there with a backhoe, but here you can find whole fallen trees in the paleosols and siltstones and conglomerates of the Chinle charnel, giant carbonized specimens six feet thick and sixty feet long.

In the evening I drive down to the badlands at the far end of Moody Canyon hoping to circle back on the Fourmile Bench Road, which turns out not to be there. On the way out to this nonroad, I meet Sioux Cochran of

Boulder Mountain Ranch, who has a permit for the Moody and Wagon Box allotment, and who's on the back of a horse that has five wild and ornery-looking cows cornered, and when I try to approach to ask some questions, the cows spook and the horse instantly puts them in check again and gives me a disgusted look, so I don't get the chance to say much and Sioux only gives me some directions and asks me to tell her husband Bob, who should be up the road, what she's up to. Further on I find Bob herding some cattle of his own, but he only sticks around long enough to let me take some pictures of him on his horse, which snorts and turns away every time I point my camera his way, and to ask me if I see any cattle with his brand, the "rocking C," to please give him a call.

I find a cairn about five feet tall, stacked up by the Purple Hills, and way out in the boondocks I turn off to a place I didn't really want to go, a short road to a water trough. When I step out of the Heap to take a picture anyway, I hear rustling in the brush nearby, like something struggling to get away, which turns out to be a silver Powerpuff Girls birthday balloon.

While I'm traveling, I watch the ridge tops of the prison walls of Wingate Sandstone that block me off from the sloping chaos just above the Escalante, hoping to see a break, but with the exception of Horse Canyon, you have to hike in all the way. Moody Canyon and Choprock Canyon are the portals to that wicked sandstone wasteland running by the river, and you must approach

Bob Cochran

them under your own power. And as much as those canyons are drawing me in, I've got my own agenda. I drive down Silver Falls Creek as far as the road will take me, spot a coyote's flash of gray fur in the headlights and chase down a kangaroo rat hopping like a wind-up toy. I believe I could keep going all the way down to the river on this pioneer road but one sign after another warns me of the dire consequences should I be caught trying to do so, and I park the Heap right in front of the last "flipper" and make camp there.

There's petrified wood here, too; one upright old stump that I initially mistook for the real thing just down the riverbed. The Chinle is a weird mix of purple and brown, perse and uranium green molded into high, macilent pedestals for Wingate boulders and a billion tiny rain pillars for pebbles. There are a great number of desert trumpet pods looking fairly comfortable in this environment, which must be much like their home planet, and they're ready to snatch my body away when I fall asleep, but if that's what it takes to build a more just and sustainable society, without need or greed or violence, where we can all work together for the common good, I guess I'll have to make that sacrifice.

But the alien pods fail that night and I awake with an evil plan. Not to drive down Silver Falls Creek, though I'm tempted, but something more sinister. I've been aching to explore the hoodooland on top of the Wingate cliffs but I didn't know how to get up there until I passed a vertical slot filled with landslide debris yesterday, and I drive back there this morning and climb up the talus fan and then start on that slide, which is damned loose and vertical, in fact probably the most vertical face I've ever gone up, and when I start dislodging boulders as big as myself, I have to laugh and wonder what I'm doing here, but by then it's too late to turn back.

Some advice for those who would duplicate my feat, besides filling out a will beforehand, which should be second nature to every experienced hiker: make sure you note the backtrail, the point where you came in, because the path you take towards the center of the bluff is going to look very different from the path you take back, and it's not as easy as it looks to get back to the edge and once you're at that edge, you're not going to be able to spot a chute recessed into the cliff wall unless you're practically on top of it. The top of this bluff is like a spine and you must follow a rib to reach the end, and if it's not the rib you wanted, you have to return to that central axis and try again because these ridges are disconnected and discreet.

Just how discreet I will find out in the next few hours. I climb across the top of the butte so I'm overlooking Silver Fall's Dry and North Forks, and then I make my way towards the end of the butte on the spine and it looks like an easy hike over tilted red flapjack stacks but it turns out not to be so because when I'm crossing the butte lengthwise there are usually no saddles between the lumps. So the hike goes like this.

1) Decide where I want to go and visualize how to get there.
2) Discover a deep crevice between the ridge I am on and the one I'm trying to reach.
3) Discover a difficult route down to the intercolline sand gully. This route will involve technical climbing skills.
4) Reject this route as too dangerous. Look for another.
5) Find a much easier path which descends to the sand gully without any obvious route up the next ridge. Assume I can find a route once I get down there. Assume that anything has to be better than the route I've rejected as too dangerous. Descend.
6) Discover after much exploration that there is absolutely no way to gain the next ridge from my present position short of flying up to it.
7) Attempt to return the way I came and when this fails, due to steepness, lack of handholds, etc., find another way back. Or die. This new route will invariably be far more life-threatening than the route I first considered.
8) When I gain the ridge, take the route I rejected earlier as too dangerous.

By cycling through these eight steps, I am able to travel about a mile towards the end of the ridge in three hours and it's easier to travel in this direction because the tops of the stacks are tilted towards me, and occasionally I can leap from the top of one down to another. But when I reverse direction, I find it's much harder to leap across that horizontal distance and also up four feet to the top of the next pedestal, and it's also usually much harder to crawl back up steep inclines that I ran down coming the other way (see step 7), and so I'm going against the grain and the return trip takes twice as long.

Towards the end, I'm discovering how to jam my hands/feet/knees/arms/body into cracks to serve as holds on rock faces and I'm making deals with the devil, stemming above forty-foot drops and leaping across even deeper chasms where I would die or be seriously injured (and, since I wouldn't be able to climb when I'm seriously injured, die) if I fell short, just to save myself twenty minutes backtracking. When I stumble on the chute again, I'm spent, and this is the most dangerous part.

More than once I find myself dangling off a tailing of rock while I try to spot the white scuff-marks from my shoes so I can see where the footholds were coming up. More than once I set some big rocks free, and I have to watch each of them skip down and bounce and spin out from the face and land somewhere very remote, and more than once I have to test the stability of an entire crumbly slope, several tons of rock, by kicking it and shoving it and then carefully setting half of my weight on it and then trusting it utterly to stay still while I cross over it and trusting it further when I crawl beneath it. I worry more about having a slide come down on me than I do about falling. More than once I question my own sanity.

As I slide down through the Chinle, I notice a storm cloud front sweeping in from the Aquarius with rain trailing down from it like fingers just brushing the tips of the buttes. I find a passageway blasted through the hollow purple slope by floodwaters, thirty feet long and about as tall as I could crouch. When I get back to the Heap and I'm gulping down water and shoveling corn chips in my mouth, I notice that the dust gathered on the back window, which came from my off-highway adventures near Boulder, has formed itself into the pentagonal hadrosaur-skin pattern of the Navajo Sandstone outcroppings.

If I'd died back on that butte, my spirit wouldn't have far to go to join the Great Western Trail. There's a ghost town named Hinesville at the head of Silver Falls Canyon, which is itself criss-crossed with prospecting roads and cairns, from the uranium boom, or at least there should be. The Wolverine Loop Road cuts over one of Hinesville's airstrips. I park the Heap just off that road, beneath another butte with a Wingate tower closed up like a red flower with one petal ready to unfold and I kick around the dead town where all the plants, the prickly pear, dandelions and thistle,

Indian paintbrush and yucca are in full bloom, looking for signs of prospectors, and I do find some: boards scattered passim, a roadbed going nowhere, earth ramps, the usual rusted cans, a half-buried fifty-five-gallon drum, chips of porcelain, a bucket of grease, an intact bell jar, but no structure except an earthen dugout still upright, and in fact no walls or roof beams or shingles from any structure that might have collapsed.

A side road takes me up to a mining camp where one large

The Burr Trail where it breaks through the Circle Cliffs past Long Canyon

Ripple rock in South Draw

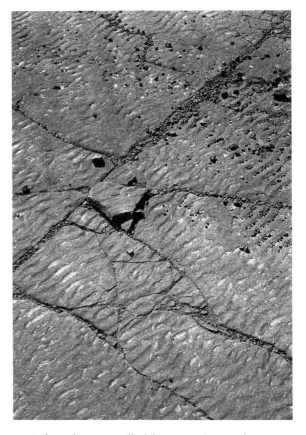

shack does still stand, though its windows are busted out, its outer walls are gone and its floor is covered with ten-penny nails and its frame creaks in the wind. Nearby are scattered Caterpillar parts and below the shack is a washed-out track not fit for man nor mule, and there's another, better track up the side of the hill, no doubt to a mine up there, and I would take it if the light wasn't slipping away and that front wasn't moving in on me like an ancient white fury.

Road to Nowhere

Ray Freeze and Carol Georgopoulos of the Utah Rock Art Association were going to lead a group to the petroglyphs past Lower Bowns Reservoir but they cancelled because the roads were supposed to be muddy and rutted and all but impassable. I didn't have the luxury of rescheduling so they gave me some directions and sent me on my way, and I'm finding the roads dry but very rough, ungraded, certainly impassable to anything with low clearance, but not the Heap.

It's a beautiful April day, the temperature in the mid-sixties, and there's a light wind blowing and shadows of cumulus clouds drifting by in no particular hurry, and to make things perfect, there's a controlled burn just above the reservoir, so I have the rich scent of ponderosa wafting over me, and it occurs to me that maybe the Indians used to burn forests just for the aroma. Soon I'm out of the woods, into scrubland past what's left of the reservoir, and then I'm headed for a big orange holy rock but the road turns, drops down a dugway to a low-flowing creek and climbs the other side, and at that point I have to walk. I find the petroglyphs, reted antelope and deer and anthropomorphs faint as old memories, pecked into a lonely outlier of rope sandstone, along with some more modern artwork and a few signatures, including multiple signs from one cowboy with too much time on his hands and a hankering for immortality but no plan on how to get it other than to chisel his name into every nook in Pleasant Creek: Walter Goodwin, Walter Goodwin, Walter Goodwin.

I sleep beneath the petroglyphs, at the base of the sandstone scarp where the brush has scratched off the desert patina, and I get an early start the next day while the Aquarius draws the morning clouds to it. Pleasant Creek Road turns onto Sheets Draw at Tantalus Flats and follows it through blow-sand drifts past a formation known as the Salmon for its shape, maybe, or more likely for its color, which is almost a match, and then it creeps around a set of flatirons and up through the benches of a ripple-rock catastrophe known as the South Draw, turning northwest and 180 degrees to its former course, to a valley that runs into the Waterpocket Fold beneath a Wingate Sandstone slab-wall, the back of Capitol Reef, beyond which four canyons cut through that fold as narrows. From my tape player, the Talking Heads narrate the journey:

> We're on a road to nowhere
> Come on inside
> Taking that road to nowhere
> We'll take that ride.

Pleasant Creek

The signs that would tell me where I am have been knocked off their posts and hidden and David Byrne is no help to me here, singing "Maybe you wonder where you are/I don't care," so I have to guess that windgap in the wall above me is Burro Creek. I park the Heap there and climb up the talus above the Chinle, over big blocks of Wingate, which the nameless ephemeral stream on this side has bored right through like they were sugar cubes and carved into legions of wedge-headed alien preda-tors, and over the lip, and then I hike down into the canyon

Detail of monster, Deer Creek Canyon

head, where its soul resides, on about a thirty percent grade, the angle of the reef.

Right off, I come to a catacomb-rock channel at the end of which is a red monster head a hundred feet high and it has a thousand eyes and mouths within mouths within mouths. All the rock in this canyon is cancellate, looks like the inside of organs, and some of it oozes calcite. Further down I can see white Navajo Sandstone on top of the Wingate but I don't get that far. I come to what I think is an abandoned meander but it's not; it's just a low ridge hiding a couple passageways that curve back up towards the top of the reef. One of them is a narrows just above a pour-off that's maybe four feet high, so I stem up to the mouth and try to squeeze through. But the opening is so tight, my equipment isn't going to fit, so the water bottle, camera bag and notebook go to the floor, and even then it's difficult. This is the narrowest slot I've ever been in, just a little wider than my rib cage. I get to a point where I have to turn my head to get through, and then the passage twists right and opens up just a little before it comes to another pour-off thirty feet high. There's a chamber up there, a loxotic light, and I manage to stem up to it and it opens up into a hallway running perpendicular to the crack-in-the-rock. Call the slot the transept and this hallway would be the nave; it's walls are maybe two hundred feet long, and two hundred feet high, with fifteen feet between them the whole way and a dead wall at the far end, just past a cottonwood sapling. Otherwise, the level floor is covered with grass and deep, dried mud, which must swallow up the debris which falls down here, as there's no rock at the base of the walls. There's no other outlet and I expect when it rains this hidden chamber fills up, and the only place it can go when it overflows is back the way I came, which, when I look at it now, is just a hole in the floor.

I've got to let my eyes adjust when I peer down into that well. Going back down isn't as easy as coming up because I'm looking down, thinking what would happen if I slipped, how the walls might crush me or snap my neck or at the least beat the hell out of me and break one or both of my legs. But sooner or later, like a cat in a tree, my stomach, the great motivator, is going to override my senses and I'm going to come down, so it might as well be sooner.

The second canyon is nothing like the first. It just runs up another pas-sageway as wide as my outstretched arms, to a rock fin that curves up from a horizontal foot to meet the wall vertically about two hundred feet above me, but below the point where they meet, there's a lateral joint I might be able to utilize to get across the head of the canyon and up on top of all this. I decide to see how far up I can get, and that's not far, maybe sixty feet, before my shoes lose their grip. From there I spot an arch, or perhaps I've even discovered it because I don't remember seeing one on my map. It is, at last, a pothole that has weathered all the way through the rock floor, a portal *down*, or in this case *up*. The opening is about twenty-five feet long and maybe fifteen feet high and the truss is about six feet thick, so it's re-spectable.

However, a problem is overshadowing my sense of accomplishment, and that is that the topside of the fin, which is about ten feet wide here, curves gently away from the cusp and then the surface drops in an intimidatingly vertical manner off either side for about forty feet, and I had to snake over to some footholds on the steep side to get as far as I did, and now that I don't see any handholds to pull myself up, I'm stuck, and not stuck in a place I can rest, either. The tips of my toes are jammed into the merest ledges and my legs are going to start shaking soon and then they're going to cramp up.

Near Tantalus Flats

The only thing I can do is try to put my leg up over the edge and start to slide and hope my clothes have enough friction and I've distributed my weight well enough that I can control that slide and direct it along the top of the fin. Otherwise I'm going to slide *off* the fin and I'll get wedged between the rock faces about thirty or forty feet down. *I seem to have been here before*, I think. I make a mental note about how tired I am of this routine and I swing my leg up, at which point, for an instant, I am only held in place by the tip of my shoe on a beveled ledge less than one centimeter wide, and then I let go and slide.

The first thing I do when I've got enough momentum is flip over so I'm sitting on the rock and I can bring my shoe soles in contact with it, but I gain speed fast, which, because this is sandstone and it has about the highest frictional coefficient of any rock on the planet, says something dramatic about how steep the fin is, and in very little time I'm going so fast I can hear the wind and my shoes are just scuffing the surface like runners and I can feel a hole being torn in the seat of my jeans.

Thirty feet down there's a ledge which is thankfully covered with dirt and brush and I crash into it and spin off in a pirouette into a stiff, spiky fremont barberry bush, which to me, with my mind on how the rock could crack my head open like an egg, feels soft as a feather bed.

No more. I want to get to the top of the ridge but I'm not going to engage in any more life-threatening behavior today. Near the outcropping I mistook for an abandoned meander, I find a fifty-degree slope, which is nothing, and I go straight up it, gain the top, where there are dozens of small windows blown through the rock by the wind. This is portentous. Far ahead of me there's a ventifact shaped exactly like an elephant's head and I make for it but it turns out there's a few chasms in the way and I have to head them all, including the canyon I was just in. Most of the walls of the slots I'm bypassing curve down and I can't see over that curve, so I really don't get a sense of how deep they are, but the walls of the canyon with the arch, and the fin in its center, both of which I am now looking down on, drop two hundred perfectly vertical feet, so with my toes on the edge, my eyes are directly over the seam where the wall meets the base. It is a hideous verticality, but the dimensions, I realize, are exaggerated by the narrowness of the canyon.

Out near the edge of Capitol Reef the wind picks up to a steady F1 velocity. If I didn't hold my notebook closed, the wind would tear pages out of it. I have encountered this kind of wind twice before—the first time about twenty years ago, in Indiana, when I was eating cornflakes on our family's screened porch and it was overcast and there was a heavy wind which picked up so rapidly that I didn't even have time to get up from my chair, to the point where small trees were tumbling past, and then died just as quickly— this turned out to be a small tornado. And the second time was at the edge

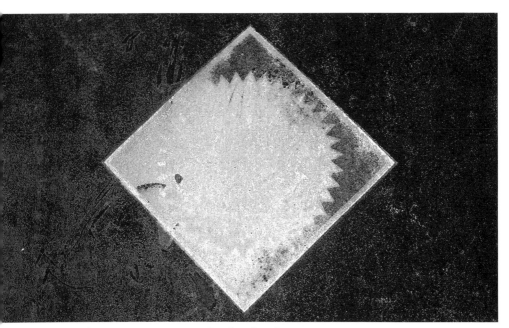

Emblem on farming equipment near Rainbow Ranch

of SP Crater down in Arizona, and that wind actually knocked the glasses off my face and carried them *up* into the sky and down into the caldera and I never did find them, which is why I have a band around my present pair of glasses.

Fortunately, deep waterpockets have been ground into the sandstone. From inside one I can hear and feel the wind rumbling against the rock. I lift my head up like a soldier looking out of a foxhole and I can see the Henry Mountains and the Aquarius Plateau and the smaller fins out west beneath the fold and a vast, tilted, howling wilderness plain.

I rest for a while and then I get out of there but I don't go back down Burro Canyon, I find a short-cut chute next to it and follow it down to the Chinle, breaking my vow because it gets steep and even the largest stones pop loose when I put my weight on them, and tear down the chute and start their own slides, so my path is fairly limited to the stunted pines I can grab at when the earth rolls out from underneath me, which it often does, and even some of those pines are loose.

The purple Chinle isn't safe either. I take an unplanned ride on my butt down a badland spur and find that it's compacted like stone and sharp as well.

When I get to the Heap, I'm a mess, but the rest is driving. The tape cycles back to the beginning.

Some things can never be spoken
Some things cannot be pronounced
That word does not exist in any language
It will never be uttered by a human mouth.

A few miles north I come to the isolated Sleeping Rainbow Ranch, an old dude ranch the Park Service, which had considered condemning the property to acquire it, ended up buying from Lurton Knee in 1978. The ranch ceased operations sometime around then and the Park Service has let the place go to seed, but Utah Valley State College is planning to fix up some of the buildings and put in another well and some solar panels to provide electricity and use it as a paleontological and archaeological research center, though as I drive through it, it's obvious from the rotting corrals and leaning shacks, the rusting farm machinery and dead cottonwoods, that the ranch is still sleeping.

Still further north, I'm on the scenic drive. Here I am viewing all this beauty, the reef and Capitol Dome and Fern's Nipple and Cassidy Arch, and I didn't pay a cent for it. Some people will go to extremes to avoid the entrance fee.

I start encountering traffic and I start seeing tourists, real humans, taking pictures by the roadside. I stop to take a few photos myself and waste some time beneath the red walls of Grand Wash, so when I finally get to Fruita at the north end of the scenic road, it's dark and the grassy campground there is packed with RVs, trailers, tents, VW vans with their tops popped. The only way I can see all this and all the people who are out in the cool evening air is by the light of a hundred flashlights and kerosene and propane lanterns and grills, and though I spend my time trying to get away from the crowds and I need to be miles away from here by morning, I feel this curious desire to pull in there and join them.

Voyage of the Damned

I kept Jerry Wyrick and Marianne Richardson—friends of mine who have come up from Arizona on their vacation in March of 2003—waiting for two hours in Panguitch when the Heap's battery died in my driveway, and now I'm going to keep them waiting again. We're in Capitol Gorge and they've started walking back from the Tanks to the car, but I had decided to keep going downcanyon because I had to see where it ended up and there was another reason—beyond the fact that the Tanks, mere oblong potholes, weren't that exciting—which was that the *official* trail ended there. A friend of mine once related to me the tale of a petroglyph panel he and a few friends

Jerry Wyrick

had spotted out by the Dark Angel obelisk in Arches National Park. There was a sign before the panel chastising them for leaving the trail but acknowledging they had discovered something priceless they never would have known about had they *not* been so adventurous, and they were expected to sign a register book, which, of course, they didn't, and they figured the Park Service wouldn't have gone to the effort of setting up the sign and the heavy post for the register unless there was something even more dazzling even further off the trail, and a little ways further there was an even larger panel with no sign before it, no register, no nothing.

This is what I expect again and I'm not disappointed. Down a few more bends from where the trail ends, there's a big overhanging brow of red rock on the north side of the canyon painted with axle grease cowboyglyphs which are high enough that the artist(s) must have used a rope or a ladder to get up there, and at the base are petroglyphs and pictographs: deer and antelope, stars and spirals, a waving hand on a wriggling line and a squatting anthropomorph wearing what truly looks like a samurai helmet.

I can see the end of the canyon from here and I have to follow it down but I'd promised I'd turn back after fifteen minutes, which have already expired, so I run to the end, or at least that's how I start out, but soon I'm just walking fast.

This trail used to be a road, and a good one. The cuts and fills are still there, as are three concrete check dams. I tell people you should never walk when you can ride and I tell them I'll hike as far as my Jeep will carry me but the fact is if I think there's something ahead worth seeing, like Indian art, an Indian ruin, an old mine, an old road, a bizarre rock formation, I'm a complete sucker for it. I'll walk twenty miles, I'll walk at night, with or without water, until I can't walk any more, though I've never had to go quite that far.

At the end of the canyon, there's an old cab sunk in the sand up to the doors, on which is written "SCENIC ATTRACTION—ENTERING—CAPITOL REEF NATIONAL MONUMENT," and there's a Park Service sign, a flippie stuck down through the sunroof like Ahab's lance in the White Whale, which reads "NO MOTOR VEHICLES."

"It tasks me," I tell Marianne later. "It heaps me."

I'm talking about a society at odds with itself, and my inability to find root causes. Dealing with individuals, I've come to believe there are ranchers and loggers who actually tried to be good stewards of the land as they understood the term and others who didn't give a damn, though I haven't found any so far who ever rode out into the wild with the intention of doing grievous harm to it, and I believe there are environmentalists who are informed and genuinely believe in what they're doing and others who have a score to settle. I've tried to apply Dutton's premise that "Nature here is more easily read than elsewhere" (*High Plateaus*, 15) to human interactions and the only answer I can come up with is a visual model: a strand of barbed wire, a double-helix, a collection of ideas snapped to opposing bases, the green myth and the cowboy myth twisted, snake like, around each other.

I spoke with A. J. Martine about this dilemma. A. J., an ecologist, is also president of Entrada, an arts organization based in Torrey, and he owns a house in Boulder. He grew up cowboying on a ranch in southern Colorado and he also tried his hand at mining before he became a BLM area manager. He was among the first managers, or perhaps he was the first, to cut back grazing on the lower Escalante, and this was working with ranchers who wanted it cut back. Like Gayle Pollock, he sees both sides of local issues.

"We've had over a hundred years of grazing and a lot of that was overgrazing," he told me at his home in Salt Lake City, "and we've had over a hundred years of fire exclusion. That's on a delicate ecosystem that really can't take that kind of pressure. If we were just beginning to move cattle onto the range today, the BLM would probably allow even less grazing than it actually does. The BLM manages for multiple use but that doesn't mean every use on every acre. But the prevailing paradigm is that we're trying to get all the ranchers off the range.

"Now some of the kids—twenty-five to thirty year olds—who got into the BLM during the supposedly 'greener' Clinton era—they're a little more outspoken and some of them *do* want to get rid of grazing on public lands. But the BLM as a whole isn't moving in that direction. They've been hunkered down the last ten years. They keep getting sued by the tails of the curve of normal distribution. When I came in as area manager about 1991, every single decision we made was appealed by one side or the other, and with our small staff, we were frozen. And that's the way it is now. Both ends of the curve are in the business of conflict and both ends, when they look at the BLM, they see big government. One side says we want to lock it up for just a few and the other says we want to open all the land up to industry. So the range is being managed to satisfy these two extremes, which means that true range management isn't happening."

Martine believed the BLM lost "credible presence" when the Clinton administration declared the national monument back in 1996. A. J. himself was asked by the BLM's acting associate state director to move up to the state office before the monument was created.

"Turns out people I'd known and trusted in the environmental community saw me working with [Republican Senator] Bob Bennett, who trusted me to be the token green and Democrat on his staff, and they thought I'd gone to the other side. So the BLM moved me up north and then Clinton rammed that monument down our throats. I thought the Clinton administration was about collaboration and communication, and that's what I'm about. I'm a facilitator, a mediator. If they'd given us some time to work with them on the monument, there might have been some cooperation, but that's when collaboration went down the toilet."

Before he was transferred to Salt Lake City, A. J. was working with Louise Liston and SUWA on the counties' RS 2477 claims, trying to avoid litigation by finding compromises that would work for everybody involved, and that all went down the toilet as well. Martine was transferred because he was about finding those compromises, and no extreme political movements ever have had much use for people in the middle.

Why is all of this important to me? Because it was more difficult to build roads here than most other places on earth, and in the beginning the terrain itself was the barrier, and now it's other people in front of the bulldozer. Everything the road builders couldn't push to the side got scraped up into a ball before their blades and they have no idea now how to move it out of the way and I don't think they're pushing up against facts or science anymore, or that it's as surficial as they'd like to believe; I think it is a full-blown myth; I think it's part of a deep structure, some elemental multitarian energy from out of the earth itself, wearing a new mask but playing out some ancient role.

Marianne is a schoolteacher nearing retirement and an ardent feminist, a little to the left on most issues, so I think I can rely on her to have some theory about why a bunch of cowboys woke up one day to find their world turned upside down, but her eyes just glaze over.

Jerry Wyrick, the gray-bearded biker, master mechanic, AMC specialist, freethinker, the guy to whom I owe all my mechanical knowledge, probably has a straightforward opinion on the matter and he could probably render it down to "bullshit."

We stopped at the plaque near the entrance to Capitol Reef which read, "The best visibility in the lower 48 states is here on the Colorado Plateau. The average summer visual range is 145 miles at Capitol Reef but a warning has been sounded; degradation of air quality mars visitor enjoyment at the nearby Grand Canyon. . . ." and at the bottom there was a photo of what we would be seeing if the air quality here was the same as it is in the Ohio River Valley, which has a visual range of nine miles.

"Bullshit," said Jerry, "pollution, my ass. The Ohio River Valley has more humidity, that's why you can't see anything."

Jerry wasn't impressed with the names, either.

"Egyptian Temple, my ass."

And he had a straightforward explanation for the geological strata we encountered: "shit happened, nothing happened, shit happened, nothing happened."

The two of them aren't as upset as I expect when I get back to the trailhead late and out of breath. They're having lunch and they're interested in what I've found. Jerry is especially interested in the car. I get the feeling that if I send them copies of the photos I took, everything will be copasetic. I get no input on the genesis of myths from Marianne so I drop it. When we finish lunch, we pack up the Mercury Sable rental car—the Heap only seats two and this thing gets twice the gas mileage—and we head over to Notom Road.

The sun is setting beneath the clouds, so the Henry Mountains are black and the shale badlands below them are bright-lit. The air is so thick with light I can almost breath that light in.

"Driving through Capitol Reef is like driving on the bottom of the ocean or driving on the moon," says Marianne.

Jerry stops to let me get a picture and I scramble around trying to get the best angle but the light shifts and fades and so it's one of those times I just have to get the scene fixed in my memory: cantlands, flatirons, hingelines, white domes, an abandoned meander, two gray shelves, green fields below me and the Unknown Mountains.

The lines of the badlands are foreshortened by the light and the range looks like flat glass shards I could reach out and touch if I were willing to walk across the valley. The axis of the Henrys is Dutton's fourth center of "maximum erosion" in the central Colorado Plateau. Almon H. Thompson dropped Grove Karl Gilbert off here from his 1875 expedition to flesh out a few nascent theories on what came to be known as "laccoliths," buried volcanic domes. In his introduction to the *Report on the Geology of the Henry Mountains*, Gilbert says,

> At the time of their discovery by Professor Powell the mountains were in the center of the largest unexplored district in the territory of the United States—a district which by its peculiar ruggedness had turned aside all previous travelers. Up to that time the greater part of the knowledge that had been gained of the interior of the continent had been acquired in the search for routes for transcontinental railways; and the canons of the Colorado Basin, opposing, more serious obstacles to travel than the mountain ranges which were met in other latitudes, were by common consent avoided by the engineers. (1)

As the Henrys were an erosional center, then, they were also the epicenter of an unknown land. When Thompson was climbing the "Dirty Devil Mountains" in 1872, he referred to the individual peaks as "First Mountain," "Second Mountain," and so on, and when he reached the Dirty Devil River soon afterward, Frederick Dellenbaugh, his young cartographer, recorded, "We had at last traversed the unknown to the unknown" (205).

Gilbert seems to have solved the mystery of these mountains in most particulars, and sometimes with mathematical precision. Dutton, Thompson, Howell, and Powell's geologist, John F. Steward, had all noted how the strata curled up around the base of the Henrys and several other nearby mountain ranges, and G.K. Gilbert spelled every detail out about how the mountains came to reside in such strata.

> It is usual for igneous rocks to ascend to the surface of the earth, and there, issue forth and build up mountains or hills by successive eruptions. The molten matter starting from some region of unknown depth passes through all superincumbent rockbeds, and piles itself up on the uppermost bed. The lava of the Henry Mountains behaved differently. Instead of rising through all the beds of the earth's crust, it stopped at a lower horizon, insinuated itself between two strata, and opened for itself a chamber by lifting all the superior beds. In this chamber it congealed, forming a massive body of trap. (19)

The weight of the overlying rock kept the surrounding sandstone from fracturing as it was lifted up on the shoulders of the buried mountains and then erosion planed off over a mile of overburden to reveal them. Such was the history of the La Sals and Abajos and Navajo Mountain as well, except the last hasn't yet freed itself from its sandstone cap. But Gilbert's schematics of how the rock above the Henry Mountains looked before they were exhumed closely match the dome structure of Navajo Mountain.

As fast as the wind turns cold, I'm back in the car.

Notom is just a collection of ranches. We pass a grave enclosed in a six-foot-by-six-foot picket fence on a hill and some barns and bunk houses and not much else. The road is gravel and clay, which hasn't escaped Jerry's attention.

"If it was rainy, this road would be a mother," he says.

A sign tells us we're on Route 1670, and there's no hunting.

"Always quick to say no, ain't they?" he adds.

We pass by a new, gray Dodge pickup with a horse trailer behind it and then a cowboy in his fifties on the horse, heading into the range and holding down his gray hat while his cow dog tracks us with his bright eyes but makes no move to intercept us.

"You know you're in the country," I tell the two up front, "when you see people hauling stuff with their pickups."

The Reef is like odd-shaped piled white plates tipped to the kitchen floor but plunging through it. *What's beneath the floor?* I wonder, *What's still down there that the sky and the rain haven't gotten to and when will it emerge?* Looking back at the Henrys, the machine generators of the unknown, I'm not sure now that Gilbert has cleared everything up.

Capitol Reef turns red and we're inside the fold, with nearly vertical banks of shale on our left cutting off my view. On the right, the rock tilts up

FIG. 3.—View of the Waterpocket Cañon and the Waterpocket Flexure. The cliff at the left is capped by the Henry's Fork Conglomerate. The arched rocks at the right are the Gray and Vermillion Cliff Sandstones.

from Gilbert, *Geology of the Henry Mountains*

until the sun slides behind the cusp and the niches and humps and clefts on the hogsback become back-lit.

"Hope we don't come up on a horse," says Jerry.

"They don't have taillights on their asses," says Marianne.

We spot an arch in the ridgetop, a squinty white eye, and then the road turns west and soon the car is laboring up switchbacks. This is the original Burr Trail, these narrow doglegs up a sandstone wedge excavated by an ancient rockslide, and it is so steep there's almost no offset from the dugway we're on to the one we just navigated, so we can look almost straight down at the shorter stretch of road we left behind three turns ago.

"Whoever came up with the idea for this road had a lot of imagination," I say.

Jerry is driving slow, taking in the view. "Please don't look," Marianne tells him, "You scare the hell out of me."

"I'm looking at those mountains over there," he says.

"Yep, I see 'em. I think it turns here."

"Then so will we."

We camp at the top of the Burr Trail, near the Muley Twist Road Charles Hall established after the San Juan Expedition had gone its way and he'd decided there was no future in the Hole-in-the-Rock route. Having hiked a portion of it, I'm not sure what the advantages were of this second road, which came up from Silver Falls and ran beneath the crest of the Waterpocket Fold through a canyon named for the effect it had on your average jackass, down Hall's Creek and the Grand Gulch and out to what became known as Hall's Crossing. It avoids the steep grade at Hole-in-the-Rock and the slickrock doom beyond it but it seems much lengthier on this side of the Colorado.

Perhaps Hall rerouted travelers through here because of the views. From the end of the road into the Upper Muley Twist, you can walk out to the Strike Valley Overlook. I met a short German tourist there once, a physicist with a profile like Charlton Heston's, who had traveled all over the western United States and believed the Overlook was one of the best views in the nation, on par with the Grand Canyon. I can only say that you will at least get a great view of the curvature of the great reef's spine and you may gain some appreciation for the land that isn't there, the missing fold above the jagged edges of bent-up earth.

Jerry and Marianne are experienced car campers. They cook some dinner on their camp stove and they're ready to call it a night and sleep on the car's comfortable front seats. They save the back seat for me but I've got to have my fire and I've got to see the stars.

Strike Valley, view to the north

Strike Valley, view to the south

In the morning we put together a plan. I convince them we should drive down Moody Creek, and then we can ride over to Boulder and down to Escalante and back up over the mountain and up to Fountain Green where I've left the Heap, many miles north. As we travel, I explain the litigious history of the Burr Trail. Jerry doesn't understand what the fuss is about and I tell him I think it's about who owns the roads and whether we, as individuals, have the right to travel as we see fit. And I tell him that right isn't in the Constitution. He doubts me on this point.

"The people that drew up the Constitution was smarter than the average toad," he tells me, but I maintain it isn't there and travelling is a privilege.

"Bullshit," he says, "It's not a privilege, it's a right. That's self-evident. If you don't have the right to travel you're a slave."

"Slaves" is how Jerry would classify most wage-earners, by the way. I think of him as a wobblie when he goes on one of his tirades, no matter where he starts, he always gets around to the unions, the grunts, the unskilled labor and the living wage, etcetera. Hit any of these buttons and he goes off like an unguided rocket. What was life like for the working man before unions? If you worked construction and you fell off the scaffolding, "you were fired before you hit the ground."

I should also point out that while we've been friends, I've never known Jerry to have what most people would regard as a "real" job, that is, regular hours, a boss, a wage, a steady paycheck and so on. But the older and further in debt I get, the less "real" jobs—where I work hard to pay someone else's mortgage—seem to appeal to me.

We philosophize on the law of unintended consequences. I don't understand how mandating higher fuel efficiency standards through regulations is going to save gasoline in the long run because if the Heap got twice the mileage from a tank of gas, I would drive it twice as far, and while Jerry fumbles for the seatbelt and the car swerves to the edge of the road, he observes how Utah's mandatory seat-belt law will have the unintended consequence of getting us all killed.

"But they'll say *statistics* show they shouldn't be dead,'" he says.

Again, if you want to get to the river, you have to hike down one of the long canyons. This keeps the weak and the lazy and those who are short on time, as we are, out of the watershed. So be it. We dine on Spam at Four Mile Bench and head back, and by dint of my mistake, we end up taking the Wolverine Loop west rather than backtracking to the Burr Trail, and we only have a quarter-tank of gas left, which makes Jerry and Marianne nervous, which puts me on edge.

"This would be a hell of a place to walk out of," says Jerry.

I assure them we'll have enough gas to make it to town. I point out the red domes on the ridgetops and the monkey drifts of old uranium mines, but

Last light on the Circle Cliffs

their eyes are stuck on the gauge until we roll into town on more than an eighth of a tank, which is cutting it pretty thick for my tastes.

Then it's south to Escalante and the ruins and Indian art at the river and back north and coffee and more sandwiches on the first turnoff on the Hogback and talk about petroglyphs.

There are petroglyphs on the sandstone bluffs along the old Route 66 alignment just outside Winslow, where Marianne lives.

"They're always near a vantage point where you could look for game," she says.

So a hunter is sitting on a ledge watching for game, Marianne's theory goes, and he gets bored and he sets to work on an image of what he'd like to see on the plain below him. Time passes faster while he's so occupied and soon enough an antelope does appear, and he goes off and kills it. Maybe this happens a few times. The hunter forgets the times he pecked an antelope in the rock and nothing happened or he ascribes the antelope's failure to appear to his own transgressions against some other superstition, and pretty soon he's got a ritual going and he seems to have gotten some control over what seemed like a random event.

We drive up the side of the Aquarius Plateau and Marianne points out a sign to me: "This highway maintained by 'Freedom from Religion.'" I tell them about the founder of that organization who lives in the valley we're leaving, an atheist who moved to Boulder long ago, when the town was practically one hundred percent Mormon, and who antagonized one of the locals to the point where the courts decided he was a terrorist and gave one man he was persecuting a big settlement against him . . . blah, blah, blah . . . "and did I tell you that the most outspoken defender of the ranchers in Escalante and their most outspoken critic both come from Berkeley and they both have environmentalist activists for girlfriends: Toni and Tori, and do you think that's a coincidence? . . . "

They're not listening, they're studying the landscape. The flank of the Aquarius flows out from beneath the cap and down the mountain in the form of ancient and not-so-ancient slides and mud spates and the highway gains its summit right over the top of them and a series of scenic turnouts take you to some of the best views you'll find anywhere in the world, guaranteed. As the sun tips to Boulder Mountain, we turn off to the Homestead Overlook and below us we have Capitol Reef and the red slash of the Circle Cliffs and the Henrys and Navajo Mountain and every sinuous red cavity in-between. The signs tell us about Clem Church, the father of Highway 12, the visionary who got the road put in between Grover and Boulder, and about the rockscape below, how Connecticut or Luxemburg would fit neatly into the space between here and the Henrys and Navajo Mountain and how nobody lives there and there are no houselights down there at night, which is fast approaching.

I usually manage to hit this stop in the last few hours of daylight, but once I came through here when the sun had just set and the light was being sapped off the Henrys and the full moon burned like the eye of a new deity, and then I saw myself inside that eye, its inside curve the night sky, the moon its pupil and I was looking through the moon at another, distant world.

Marianne tells me about the conflagrations down in Arizona the previous year, which left much of the northern portion of that state blackened and just as dead as the landscape before us and I try to think of how to communicate what I saw that night, long ago, but the words don't come then. We have miles to go, we three misfits, and we set out again, making for the end of Highway 12 and beyond.

The Crooked Road

The Heap comes down the mountain at three centerline slashes per second. Down past snake-arrow signs, through the aspen forest still filled with deep

Petroglyph, Capitol Reef

shadows from the night. Down steep grades on Clem Church's road, through Bowery Flat and 4WD Creek, past Pleasant Creek and Wildcat Ranger Station, Chokecherry Creek and Singletree Creek. Down into Wayne County, while I'm thinking about a road to a Navajo Sandstone nowhere, thinking about still ripples in the rock and still animals and a sleeping land, watching for deer, thinking about the toolbox in the bed waiting for me to crash so it can fly forward and separate my skull from my spinal column.

I'm thinking how this road never would have been built if it hadn't been for the federal government and how that same government also helped many people in the towns along Highway 12 make it through the Great Depression. How the money has always flowed in from the east, and I'm wondering if the locals should be surprised that control is flowing in from the same direction.

Highway 12 twists to the toe of landslides, the bottom of the mountain. It leaves Dixie National Forest and then comes into Grover, which is just scattered ranches for sale and second homes, no center, with another Wide Hollow Reservoir above it. The Great Western Trail joins the Highway from the south and another road cuts off for Teasdale past the ragged edge of another Cockscomb built of Moenkopi and Navajo Sandstone. On that road are more ruins of defunct ranching operations and more old farming machinery and other junk which is pleasing to my eye but ugly to most others, and trailers and ranches on the edge of town with hoodoos in their backyards. That road comes through the heart of Teasdale, right by the cultural center with its weird, domical brown roof, by a pasture with one white and one black horse in it, out towards Torrey, but it ends at a T at Highway 24 before the throne of Thousand Lakes Plateau.

I turn off before I get to Teasdale and drive down a road of deep mud from the spring thaw to Fish Creek with two white dogs and a black sheepdog barking wildly and crossing in front of the Heap, and at a turnaround I find pictographs on the white Navajo Sandstone. There are several headless

The Henry Mountains from Highway 12 on the slope of the Aquarius Plateau

sheep, antelope or deer and there are wedge figures with sashes and jewelry and a familiar totem, the same kind of horned figure that guards over Calf Creek. All of this art is shot up badly and crisscrossed with cowboy-glyphs from as far back as the 1880s, and a few brands:

7   ⓦ   Ā   𝔏

Beyond the Aquarius Plateau the land is turned outward and the magic begins to dissipate. This is still remote country but it's connected to the outside world. It makes sense. Highway 12 itself Ts to Highway 24 short of mile marker 124, about a mile east of Torrey. At its end are a gas station and a cemetery.

Mountain of Bones

I've been on the chalky headland of Powell Point for about an hour, letting the view soak in, pacing the rim of a thousand-foot drop, studying, through binoculars, the totems of Bryce Canyon and the red wounds beneath me where the forest cover and loose earth have been excoriated, the transition in the aspen crowns from green to orange and yellow where death has crept down the mountain, and the skyline, the lip of the Grand Canyon a distant,

Fading and shot up wedge figures at Fish Creek

cryptic blue, and the black mound of Navajo Mountain at the bottom of the Straight Cliffs.

Dutton, as I've said, describes the thirty-mile-wide basin of the Paria Amphitheater, headwater of the Paria River, as a radially expanding wave of disintegration and negative causality with its nexus at the Paunsaugunt fault intersecting another such wave of erosion propagated from the center of the Circle Cliffs, and that intersection lies right where I stand, on what he calls the "Parthenon" at the southern extreme of the Escalante Mountains (*High Plateaus*, 253, 297).

Last night I slept at Griffin Top, at ten thousand feet, next to piles of lumber cut by Stephen Steed's men and I watched Orion with his sword of newborn suns spin on the hinges of the night into the western horizon, where those stars were extinguished by the crowns of spruce.

When I woke up this morning, the water I'd left in the frying pan had frozen into a puck. I didn't get up until about 11:00, when sunlight finally crossed my sleeping bag and the wind snapped an icicle off the water jug spout and it stuck into the ground like a needle.

I drove the ridge of Barney Top on a jarringly rough road, FS 143, past a radio tower, over patches of snow and, later, mud, to the turnaround where

I had to hike in to the Table Cliffs, setting one big old spruce, which had toppled over the edge of a two-hundred-foot declivity but was still hitched by two roots and a couple crumbly rock bosses, free to the caprices of gravity along the way. And here I am, confronted by a huge, silent blue block of scenery.

I don't snap many photos because my camera's lenses reduce jagged horizons to wavy lines, and I drive back down Pine Canyon, past Pine Lake where the ghosts of Widstoe still cross to the Great Western Trail, down to John's Valley and back up to town. There I pay a brief visit to Bruce Osojnak and his brother Keith, who tell me why I'm getting A.M. broadcasts from Portland and Los Angeles and the Navajo chants from the reservation in Northern Arizona at night: because the ionosphere solidifies in the evening and the A.M. waves "skip" down off it.

I take the old road out of Widstoe, up Sweetwater Canyon, from which the blessings of spring water still flow to a few fields in John's Valley, up the switchbacks with the Heap growling in second, grinding gravel and spitting out dust for purchase, over the saddle again—the intersection of FS 143 to Barney Top and FS 140 to Griffin Top.

A man named Heber Hall grew up near here and his family came through this pass in a wagon back in 1927, when he was a child, and Hall asked his mother if he was seeing the entire world from there. He records, "Until

Thousand Lakes Plateau

today, I had believed the winds, rain, snow, sleet, hail, all the weather had its origin from the top of the Boulder Mountain" (Hall, 42).

More switchbacks and I come down through Main Canyon, where there's a line of old shacks, the remains of the McNelly Ranch, and a burnt-up lumber mill, quite possibly the one owned by the Steeds. Whether there was ever a roof over the blackened machinery and the rusted framework around the saw blade, I can't say, but I can say it was a fair-sized operation, employed a few men. There are piles of refuse scattered about and fifty-five gallon drums, and there's a safety-yellow International Loadstar 1600 hood here and a seized-up block of metal that was once an International tractor, with the tires melted off the rims and a radiator grill of inch-high slats with flecks of paint still adhering to the metal. There's a hauling truck with its tires still inflated and there's a bulldozer with gleaming hydraulic arms extended and two rotting piles of lumber stacked taller than me. All this, I would argue, once represented a sizeable business.

I drive into Escalante, buy some provisions, some batteries and film and some canned corn. I'm on the Fremont diet now; my boss got his deer this season and I got venison and I brought along a bag of pinyon nuts.

I head up Hell's Backbone Road to the bridge where, by coincidence, I meet Reese Stein, writer for *Utah Outdoors* and anchorman for Channel Two in Salt Lake City, and his wife and a couple of their friends who are on a road trip over the Backbone from Escalante. They're eating lunch off their tailgate by the bridge and I'm out on a precipice, a knife-edged ridge with hundred-foot drops off either side, taking pictures of cross-bedded ravines and crystalline fractures and sheer verges, with my foot over the edge to show scale, when they call me over to join them. We talk about Highway 12, about the corners of this country which are still unexplored and the lack of tourists. Stein and I are both put off by the crowds around Moab. He's been coming here for twenty years, to a place more familiar to Europeans and the Japanese than most Utahns. He tells me, "When I visited Calf Creek once, back in the eighties, five of the ten campgrounds were occupied and four of those were by people from outside the United States."

They feed me crackers and cheese and Stein gives me a few tips about where I might find petroglyphs around the Escalante River, and then some parting advice: "Be careful. People make me nervous when they're traveling by themselves." And I tell him "Sometimes I make myself nervous."

Stein and company head for Boulder and I drive back and catch Posey Lake Road over the west shoulder of the Aquarius Plateau, the highest forested plateau in North America.

Road to Boulder Top

Dutton describes the lakes on the Aquarius' summit as "broad sheets of water a mile or two in length" (*High Plateaus*, 286). Today I see no such bodies of water. Cyclone Lake, which I remember as a long, liquid swath of mirrored sky, is a puddle in a marsh. Further on, other lakes which "never dry up," according to Dutton, are entirely missing, replaced by black ulcers of dried mud. Roundy Reservoir is gone and Big Lake is neither big nor even a lake.

The shadows spread but I keep driving. I try to get to Boulder Top but it's too muddy on this side of the plateau, so I turn west, take FS 140, heading for Griffin Top, detouring on side roads when I get the opportunity. I search for the "sinkholes" which are supposed to be around here somewhere and don't find them, but I do find an elk carcass in a field of grass hummocks, its head and upper spine broken free, the skin shrunk to the upper jaw so it appears to be grimacing. Further on, I find disarticulated cow bones: femurs and scapulas and a complete cow skeleton not far from the road, with a bullet-sized hole through its skull.

Coyote Hollow, one of the headlands of Antimony Creek, is a short-grass steppe capped by a Montana sky. I find a clearing in the woods at its

Cyclone lake on the Aquarius Plateau

southeastern end and set up camp there and watch the sun sink into the hills, watch the shadowline seep over the gentle folds like rising black water and the light in the west fade in bands to darkness. I read the names on my map by the fire's blue flame: two Mud Lakes, Bug Lake, Stink Flats, Five Lakes and Four Lakes, Guddyback Lake, Twitchell Creek and Griffin Creek, Auger Hole Lake, Barney Lake, Black Lake and the Black Stairs, Lightning Lake, Lost Lake and Bone Flat. I plan the next day's itinerary.

The moon casts achromic light on the meadow and lampblack shadows too. I walk away from the campfire, to the edge of the woods, and study the rounded knobs and the bluffs to the east. I listen for coyotes but I never hear them on the Aquarius Plateau.

Next day, on my way down from the plateau, heading for Bicknell, I'm motioned to stop by the driver of a white pickup in the oncoming "lane." He's middle-aged, wears an orange cap and vest. "Where're they at?" he asks.

I tell him what I'm up to. I've seen a few deer around, one buck, but no elk at all, and that's the season we're in. He doesn't seem disappointed; he's been up here about as long as I have and he's caught sight of the Heap now and then and he knew we probably weren't after the same thing. I tell him where

I'm going and he lets me know what I'm in for: washboard. And he asks me to pass a message along to the Forest Service: "Please grade FS 154."

I don't want any special treatment, but if it's up to a vote, I'll second that motion. The Heap gets hammered and the metal fatigued side-view mirror bracket, which I bought maybe two years ago, snaps. There's one point where the Heap continues, counter to all steering inputs, in the direction of a roadside ditch, but it comes around just before taking the plunge.

Today my way takes me over the Awapa Plateau, the lowest of the High Plateaus. Dutton describes it as

> . . . a dreary place. Upon its broad expanse scarcely a tree lifts its welcome green, save a few gnarled and twisted cedars. Its herbage consists only of the ubiquitous artemisia and long nodding grasses. Not a spring or stream of water is known upon all its area, except at the lowest part. . . . A ride across it is toilsome and monotonous in the extreme. It takes us over an endless succession of hills and valleys, clad with a stony soil, usually just steep enough to worry the animals, but not enough so to require us, or to even encourage us, to dismount. (*High Plateaus*, 273)

Except for the condition of the road, I enjoy traveling over the Awapa. It *is* an endless succession of hills and valleys, and there's still little vegetation and there are no trees, but there are rocky bluffs spread over it—Timbered Knoll and Smooth Knoll, Bald Knoll and Flossie Knoll—and there are old cairns piled on top of some of them, and each rise brings into view the convergence of the snow-capped northern Sevier Plateau and the Wasatch Plateau and Thousand Lake Mountain and the bright red tear of sandstone above Bicknell. The land here is sullen and restless at once and the hills are like waves rolling from the storm of mountains on the horizon.

In the evening, I return from town and drive to the top of Boulder Mountain. The road cuts diagonally up the black eminence of Rock Spring Ridge, gaining the top of a flat in a sideways manner, then doglegging back around Lookout Peak and up to Cook Pasture where a winter gate will close the Mountain off to visitors from November 1 until June 15. That's in about three weeks. From there, the road chops up through another lava bulwark right to the top of Boulder Mountain.

Glaciers flowed off the Aquarius's peaks a few tens of thousands of years ago and nearly leveled them. The surface of the Aquarius's lava cap has been scalloped into drumlins and kettles and the loose rock has been dredged up and spread over the plateau and the surrounding country as erratics. Stands of Engelmann spruce lean from kames over open country as if from islands, and there are whole forests in the blue hollows.

The clouds are flat like ice sheets and the autumn sky is a jet blue. I can almost feel the sun's rays shifting south. I'd almost expect to see the brighter stars during the day, and now night is falling.

I've got the summer top on the Heap, and it has no doors. I study the map for a few minutes. The main road will take me all the way across the top, to Bown's Point, about sixteen miles away, where I can camp and watch the sun rise out of the skelic rockscape to the east, out of what Dutton called the Dreamland.

The road starts out level and smooth, and I make time. I pause at Bluebell Knoll which is just another forested knob barely higher than its neighbors, but is also, at 11,322 feet, the highest point on the plateau, and I go on, past the barren depression which used to be Elbow Lake, through East Boulder Draw and Stink Flats and Stink Draw, which thankfully don't smell this evening. The sunlight contracts into slivers and fades out, and then the rim of a harvest moon, an airless, waterless skeleton world, breaks over the threshold directly in line with the road. Its yellow skull face is looming, incandescent. I can clearly make out Tycho Crater and the coastlines of the Ocean of Storms and the Seas of Tranquility and Crisis.

The road deteriorates and the trip turns into a mud slog. The Heap is starved for air. The vacuum gauge, which normally reads seventeen inches at idle, is stuck at twelve. I spin the tires through snow fields and somewhere around Pleasant Creek Meadow I come to a hundred-foot-long snow bank, with tree lines extending out from either side. There are ATV tracks on top of it but in three attempts I can only get the Heap up about a third of its length. This is the end of the road.

The Andrus Expedition made it further. They gained the plateau in early October of 1866 and traversed Boulder Top, which Woolley described as "comparatively flat, (with) numerous Small lakelets, Groves of Pine timber, growing less dense as we proceed," and then they circled back to Bown's Point, where they saw

> the Colorado Plateau Stretching as far as the Eye can see a naked barren plain of red and white Sandstone crossed in all directions by innumerable gorges . . . . Occasional high buttes rising above the general level, the country gradually rising up to the ridges marking the "breakers" or rocky bluffs of the larger streams. The sun shining down on this vast red plain almost dazzled our eyes by the reflection as it was thrown back from the fiery surface.

And, more to the point of their mission:

> To N of East and distant about 15 to 20 miles appear the breakers of two larger streams one coming from the N.E. Supposed to be the Green River the other

coming from the ESE Supposed to be Grand (Colorado) River. (Crampton, 156)

Here, according to historian C. Gregory Crampton, the expedition mis-identified the Fremont River as the Green River and upper Hall's Creek with the Colorado, while the actual confluence of the Green and Colorado that they were looking for is about eighty miles away, in what's now Canyonlands National Park. Believing they'd completed their mission of exploring the territory from the Kaibab Plateau to the mouth of the Green River and accurately charting the only Indian trails to cross the Colorado River, they reversed course and crossed back over Boulder Top and over the Awapa Plateau, which Woolley described as "barren, destitute of water" (Crampton, 158). From the Aquarius to the abandoned town of Circleville they encountered no natives, only old trails and "rude breast works of rock" and the remains of cattle stolen from nearby ranches. However, the expedition did also fulfill its mission of "chastising" the hostile Indians, not through violence but with a little dangerous knowledge—descriptions of "green grassy meadows" and "extensive range for stock," "level," "fertile" land that was "easy to irrigate" quickly drew settlers into the High Plateaus; and they effectively separated the Utes and Paiutes from their own home-lands.

The temperature has probably dropped into the thirties. I race back through draws, over low hills with the moon over my shoulder lighting the thin ice coating, the spruces, and the land. The frozen mud holes splinter when I ride over them. I look around for a spot to camp, a sheltered place where the ground is dry, but see nothing, and I finally decide to get off the mountain. Coasting down the dugway with the canyon winds, I have the Awapa Plateau spread before me to the mountains and the Parker Range, where it falls off to Grass Valley. The plain shifts subtly in the moonlight, shadowed crests pulsing and seething with the night's energy.

I set out my bag in a dell at the edge of that vast terrace, at an old hunting camp with a log tied crossways between two trees. Deadwood is plentiful and I'm not stingy with it; the logs pop in the heat and the fire spits six feet into the cold air. I walk out into the open for a final look at the Milky Way, rachis of the sky, and I find another fire pit with a charred rib cage in it.

Again, in the morning I can't force myself out of my sleeping bag until I have sunlight on my face. Packing my outfit takes about half-an-hour and then I'm off for Dark Canyon, just over the flank of Boulder Top, at the base of a shelf of volcanic rock. The road is rough and the Heap has to crawl, but it's worth the effort. I pass a line shack rotting from its earth

Awapa Plateau

foundation, descend to the floor on a narrow switchback and I come to a hidden corner of paradise—a green meadow enclosed by volcanic cliffrock and ponderosa and aspen—with cows grazing along its whole length and old fenceline strung all over, shacks leaning away from the mountain with their sagging wood walls bleached out and a two-story line camp at the field's edge with a new roof, a swing set out back, a hose with a sprinkler at its end and a still-functional Ford tractor from the fifties or early sixties parked in the yard.

This, I imagine, is what Boulder must have been like a hundred years earlier—a green swale hidden in a rock pocket. I knock on the door but there's nobody home, so I peek in the windows and poke around the collapsing shacks.

I drive back past aspens bowed over the road, up to the top of Boulder Mountain, and I try to get out to its rim, to reach one of the promontories from which Dutton surveyed the wasted immensities of rock beyond the plateau, but the side roads have all been torn up to prevent the hillsides from eroding into the empty lakes and killing the dead fish. I drive past flag trees and scrags and the remnant of Raft Lake, past an elk jawbone and a femur, over the still-frozen road, through brown fields of galleta grass laying on the land like a shriveled deer hide, past the dead black beds of the Twin Lakes, past more scatterings of cattle bones, and I don't seem to be coming any nearer the edge.

I park the Heap and walk east, over an old rock bar and then into a draw. Beyond a lava plug and the plateau's cap, there's the vesticated red desert, Tantalus Flat, the Waterpocket Fold, and above that are the Henrys, the Unknown Mountains, bright gray now with the sun filtered through the sky's red edge, though in the morning, with the light behind them, they become a flat black plane of night, an open portal off the earth.

Dutton was on the south edge of Boulder Mountain when he wrote the following description, but he might as well have been where I am now:

> It is a sublime panorama. The heart of the inner Plateau country is spread out before us in a bird's-eye view. It is a maze of cliffs and terraces lined off with stratification, of crumbling buttes, red and white domes, rock platforms gashed with profound canons, burning plains barren even of sage—all glowing with bright color and flooded with blazing sunlight. Everything visible

Dark Canyon

tells of ruin and decay. It is the extreme of desolation, the blankest solitude, a superlative desert (*High Plateaus* 286-287).

I rest at the edge of the pseudo-mountain, watch the desert burn, look for Highway 12, the road which brought me to the side roads which carried me here, but my view is blocked by lava breaks and spruces and the plateau's curve. My watch says it's exactly three o'clock, but it actually stopped at that time this morning. I don't know what the hour is, but it's late and I have to work tomorrow, so I go back to the Heap and I drive down from the plateau, watching for the roads which will carry me home.

Bibliography

Abbey, Edward. *Desert Solitaire: A Season in the Wilderness.* New York: Ballantine Books, 1968.

———. *Slickrock: The Canyon Country of the Southwest.* San Francisco: Sierra Club, 1971.

Allen, Steve. *Canyoneering 3.* Salt Lake City: University of Utah Press, 1997.

Alvey, Edson B. "Place Names in the Escalante Area." Unpublished, 1982.

Anderson, Shea. "A Pothunter Is Nailed at Last." *High Country News,* September 4, 1995.

Ambler, Richard J., and Mark Q. Sutton. "The Anasazi Abandonment of the San Juan Drainage and the Numic Expansion." *North American Archaeologist* 10, no. 1 (1989).

Bensen, Joe. *Scenic Driving Utah.* Helena: Falcon, 1996.

Bergera, Gary James. "The Murderous Pain of Living: Thoughts on the Death of Everett Ruess." *Utah Historical Quarterly* 67, no. 1 (1999).

Blackett, Robert E. "A Preliminary Assessment of Energy and Mineral Resources within the Grand Staircase-Escalante National Monument." *Utah Geological Survey,* Jan. 1997.

Breed, Jack. "First Motor Sortie into Escalante Land." *National Geographic,* Sept. 1949.

Butler, B. Robert. *Quest for the Historic Fremont.* Occasional Papers of the Idaho Museum of Natural History, no. 33. Pocatello: Idaho State University Press, 1983.

Cannon, Brian Q. "Struggle Against Great Odds: Challenge in Utah's Marginal Agricultural Areas, 1925-29." *Utah Historical Quarterly* 54, no. 4 (1986).

Chidester, Ida, Eleanor Bruh, and Alice Haycock. "Golden Nuggets of Pioneer Days, A History of Garfield County." *Garfield County News,* 1949.

Desert varnish in Bull Valley Gorge

Cope, Maurice Newton. Autobiography. Unpublished, 1973.

Crabtree, Lamont. *The Incredible Mission*. Self-published, 1980.

Crampton, Gregory. "Military Reconnaissance in Southern Utah, 1866." *Utah Historical Quarterly* 32, no.2 (1964).

Davis, John Henry. "Among My Memories: A Life History and Stories of John Henry Davis." Unpublished.

Dellenbaugh, Frederick. *A Canyon Voyage: The Narrative of the Second Powell Expedition down the Green-Colorado River from Wyoming and the Explorations by Land in the Years 1871 and 1872*. New Haven: Yale University, 1962.

Dutton, Clarence. *Tertiary History of the Grand Canyon District with Atlas*. New York: Peregrine Smith, 1977.

————. *Geology of the High Plateaus of Utah*. Washington: U.S. Government Printing Office, 1880.

Foreman, David. *The Big Outside: A Descriptive Inventory of the Big Wilderness Areas in the United States*. New York: Harmony Books, 1992.

Frye, Bradford J. *From Barrier to Crossroads: An Administrative History of Capitol Reef National Park*. Volumes I and II. Cultural Resources Selections 12. Denver: Intermountain Region National Park Services, 1998.

Geary, Edward A. *The Proper Edge of the Sky: The High Plateau Country of Utah*. Salt Lake City: University of Utah Press, 1992.

Gilbert, G. K. *Report on the Geology of the Henry Mountains*. Washington: U.S. Government Printing Office, 1877.

Gratton-Aiello, Carolyn. "Senator Arthur V. Watkins and the Termination of Utah's Southern Paiute Indians." *Utah Historical Quarterly* 63, no. 3 (1995).

Gregory, Herbert. "Diary of Almon Harris Thompson." *Utah Historical Quarterly* 7, no. 1 (1939).

————. *The Geology and Geography of the Paunsaugunt Plateau*. Washington: U.S. Government Printing Office, 1951.

————. *The Kaiparowits Region: A Geographic and Geologic Reconnaissance of Parts of Utah and Arizona*. Washington: U.S. Government Printing Office, 1931.

Grey, Zane. *Wild Horse Mesa*. Thorndike: Thorndike Press, 1993.

Haas, Jonathan, and Winifred Creamer. "The Role of Warfare in the Pueblo III Period." In *The Prehistoric Pueblo World, A.D. 1150-1350*, edited by Michael A. Adler. Tucson: University of Arizona Press, 1996.

Hall, Heber H. *Going Home, As Momma Said*. Salt Lake City: Self-published, 1995.

Hansen, Andrew J. "Tropic: How She Came Into Existence." *Cope Courier* 4, 1974.

Haymond, Jay. "Interview with Melvin Alvey." Utah State Historical Society, Aug. 28, 1998.

————. "Interview with Dell LeFevre." Utah State Historical Society, Aug. 26, 1998.

————. "Interview with Wallace Ott." Utah State Historical Society, Oct. 14, 1998.

————. "Interview with Afton Pollock." Utah State Historical Society, Sept. 17, 1998.

———. "Interview with Jerry C. Roundy." Utah State Historical Society, August 6, 1998.

Henderson, Randall. *On Desert Trails, Today and Yesterday*. Los Angeles: Westernlore Press, 1961.

Holland, Marsah. "Interview with Bob and Mira Ott." Utah State Historical Society, June 13, 2000.

Holt, Ronald L. *Beneath These Red Cliffs*. Albuquerque: University of New Mexico Press, 1992.

Hunt, Charles B. *Geology of the Henry Mountains, Utah, As Recorded in the Notebooks of G. K. Gilbert, 1875–76*. Boulder: Geological Society of America, 1988.

Kelsey, Michael. *Hiking and Exploring the Paria River*. Provo: Kelsey Publishing, 1998.

King-Ence, Marjorie. *Irene, Kings, and Boulder*. St. George: CFP Books, 1996.

Lambrechtse, Rudi. *Hiking the Escalante*. Salt Lake City: Wasatch Publishers, 1985.

Ludmer, Larry H. *Utah Guide*. Cold Springs: Open Road Publications, 1999.

Madsen, David. *Exploring the Fremont*. University of Utah Occasional Publication 8. Salt Lake City: Utah Museum of Natural History, 1989.

Miller, David E. *Hole-in-the-Rock: An Epic in the Colonization of the Great American West*. Salt Lake City: University of Utah Press, 1959.

Muench, Joyce R. "On Top of Utah." *Westways Magazine*, 1966.

Munson, Voyle L. "Lewis Leo Munson: an Entrepreneur in Escalante, 1896-1963." *Utah Historical Quarterly* 64, no. 2 (1996).

Neilsen, Mabel W., and Audrie C. Ford. *John's Valley The Way We Saw It*. Springville: Art City Publishing, 1961.

Newell, Linda K., and Vivian L. Talbot. *A History of Garfield County*. Salt Lake City: Utah Historical Society, 1998.

Ott, Layton J. "A Sketch of the Life of Elijah M. Moore." Unpublished, 1939.

Proussevitch, Alex, and Dork Sahagian. *Neogene Uplift History of the Colorado Plateau from Vesicular Basalts*. Boulder: Geologic Society of America, 2002.

Powell, Christa, and Buck Swaney. "Divided Highway: The Politics of the Roadless Debate." In *Contested Landscapes*. Salt Lake City: University of Utah Press, 1999.

Powell, John Wesley. *Canyons of the Colorado*. New York: Argosy-Antiquarian Ltd., 1964.

Powell, John Wesley. *The Exploration of the Colorado River of the West*. New York: Penguin Books, 1987.

———. *Report on the Lands of the Arid Region of the United States with More Detailed Account of the Lands of Utah with Maps*. Washington: U.S. Government Printing Office, 1879.

Richardson, Elmo R. "Federal Park Policy in Utah: The Escalante National Monument Controversy of 1935-1940." *Utah Historical Quarterly* 33, no. 2 (1965).

Rivers, K. E. *Standing Rocks and Sleeping Rainbows: Mile by Mile through Southern Utah*. Ketchum: Great Vacations, 1999.

Highway 12 at Haymaker

Roundy, Jerry C. *Advised Them to Call the Place Escalante*. Springville: Art City Publishing, 2000.

Ruess, Everett. *The Wilderness Journals of Everett Ruess*. Layton, Utah: Gibbs Smith, 1998.

Rusho, W. L. *Everett Ruess: Vagabond for Beauty*. Layton: Gibbs Smith, 1983.

Schreiber, Stephen D. "Engineering Feats of the Anasazi." *Anasazi Architecture and American Design*. Albuquerque: University of New Mexico Press, 1997.

Scrattish, Nick. "The Modern Discovery, Popularization, and Early Development of Bryce Canyon, Utah." *Utah Historical Quarterly* 49, no. 4 (1981).

"Sierra Club vs. Hodel." Deposition of H. Dell LeFevre, May 13, 1987.

Southern Utah Wilderness Alliance Newsletter, Summer 1999.

Sowell, John. *Desert Ecology: An Introduction to Life in the Arid Southwest*. Salt Lake City: University of Utah Press, 2001.

Stegner, Wallace. *Beyond The Hundredth Meridian: John Wesley Powell and the Second Opening of the West*. New York: Penguin Books, 1954.

Stuart, David E. *Anasazi America*. Albuquerque: University of New Mexico Press, 2000.

Subcommittee on National Parks and Public Lands, of the Committee on Resources, House of Representatives, 105th Congress. "Establishing the Grand-Staircase Escalante National Monument Oversight Hearing, Serial 105-20." Washington: U.S. Government Printing Office, 1996.

Taylor, Mark A. *Sandstone Sunsets*. Layton: Gibbs-Smith, 1997.

Terzaghi, K. "Stability of Steep Slopes on Hard Unweathered Rock." *Geotechnique* 12 (1962).

Tindall, Sarah E. "The Cockscomb Segment of the East Kaibab Monocline: Taking the Structural Plunge." In *Geology of Utah's Parks and Monuments*, Utah Geological Association Publication 28. Salt Lake City: University of Utah Press, 2000.

Tom, Gary, and Ronald Holt. "The Paiute Tribe of Utah." In *A History of Utah's American Indians*, edited by Forrest S. Cuch. Salt Lake City: Utah Division of Indian Affairs, 2000.

Utah Wilderness Coalition. *Wilderness at the Edge*. Salt Lake City: UWC, 1990.

Van West, Carla R. "Agriculture Potential and Carrying Capacity, Southwestern Colorado, A. D. 901 to 1300." In *The Prehistoric Pueblo World A. D. 1150–1350*, edited by Michael A. Adler. Tucson: University of Arizona Press, 1996.

Wannamaker, Philip E., et. al. "Great Basin-Colorado Plateau Transition in Central Utah: An Interface between Active Extension and Stable Interior." Salt Lake City: Utah Geological Society and American Association of Petroleum Geologists, 2001.

Warner, Ted. *The Domínguez-Escalante Journal: Their Expeditions through Colorado, Utah, Arizona, and New Mexico in 1776*. Salt Lake City: University of Utah Press, 1995.

Watson, R. A., and H. E. Wright. "Landslides on the East Flank of the Chuska Moutains, Northwestern New Mexico." *American Journal of Science* 261 (1963).

Widstoe, John A. *Success on Irrigation Projects*. New York: John Wiley & Sons, 1928.

———. *Dry Farming. A System of Agriculture for Countries Under a Low Rainfall*. New York: MacMillan Company, 1913.

Winkler, Albert. "The Circleville Massacre: A Brutal Incident in Utah's Black Hawk War." *Utah Historical Quarterly* 55, no. 1 (1987).

Woolsey, Nethella G. *Escalante Story*. Springville: Art City Publishing, 1964.

Note on the Author

Christian Probasco is a travel writer who lives in Las Vegas with his wife Sarah. He studied English literature, philosophy, and creative writing at the University of Utah. He is one of Brigham Young's many great, great, great, great grandsons.

Christian is deserticulous. He was born in Twenty-nine Palms, California, a lonely Marine Base in the Mohave Desert's heart and grew up in Valparaiso, Indiana, longing for the arid, desolate western wastelands, not realizing how deeply, until he moved to Utah during his senior year of high school.

Photo opposite: Half-Dome and shadow of author

Index